# THE MYTH OF THE MASTER RACE:
## Alfred Rosenberg and Nazi Ideology

# THE MYTH
# OF THE MASTER RACE:
## Alfred Rosenberg
## and Nazi Ideology

## Robert Cecil

We had fed the heart on fantasies,
The heart's grown brutal from the fare,
More substance in our enmities
Than in our love. . .
W. B. Yeats, *The Tower*

red-rag and pink-flag
blackshirt and brown
strut-mince and stink-brag
have all come to town
e. e. cummings, *selected poems*

## Dodd Mead & Company, New York

© Robert Cecil 1972
All rights reserved

No part of this book may be reproduced in any form
without permission in writing from the publisher

ISBN: 0-396-06577-5
Library of Congress Catalog Card Number: 75-39009 *10 . 5. 72*
Printed in Great Britain

# Contents

54890

# Illustrations

The Author and Publishers wish to thank the following for permission to reproduce these illustrations:
*Radio Times* Hulton Picture Library for figs 1 and 17; Bilderdienst Ullstein, Berlin for figs 6, 7, 10 and 16; Bilderdienst Süddeutscher Verlag, Munich for fig 8; Wiener Library, London for figs 11–15; Zeitgeschichtliches Bildarchiv (Heinrich Hoffman) for figs 3, 4 and 9.

# Preface

I have been motivated to write this book both as a student of human nature and as a student of history. I have long been interested in man's capacity to retain in his mind two or more incompatible ideas and, indeed, to pursue contradictory courses of action. The Nazis illustrated this tendency to an alarming extent. One has only to think of Himmler, who coldly destroyed so many human beings, but had an aversion from blood sports; or of some of his concentration camp commandants, who in their private lives were good fathers and husbands. It seemed to me that Alfred Rosenberg deserved to be included in this rogues' gallery. His career provides a classic example of a man who openly contemplated a brutal and inhuman fate for large groups of his fellow creatures; but when given the chance to cooperate in carrying his lethal programme into effect shrank from doing so.

There is no life of Rosenberg in English or German; nor has the memoir which he wrote in prison at the end of his life been translated in full into English. In 1949 a fragmentary version of it was produced with a commentary calculated to make him appear more as a monster than as a misguided human being.* This was an understandable response on the part of the commentators to the cataclysm that had so recently ended, but it deprived the character of Rosenberg of all variation of colour and thus of interest. More time has now elapsed and one can study the Nazi leaders as members of the human race without being suspected of having sympathy with their inhuman aims. Indeed, if we assume that thoughts of racial superiority, leading inevitably to racial hatred, can only arise in the minds of monsters, we shall make little progress in understanding the sad history of our planet in the years since 1945. The primary task of the biographer is to understand, rather than to condemn.

My interest in Nazism was first aroused when, as an undergraduate, I was in Bavaria in the summers of 1933 and 1934. Apart from a short stay in Bonn in 1935, I did not return to Germany until 1955, when I lived there for four years. In the

* *Memoirs of Alfred Rosenberg*, ed. S. Lang and E. Schenk (New York, 1949).

two intervening decades there had passed over the country – and indeed over Europe – a typhoon of terrifying violence; yet in the Federal Republic in 1955 calm and prosperity prevailed and it was already difficult to comprehend the fate that had earlier overtaken the orderly, industrious and cultured people of Germany. Many of them preferred to regard the whole disastrous episode as a night-mare, which they had never really experienced, or had taken no active part in. This did nothing to elucidate the vexed problem how the people of thinkers and poets (Dichter und Denker) had temporarily become transformed into the people of judges and executioners (Richter und Henker). As Kurt Sontheimer has written, 'The National-Socialist state appeared to be a sort of accident in German history, a fiendish entanglement for which in the end only Adolf Hitler could be held responsible, while the German nation and political parties, the civil servants, the univer-sities, the churches and other social institutions, although they had all contributed to the failure of the Weimar Republic and the rise of National-Socialism, were seemingly not responsible at all.'*

We know, of course, that the NSDAP never secured a majority of votes in free elections, but we also know that in April 1932 some 13,417,000 adult Germans wanted Hitler to be President and that in July of that year 13,745,000 voted for the NSDAP. It had by that time become impossible to govern the Reich without the Nazis. How had this come about in a country with free institutions? What was the attractive force of the Party? Much has been written about its organisation and skilful propaganda; less has been written – at least in English – about the message. The medium was not the message either before 30th January 1933 or afterwards. A great deal has been written in many languages about the actual course of events and the stages by which after 1933 the successful NSDAP fastened its yoke upon the German people; but much less has been written about the state of mind of the Germans that led so many of them to cooperate in this process. It was a state of mind receptive to ideological penetration, even by ideas as crude as those propagated by Rosenberg.

Works in English on Nazi ideology have been few and far between.

* *Political Quarterly*, Vol. 40, No. 3: 'Anti-democratic Tendencies in Contem-porary German Thought', K. Sontheimer.

There are, of course, the masterly volumes of Hannah Arendt and Ernst Nolte, which treat the phenomenon of Nazism-Fascism in an European context.* This treatment is highly instructive, but necessarily stresses what Nazism had in common with European Fascism as a whole, rather than tracing its derivation from specific elements in German thought and history. The broader canvas of these authors is scarcely compatible with detailed study of the vicissitudes of Nazi ideology modified, as it was, by the tactical expedients adopted by Hitler in order to achieve ascendancy first in Germany and then in Europe. This task remains to be done; I make no claim to have attempted it. To have done so would have led me far beyond Rosenberg who, although the chief theoretician of the NSDAP, was in some respects atypical of the Nazi leadership, which included a high proportion of swashbucklers and opportunists, like Goering, who tended to reach for his gun when ideology was mentioned.

Nor do I lay claim to having written the definitive life of Rosenberg; in order to have done so, access would have been necessary to sources of information that at present remain closed. These lie not only in the USSR, including the former Baltic States, but also nearer home. Rosenberg's surviving wife and daughter, for understandable reasons, avoid contact with those seeking information about him. There is believed to be in existence a substantial section of his diary, which has not yet been made available to research. I have had access only to two published extracts.† Finally, there is no fully satisfactory German text of his posthumously published memoir, an English version of which has already been mentioned. A note on two texts published in Germany in 1955 and 1970 will be found in an appendix.

Despite these handicaps, I believe that enough authentic, firsthand information is available to make it unlikely that the main events of his life, and the delineation of his character that I have adopted, will be superseded. For the benefit of those primarily interested in the biographical material, I might add

---

\* *The Origins of Totalitarianism,* H. Arendt (London, 1958); *The Three Faces of Fascism,* E. Nolte (London, 1965).

† *Das politische Tagebuch Rosenbergs,* ed. H. G. Seraphim (Munich, 1964); *Der Monat,* No. 10, (Berlin, 1949), ed. R. M. W. Kempner.

that this is chiefly to be found in Chapters 1-3, 6 and 8-10. Certain aspects of Rosenberg's political activity have been dealt with in greater detail elsewhere: the Foreign Policy Office of the NSDAP by Professor H. A. Jacobsen; the Rosenberg Chancery, which tried to exercise control over cultural life, by Dr Reinhard Bollmus.*

In conclusion, I should like to thank all those who have helped me in my work, assuring them that any errors of judgment or of fact are mine alone. I wish particularly to mention Professor Jacobsen, who gave me initial encouragement and access to his Rosenberg Archive; Professor Laqueur and the staff of the Institute of Contemporary History; Mons. J. Billig and the staff of the Centre de Documentation Juive Contemporaine; and Herr Claus Baersch, who kindly undertook research for me in Munich. In addition, I have had much willing cooperation from members of the staffs of the Royal Institute of International Affairs, the Imperial War Museum, the Institut fuer Zeitgeschichte in Munich and the Bundesarchiv in Koblenz.

Robert Cecil

Graduate School of Contemporary European Studies
University of Reading

---

* *National-Sozialistische Aussenpolitik (1933-38)*, H. A. Jacobsen (Frankfurt, 1968); *Das Amt Rosenberg and seine Gegner*, R. Bollmus (Stuttgart, 1970).

# 1 Antecedents and Life in Russia

Anyone who studies the lives of the Nazi leaders must be appalled by the fact that men of such debased character, many of them also of very mediocre ability, could in so short a period of time have gathered so much power into their hands. History records numerous examples of men who, unexpectedly invested with great responsibilities, grew in stature as they mastered their new tasks. Nothing of this kind can be claimed on behalf of the Nazi leaders, with the exception of Speer and perhaps, until the last years of his life, Hitler himself. During the expansive period of Nazism the substance of power partly masked the native inferiority of the leaders who exercised it. When they had squandered away their power, they stood revealed with all their defects both as political figures and as human beings. There is abundant testimony to the lamentable appearance presented by the war criminals, with the possible exception of Goering, in the dock at Nuremberg – balloons so deflated that it seemed impossible they could ever have soared so high.

There can be no question of claiming on behalf of Rosenberg that he was an exception to this general statement. In terms of practical ability, he was the inferior of many of his colleagues; there were markedly unattractive features of his character. One may study the photograph taken of him after death by the rope. The eyes that had looked on the world with so deep a sense of personal insecurity and so little discernment of its realities, are closed for ever; but the thin-lipped mouth still bears witness to a lack of all the more endearing human emotions. Almost all who met him alluded to the coldness and asperity of his nature, which robbed human contacts of their warmth. Yet it must be added that the characteristics that kept him at a distance from his fellow

Nazis also held him back from sharing in some of their more atrocious vices. Power came late into his hands; when it came, he used it with a certain restraint – so much so that most of his fellow bosses damned him as a weakling. Most of them enriched themselves without scruple; Rosenberg certainly achieved a standard of living well above that to which he had been born, but it was modest in relation to the opportunities of opulence that existed in the Third Reich.

A German, now dead, who worked for some years under Rosenberg, left among his private papers a character study of his former chief. The writer, after collective condemnation of the Nazi leaders, continues: 'Alfred Rosenberg was one of the few exceptions. He was, and remained, a decent man, who to the last was honest and kept his hands clean. But he, too, was by no means an outstanding figure.... He had many characteristics that go very ill together. The human kindness, incorruptibility, simplicity, and indeed childishness, of his nature contrasted with a lack of resolution and courage of his convictions, which made him the prisoner of others' disdain.... He avoided unpleasantness with a timidity that bordered on cowardice. Indeed I have actually seen him, in his relations with people, show cowardice without being himself aware of it. And yet he went fearlessly to his death and did not try to escape [i.e. by suicide] the long period of tribulation that preceded it.... His closest collaborators, who had known him for years, called him the Sphinx, on account of the opaqueness of his character and lack of initiative and capacity to express himself clearly – he was quite incapable of issuing clear orders. He, too, came to grief on the rock of the incomprehensible "leadership principle" that made a god out of Hitler, whose word and command had to be obeyed unconditionally. Anyone who for years had known Hitler, the man, and then bowed down to him, as before a higher being, must himself have had something seriously wanting in his nature.'[1]

To affirm that Hitler was the evil genius of the subordinate Nazi leaders does not, of course, exonerate them; nor does it add much to Hitler's stature. He was the sun around which they all revolved. He was necessary to them, because they had invested him with the popular myth and charisma by means of which he had then imposed himself upon the German people. The spurious attributes of divinity, in the production of which Rosenberg played his full part, were the true foundation of Nazi power, because they knit together Fuehrer, leadership cadre and Volk in one indivisible whole. The coercion of the police state, which held the structure rigid, could only have come into existence on this basis. Hitler was necessary not only to the maintenance of the state, but also to the survival of the subordinate leaders; their loyalty to him was the sole factor preventing them from destroying one another in internecine strife, which could at the same time have destroyed the body politic on which they battened. The struggles for power and precedence that characterised the Third Reich were kept within bounds only by the need to keep the Fuehrer's good will and to keep his state in being.

It will be clear, however, that this superficial unity of purpose was precarious and was preserved at the cost of a constant state of tension. One aspect of this tension was the envy, hatred and malice that formed part of the atmosphere in which the Nazi leaders lived and moved. This applied not only among those who were their victims and under their command; within the innermost circle of the Nazi elite the atmosphere was the same or worse. The virtues of honour and loyalty, exalted in the legend inscribed on the daggers of SS, found no place in the lives of the leaders. Hitler's intimate group, as revealed to us by Goebbels, Speer and others, was a viper's nest of delation, detraction and vicious gossip, as the leading contenders manoeuvred ceaselessly for power and influence at one another's expense, and at the same time wiled away the tedium of the Fuehrer's vegetarian lunches at the Wolf's Lair, or the late sessions over coffee and cakes on the Obersalzberg.

Nobody's reputation suffered more from this practice than did that of Alfred Rosenberg. Of those who had been prominent in the NSDAP in its infant years (1919–20) he was the only one who was still prominent twenty or more years later. He was, after Roehm and Strasser had been murdered and Streicher disgraced, the oldest, in terms of service, of 'the old fighters' (alte Kaempfer). He was passionately proud of this and showed his resentment of those who had entered the fight more recently and come off with a larger share of the swag. For his position never became powerful enough to make him immune, even for short periods, from the persistent denigration of those who wished to make him a figure of fun and keep down his influence.

Partly because he was less successful, partly because he was less corrupt, he retained something of the idealism which, however misapplied, had marked the early years of the NSDAP. As a recent writer has put it, 'It was Rosenberg's tragedy that he really believed in National-Socialism.'[2] As the party after 1933 gorged itself on the fruits of power, Rosenberg filled the role of the Old Testament prophet, rebuking his people for whoring after strange gods. Even the Fuehrer cult, which was an essential part of the ideology, seemed latterly to Rosenberg, the ideologist, to be in danger of exaggeration. He generated around him a feeling of cold disapproval which provoked retaliation. Hitler, he wrote in his memoir, 'had very fine antennae and knew by my silence about something that I rejected it more profoundly than if I had debated it'.[3]

Rosenberg in later life seldom debated anything when face to face with Hitler; his character was a weak one. Like his even less successful rivals, Bernhard Rust and Hans Kerrl, he suffered the pains of a weak man in an exposed position. At Hitler's rude Merovingian court he went through life with the insecurity of a new boy at his first school, inviting tormentors. It began early; no sooner was Hitler immured in Landsberg in 1924 than Streicher, Esser and Hanfstaengl attacked Rosenberg, who had been designated to lead the banned party in the Fuehrer's absence. It continued to the end, with the bully boys, Bormann and Erich Koch, conspiring to make his task as Minister for the Eastern Occupied Territories an impossible one.

One of the most ingenious institutions devised by the SS for discovering human weaknesses, which could later be exploited, was the clinic Hohenlychen, where party leaders could place themselves under the care of Himmler's friend and doctor, Karl Gebhardt. All concerned expected to benefit – in different ways – by the arrangement. Rosenberg was for three months at this clinic in 1935 and again for six weeks in 1936. At the end of the second period Gebhardt sent to the Fuehrer's adjutant a report in which he sought to explain the constant minor ailments plaguing his eminent patient. After commenting on the difficulty of making contact with Rosenberg and drawing him into the social and remedial activities of the clinic, Gebhardt continued: 'As a doctor, I have above all the impression that his delayed recovery ... is in large measure attributable to this psychic isolation.... In spite of all my, if I may say so, tactful efforts to construct a bridge, these miscarried.... Due to the way in which the Reichsleiter is spiritually constituted and to his special position in political life ... he can only be freed from restraint if he can open his mind to those who are at least entitled to speak with him on equal terms and out of similar intellectual capacity, so that in this way he can find again the calm and determination necessary for action and, indeed, for everyday life.'[4] Nobody more needed friends to whom he could unburden himself; but he found none in high places and in the lower ranks none measured up to his sense of his own importance.

Leaving aside the quirks of his psychology, it must be said that Rosenberg first entered the NSDAP with serious handicaps, which he never succeeded in overcoming. He was a would-be intellectual in a group of instinctive and self-proclaimed anti-intellectuals. The young Nazi party was largely composed of 'outsiders', but by birth and up-bringing Rosenberg was further 'out' than most. His family came from Estonia, which was one of Russia's Baltic provinces until 1918. A substantial number of leading Nazis had been born, like Hitler himself, beyond the frontiers of the Reich; but it was in South Germany that the NSDAP took root and it was there that the sombre virtues of the Baltic Germans had least appeal. Hitler at one of his private luncheons made a revealing criticism of Rosenberg's editorship of the *Voelkischer Beobachter (VB)*: 'His contempt for mankind was only increased when he found that the more he lowered the intellectual level of the journal, the more the sales increased.... I often find it difficult to get on with our Baltic families; they seem to possess some negative sort of quality, and at the same time to assume an air of superiority, of being masters of everything, that I have encountered nowhere else.'[5] Rosenberg tried his hand at almost everything and was master of nothing. For this reason Goebbels' comment on him was the most wounding: 'Rosenberg almost managed to become a scholar, a journalist, a politician – but only almost.'[6]

Even his name was a handicap; while Rosenberg was quite a

common Gentile name on the shores of the Baltic, its connotation in many parts of the Reich was predominantly Jewish. The young NSDAP was not only anti-semitic; it was also profoundly dedicated to the experience of the front-line soldier in the First World War. But Rosenberg had spent the war years as a student in Russia and only came to live in Germany when the war was over. As late as 1930 no less formidable a colleague than Hermann Goering spread in the corridors of the Reichstag the rumour that Rosenberg had been in Paris during the war, and his opponents made no bones about accusing him of having been a spy for the Entente. Because of these attacks at home and fear of reprisals against relatives remaining in Russia, Rosenberg in his active years was reticent about his life before joining the NSDAP; he wished to focus attention on the 'time of struggle' (Kampfzeit). At the end of his life in Nuremberg gaol he drew back part of the curtain, but much of what he revealed about his origins in his last memoir cannot now be verified.

Rosenberg's own account of his ancestry was that his forbears had left Germany in the eighteenth century and gone to Riga, before later establishing themselves in the provincial capital of Estonia, then called Reval.[7] He described the father of his maternal uncle, Leonid Siré, as being 'of pure German blood'.[8] In 1937 the German Foreign Office refused to grant German nationality to Leonid's sons, two of whom were studying in Germany; but two years later officialdom relented.[9] Rosenberg's maternal aunt, Emmy Siré, married Theodor Eck, who was of German nationality and in 1924 became honorary Consul in Baku.[10] Their son, Herbert, who was born in Tiflis in 1904, later established his Aryan descent to the satisfaction of the Nazi authorities.[11]

A very different version was given out by a journalist named Franz Seell, living in Reval, who claimed to have examined records there and to have interviewed members of the Siré family. According to Seell, Rosenberg had not a drop of German blood in his veins: his grandfather, Martin Rosenberg, born in Riga in 1837, was a Lett; his mother, born Elfriede Siré in St Petersburg in 1868, was French. Worse, Martin Rosenberg's grandmother was alleged to have been Jewish.[12] These statements remain unproved. If the last-mentioned was correct, Rosenberg would have been debarred from holding senior rank in the SS, since he could not have proved Aryan ancestry back to 1750, even if he had succeeded in establishing that his grandfather, though resident in Latvia and technically registered as Lettish, was of German descent. As regards the Siré family, many Huguenots had moved to North Germany after the revocation of the Edict of Nantes by Louis XIV and some of these went further East. In fact, Rosenberg never joined the SS, to which he was unsympathetic. He was for a time a contributory member (foerderndes Mitglied), but in June 1934, in spite of reminders, he allowed his subscription to lapse.[13] When he first entered the Reichstag in 1930, he declared, like all the other Nazi members, that he had no links or connections with Jews; but this evidence is also inconclusive.[14]

It may well be asked whether the fact that Rosenberg made so little effort to shed clear light on his own lineage is not in itself ground for suspicion. Part of the answer must be that, within a few years of his coming to Germany, it became essential, in the interests of the members of his family who had stayed behind, that he should make public a minimum of information about them. From the time of his arrival in Munich at the end of 1918 he plunged into anti-Bolshevik journalism and his close association with Russian émigré groups and the *Voelkischer Beobachter* (*VB*) soon made him a marked man in the eyes of the authorities in the USSR. In 1925 Theodor Eck, in spite of his consular status, was temporarily arrested in Baku and his daughter, who was married to a Soviet citizen, was sent to Siberia with her three-year-old child.[15] Long before the NSDAP sprang into prominence, Rosenberg must have assumed that any news of his family would make them objects of the attentions of the Soviet secret police.

His paternal uncle, Alexander Rosenberg, had become a doctor and gone to Odessa, where Alfred's elder brother, 'Janny', joined him and became a military surgeon. At some date before 1937 'Janny's' house was confiscated and one of his daughters was arrested for the offence of carrying on a correspondence with her uncle 'Freddy' in Germany.[16]* Alfred's other paternal uncle, Karl Rosenberg, had remained in Reval, where he was accountant

---

* The statement in *Letzte Aufzeichnungen*, written in 1945–46 in captivity, that 'Janny' died unmarried in 1928 seems to have been a deliberate attempt to mislead the Russians.

and book-keeper in a bank. In autumn 1939, when the Russians were taking their share of the spoils of the Molotov–Ribbentrop pact and moving into the Baltic States, Alfred Rosenberg was active in evacuating this branch of his family. He wrote to the German Minister in Reval that, if the Red Army marched in 'every relation bearing my name must count on certain destruction'.[17] In October, however, they arrived in Stettin and, through the help of Gauleiter Greiser, were found accommodation in Warthegau, the Reich province which had been carved out of Poland.

Whatever the truth may be about Rosenberg's origins – and it now seems unlikely that the full story will become known – there is no doubt at all that he thought of himself as a Baltic German and was regarded by most of his contemporaries as a typical one. For him the German eastward drive (Drang nach Osten) had given to European history its meaning and sense of purpose. The twin prongs of this drive had been the Hansa cities, including Riga and Reval, which had dominated the Baltic commercially, and the Order of the Teutonic Knights, who had carved out their principality among the heathen tribes and brought political order to those benighted lands. Later, in the eighteenth and nineteenth centuries, while the House of Brandenburg was consolidating its power along the southern shores of the Baltic, Russian Governors and great landowners encouraged the immigration of thrifty, hard-working German Protestants as traders, farmers, craftsmen and artisans.

These waves of settlers, among whom Rosenberg's forbears may well have been numbered, retained a strong sense of their superiority to the native inhabitants of their adopted land. Among Catholic and Orthodox Slavs, the Protestant Germans felt themselves to be a race apart, blessed by greater economic success and higher cultural standards. They needed to feel superior, because a minority in a strange land preserves in this way its exclusiveness and solidarity. In the second half of the nineteenth century these emotional attitudes were intensified, as the Baltic Germans came to fear the higher reproduction rate of the Slavs and the threat implicit in Pan-Slavism. They began to suffer political and economic discrimination against their minority interests. Many of them were prosperous and Rosenberg wrote in later life that the revolutionary movement in Latvia in 1905 had been mainly directed against the Baltic Germans.[18] Over the same period their pride had been aroused by Prussia's achievement in unifying the Reich; they felt that they, too, were heirs to this great heritage. To these slowly submerging islands of Germanism, hereditary endowment seemed to be the touchstone of everything honourable and enduring; above all, the race must be maintained.

Rosenberg's romantic attitude to Germany, which had very little to do with the Reich of Wilhelm II, is well depicted in an article that he wrote for the *VB* some two and a half years after he had taken up residence in Munich: 'On the hill the knight with his followers built a stout fortress for himself. Settlers flocked round it, seeking protection; houses were built, ramparts and walls constructed and moats dug. A sense of community existed between the knight and the citizens – individuality combined with communal feeling. Above the maze of small houses the cathedral thrust up its head towards the heavens. A great architect designed it. Thousands hewed the stone, hundreds of thousands gave what they most valued and then in this great house performed their devotions: individuality and race-soul.'[19]

He held passionately to these convictions and prejudices, which with local variations were shared by many groups of racial Germans (Volksdeutsche) outside the eastern borders of Bismarck's limited Reich. In his *Myth of the Twentieth Century,*\* which was fermenting in his mind before he left Russia at the age of twenty-five, he asserted that Russia owed everything to the beneficent influence of the Vikings, Hanseatic League and immigrants from the West. When in 1917 the whole system collapsed, he had no difficulty in analysing what had happened: 'Bolshevism meant that the Mongols had got the upper hand over the formative culture of the Nordic peoples.' The Revolution spelled defeat for Nordic blood in its struggle for the soul of Russia, which had fallen back into the destructive grasp of the Mongols, aided by 'Chinese and people of the wastes, Jews, Armenians, and the Kalmuck Tatar, Lenin'.[20] Racial chaos had taken over and, if the same thing should happen in Germany, it would be the end not only of Germany, but of all Western civilisation.

\* Quotations from 1938 edition, unless otherwise indicated.

The *Mythus* (to give the book its short German title) did not begin as a politico-racial polemic; Rosenberg admitted in his autobiographical work that, where politics were concerned, he was a late developer. The central core, from which the *Mythus* grew, was 'thoughts about form in relation to art'.[21] Baltic Germans, he explained, were chiefly under German cultural influence; Weimar meant more to them than Potsdam. At one period, before he left Russia, Rosenberg aspired, like Hitler, to be an artist. Many years later in Nuremberg gaol, as he looked back, it was the scenic and historical features of Reval, where he was born on 13 January 1893, that he lovingly recalled. He saw again the harbour filled with fishing vessels, the fortified Sea Gate and, behind it, the tiles of the houses with scrolls of woodwork over the doors. Above them rose the three symbols of the German community: the slender spire of the Protestant Church of St Olai, the twin gables of the Hall of the German merchants – the Schwarzhaeupterhaus – and the castle of the Teutonic Knights with its tall tower – Tall Hermann – from which the Knights could look west to their castle at Hapsal and South to that at Fellin. The German soldiers who arrived in 1918, he related, thought they must be in Wismar or Luebeck, not in Russia.[22]

His grandfather, Martin, was a master shoemaker and elder of his guild, who moved from Riga to Reval in the 1860s, married Elisabet (née Stramm) and had three sons and two daughters. The second son, Waldemar Wilhelm, married Elfriede Siré, whose father owned a dyeing works. She died aged twenty-four less than two months after Alfred's birth and he was mainly brought up by his two paternal aunts. Waldemar, after apprenticeship to a merchant, became director of the local subsidiary of a German firm. He had an illness of the lungs and his son remembered how he coughed every morning, before going off to work, and how he seemed 'almost entirely withdrawn from human contact'.[23] He died at the age of forty-four, and Alfred spent the first Christmas after his death with his mother's family in St Petersburg.

Waldemar never went inside a church and it is probable that Alfred's upbringing contributed as much as his temperament to making him in later life an active anti-Christian. He himself laid special stress on his confirmation, which took place in the Church of St Olai in 1909. The Protestant Pastor, Traugott Hahn, was an impressive figure with 'a mane of waving, white hair and benevolent, but severe, blue eyes; his children and his son-in-law used reverently to kiss his hand like that of a patriarch'.[24] But a spirit of contradiction was roused in young Alfred, when he heard the Pastor condemning 'green youths' who dared to adopt a critical attitude towards the Bible. He rebelled, too, when he heard a lecture by 'some kind of Jehovah's Witness', who took literally Old Testament prophecies, such as those in the Book of Daniel.

Rosenberg's later narrative brings out a strain of opinionated recalcitrance, which evidently marked his character even as a boy. When in confirmation class Pastor Hahn told him to kneel, he wrote, 'this kneeling down stirred up something in me which could never afterwards be calmed'. As a confirmation present, his guardian gave him a thick illustrated book, bound in black and gold, on German missionary work overseas. This repelled him: 'I could not grasp what these mud and straw huts and these black women and children could have to do with *my* religion.'[25] Hahn related how in the South Seas a Mission House had been saved from destruction, because the natives, who were about to attack it, were terrified to see outstretched above it God's protecting hand. For Rosenberg this 'belief in hallucination' was cut from the same cloth as St Paul's vision on the road to Damascus.

Alfred's school days seem, in retrospect, to have meant more to him than his home life. He attended the Petri-Realschule, that is, a school at which no Greek was taught and the leaving examination gave access only to a Technical University. In his school-year there were thirty or more Baltic German boys, four Russians, three Poles and two Estonians. Both the Russian and German languages were used in the school, but only two of the teachers were Russians. Young Alfred attached himself particularly to one of the German masters, who taught history and geography and, by taking him to visit local archaeological sites, awakened in him an enduring interest in prehistory. He also retained feelings of gratitude to the art master, an Estonian painter, named Wilhelm Purvit. In 1942, when burdened with Ministerial duties, he found time to write to Purvit to congratulate him on his seventieth birthday.[26] Purvit had encouraged him to wander round the old part of Reval with his sketch book. Within a few years a young man in Vienna, named Adolf Hitler, would be doing much the same thing.

Young Rosenberg was not only keenly interested in the outward traces of ancient Germanic civilisation, he also developed an enthusiasm for the old sagas and such heroic narratives as the *Hildebrand Lied*. For literate Nazis the favourite saga was the *Edda,* which described how, 'All those men who have fallen in fight and have borne wounds and toil unto death, from the beginning of the world, are come to Odin in Valhalla.' It was a world without priests or morals, where only deeds of daring counted. 'Possessions perish, clans perish, you yourself will perish likewise. One thing I know that lives eternally: the fame of dead men's deeds.'

Apart from this mythical world, there was a modern myth-maker who, as Rosenberg later wrote in his memoir, was 'the strongest positive impulse in my youth':[27] Houston Stewart Chamberlain. This renegade Englishman was the son of an Admiral and was born in Portsmouth in 1855, but he was mainly brought up in France and Germany and, after a first visit to Bayreuth in 1881, came under the spell of Richard Wagner, whose daughter he married in 1908. He devoted himself passionately to the Second Reich and became a friend of Wilhelm II, who was captivated by his book, *The Foundations of the Nineteenth Century* (1899). He regarded European history as the struggle of the German people against the debilitating influences of Judaism and the Roman Catholic Church and he pillaged literary and historical sources for material to support his thesis. He was enabled more readily to do this by adopting a purely subjective concept of race; as he wrote of his own book, 'Without troubling myself about a definition, I have depicted in the resplendent pages of human history how men carry race in their own breast and in the great deeds of genius.'[28] In other words, what he strongly approved of was, *ipso facto*, Germanic; what he profoundly rejected was, in accordance with the same definition, Jewish.

In the autumn of 1909, some months before Rosenberg's seventeenth birthday, he went with an aunt to visit his guardian, where several other relatives had foregathered and were gossiping together. The lad was bored, went to a book shelf, picked up a catalogue and read: '*The Foundations of the Nineteenth Century:*

H. S. Chamberlain.... I felt electrified; I wrote down the title and went straight to the bookshop.' The book was not in stock, but in due course two volumes arrived from Germany. 'Another world rose up before me: Hellas, Judah, Rome. And to everything I assented inwardly – again and yet again. And then I ordered Wellhausen's *History of Israel and Judah*, Bernhard Stade's *Bible Research* and other books of this kind.... The political events that happened later therefore seemed to me a necessary corollary.'[29] So began an influence which remained strong within him throughout his life. In October 1923 he accompanied Hitler to Wahnfried, Wagner's old house at Bayreuth, where his widow, Cosima, was still living with her son-in-law. Chamberlain was paralysed, but something in him responded to Hitler, to whom he wrote next day, 'At one stroke you have transformed the state of my soul.'[30] As for Rosenberg, he had already at that date partly finished the book which, he intended, should do for the Third Reich what Chamberlain's book had done for the Second.

Sailing in summer and skating in winter were young Rosenberg's outdoor occupations; apart from an atmosphere of ill health and deprivation in the house of his widowed father, the boy seems to have had the normal upbringing of a child of the lower bourgeoisie with no more than average talents. It was on the skating rink that he met his first love, Hilda, who was wearing a brown costume and fur jacket and a hat with a feather in it. Hilda's father, Josef Leesmann, owned a local canning factory and belonged to a higher stratum of the bourgeoisie; he was proud of his title Kommerzienrat ('Trade Councillor'), which was a title acquired by purchase. Hilda, who was the older by one year, studied dancing, played the piano and introduced Rosenberg not only to the music of Russian composers, such as Borodin, but also to Tolstoy's *War and Peace,* and *Anna Karenina.* One day she brought him a copy of Nietzsche's *Thus Spake Zarathustra;* he admits in his memoir that he could not make much of it. The book that moved a whole generation in Germany 'left him cold'.[31] Later he tried to assimilate Nietzsche, but succeeded only in distorting him.

As a boy, he had already begun a course of reading that was highly selective and informed by strong prejudices. What we know of the reading habits of Hitler indicates a similar process.

Hitler and Rosenberg both found in the world around them much that aroused their distaste and contempt; both sought in the past signs of a redemptive force that, they hoped, would dominate the future. As heirs to German blood living as young men outside the confines of the Second Reich, both identified this force with a racial factor that, in their view, had intermittently emerged in history and then, in the face of hostile influences, subsided again. Both men admired H. S. Chamberlain, who had given to these hostile influences the general designation 'chaos of peoples' (Voelkerchaos). In mixed races, according to this theory, the worse characteristics drove out the better ones, to which the term Ayran (or sometimes Nordic or Germanic) was applied. Nobody explained to Rosenberg at an impressionable age that the word 'Aryan' applied not to race, but to language. In the words of Max Mueller, 'Aryans are those who speak Aryan languages, whatever their colour, whatever their blood. In calling them Aryans we predicate nothing of them except that the grammar of their language is Aryan. . . .'[32]

Rosenberg at a comparatively early age became interested in philosophy, which lay outside his prescribed studies. At first he studied chiefly Schopenhauer, who was also much admired by Hitler, and Kant, the Koenigsberg Professor, who was something of a 'hero of culture' to all North Germans with academic pretensions. While still a young man, Rosenberg also began to read Indian philosophy and religious literature; here he parted company from Hitler, whose interest in India was always restricted to the means by which the British had for so long maintained their rule there. But Rosenberg read – and presumably misunderstood – the Vedas and other Indian religious writings, which he ascribed to 'the time of the immigration of the warlike Aryans'. He naturally admired the caste system, which in his view enabled the Aryans to rule the roost, until at last 'the organic circle of life, applying not only to the Aryan Indians, but also to the indigenous inhabitants, broke down'.[33] The ruin of the good blood meant the ruin of all; Voelkerchaos had come again.

Rosenberg, who always regretted that he had not learnt Greek at school, also shared Hitler's enthusiasm for ancient Greece. At the end of his life he wrote: 'The German has always sought Greece from the time that he first came consciously into contact with the Greek heritage. . . .'[34] The opportunity to emphasize this link was seized upon by the Nazis with mystical enthusiasm at the time of the celebration in Germany of the Olympic Games in 1936, to which Hitler's friend, Leni Riefenstahl, devoted one of her most spectacular films. Rosenberg has described how in his own studies he tried to polarise the affinity between Germany and Greece by placing the *Nibelungenlied* alongside the *Iliad* and also comparing the principles underlying the construction of Greek temples with those of medieval cathedrals. From his youth up, he was obsessed by the need to convert into theory the knowledge gleaned from his selective reading; but he never acquired the assiduity and objectivity necessary for true research. He remained all his life a 'deeply half-educated man'.[35]

At seventeen he passed his school-leaving examination and went to the Technical University at Riga to study architecture. At about the same time Hilda was sent to the Dalcroze school of rhythmic dancing in Geneva and later moved to Paris to be trained as a ballet dancer. She must have done much to stimulate Rosenberg's interest in cultural life, which was more all-embracing at this period of his life than at any time after he settled in Munich and became finally separated from her. In Riga he turned his attention to the question of joining one of the student societies. There were three student societies favoured by German-speaking students in the University; the most aristocratic of these went in for duelling. Rosenberg decided against this one and instead joined the Corps Rubonia, in which he met some of those who remained his friends later in Germany, including another artist, Otto v. Kursell, and Arno Schickedanz. In the Corps he was nick-named 'The Philosopher' and it was not long before he was called upon to give a lecture; he chose as his subject, 'The Jewish Question'. In retrospect, he regarded his treatment of the subject as inadequate; anti-semitism was latent in Riga, but acts against Jews were undertaken more out of high spirits than 'from any deep understanding of the problem'.[36] In the polyglot community of Riga there may have been some discrimination against Jews, but they were spared so far the full impact of the racialist idea that a man could demonstrate his essential Germanness by acts undertaken against Jews, the anti-race (Gegenrasse). F. T. Hart, the official biographer of Rosenberg, conceded that he only heard of the new race teaching when he came to Germany.[37] In 1931 Rosenberg and his friends initiated an enquiry among racially acceptable alumni of the Corps about the attitude to be adopted towards their less fortunate brethren. One reply bluntly contended that the affairs of the Corps should not be mixed up with questions of race; another wrote to remind Schickedanz that the Rubonia used to admit not only Russians, Letts, Estonians and Turks, but even Jews.[38] Such was the Golden Age before 1914.

In the summer of 1911 Rosenberg went for the first time to South Germany with his two paternal aunts.* They spent most of their time at the spa of Woerrishoefen, where Rosenberg wandered through the woods and read more Indian philosophy; they also visited Munich, Weimar and Nuremberg, where his life ended thirty-five years later. He claimed in his memoir that he almost decided to study in the Reich, but allowed himself to be persuaded to return with his aunts to Riga. An experience when visiting the famous baroque monastery of Kloster Ettal, near Oberammergau, gave him a horror of Roman Catholicism, which he vividly recalled nineteen years later in a conversation with Hitler. He had seen behind protective glass the skeleton of a saint with gold rings on the bones and a gold crown on the skull. This, to him, was 'an Ashanti religion', far worse than anything to be seen in Russia.[39]

His only other trip abroad as a young man was a three weeks visit to Paris to see Hilda in the summer before the war; it was presumably this visit that later gave colour to the charge that he had been a French agent. The young couple spent most of their time visiting Notre Dame and other old churches in Paris, as well as the Louvre and other famous galleries and museums. Rosenberg got home well before the frontiers closed and the great armies mobilised, but Hilda almost left it too late and she had to leave some of her luggage behind. On 10 April 1915 in Riga they got married, in spite of the reluctance of her father to acquire a son-in-law who had not finished his studies.[40] It was from the start a disjointed marriage; they spent the summer together and she then returned to her father's house in Reval, while he went back to Riga.

---

* The statement in *Letzte Aufzeichnungen* that they went to Munich because Alexander Rosenberg had just died there was presumably another attempt to mislead the Russians.

Later that year, when German advances threatened the Baltic provinces, the University was evacuated to Moscow, whilst Hilda's father moved his business to St Petersburg, so they still could not lead a normal married life. They came together again in the summer of 1916 in a rented cottage at Sichodnya near Moscow; it was here that work on the *Mythus* was first begun. Their lives were still untouched by politics; Rosenberg's reading at this time consisted of Dostoievsky, Goethe and Balzac. In Moscow he had rented a room cheaply from a Russian couple, so that he could save money to take lessons in portrait painting. Students, unless Reserve Officers, were not being called up. In St Petersburg Hilda was teaching the Dalcroze method of dancing, and beginning to suffer from the severe climate. The Russian revolution cast no shadow before it, so far as Rosenberg was concerned. He recorded later in his memoir, 'If I am to be honest, I must say that it was only at a very late stage that the social question in Russia began to occupy my mind.'[41]

In one of his early books he described the impression made on him by the first risings. 'In 1917 I was living in a settlement of villas one hour by train out of Moscow. At the end of February came news of attempted strikes and bread riots and one day it happened – revolution. I went early one morning to Moscow. . . . Hundreds of thousands of people filled the squares and streets, hysterical joy reigned, people wept on the shoulders of complete strangers, the psychosis had gripped millions. . . .'[42] Although elsewhere he wrote of the relief generally experienced when Tsarism and 'corrupted officialdom' were overthrown,[43] he seems from the start to have resented the anarchy implicit in the revolutionary situation. During the summer a more personal episode occurred, which gave a specific direction to his subsequent judgments and confirmed his prejudices. As he was reading in his room, 'a stranger entered, laid a book on the table and silently vanished. The cover of the book bore in Russian the words from the twenty-fourth chapter of Matthew: "He is near, He is hard by the door".'[44] The author of this book, which came into the young student's hands in so solemn a manner, was Sergei Nilus; its appendices included the famous anti-semitic forgery, *The Protocols of the Wise Men of Zion,* which made so great an impression on Hitler and many others, as well as upon Rosenberg, who later re-edited it.\* A fuller discussion of this important document will be found in Chapter 4. That it should have come as a revelation to Rosenberg need not surprise us. He was a dreamy young man, politically immature, but rooted in the prejudices of the community in which he had been brought up. He found himself in the capital city of a great Empire which seemed suddenly in the throes of disintegration. Nothing could be more natural than that he should accept at face value the facile explanation that the collapse, the social and economic causes of which were obscure to him, was due to a vast subterranean conspiracy, organised by Europe's perennial scapegoats, the Jews.

If this was indeed his reaction, the question may be asked, why this episode finds no place in his published writings. The probable answer is that what he wrote as a young man in Munich contains very little autobiographical material; later, as the counter-attack was mounted against the peddlers of this forgery, he must have become increasingly reticent about its influence on him. It is one thing to experience a political revelation in one's youth; it is quite another to confess, as an established political commentator, that one was taken in by a fraud. In December 1939 he sent Rudolf Hess a copy of the *Protocols,* adding, 'By the way, I advise you not to make use of the *Protocols* themselves. . . . Such use could only involve a long series of debates, which are not to be desired and could in any case lead to no result.'[45] After the conquest of Poland there was an odd echo from the past; a certain Sergius Nilus, claiming to be the son of the propagator of the famous forgery, wrote to Rosenberg from Warsaw, offering his help in purging Poland of Jews.[46] The letter appears to have gone unanswered.

Later that summer Rosenberg's mind was distracted from politics and architecture by the state of his wife's health. The hard winter and poor food had brought on the first symptoms of the disease of the lungs that would in due course prove fatal. Her family had packed her off to Crimea to recuperate and Rosenberg, his studies nearly at an end, decided to follow. Though neither of them knew it, these few weeks were to be the Indian summer of their life together. They went on an excursion to Yalta, where the fate of the Third Reich was one day to be decided, and

\* *Die Protokolle der Weisen von Zion und die juedische Weltpolitik* (Munich, 1923).

at New Simeis watched the moon rise over the Black Sea. He remembered that a Greek colony had once flourished there and that Gothic tribes had survived in the peninsula until the sixteenth century. He was eagerly studying Houston Stewart Chamberlain's books on Goethe and Kant, and read aloud most of the latter to his ailing wife. But the government of Kerensky was more and more precarious and they finally decided it would be safer to go back to Reval.

The journey across Russia and back made a great impression on Rosenberg. 'Travelling on into limitless space, one could feel the immensity of the East in one's whole body.'[47] It was this experience that later convinced him, unlike the other Nazi leaders, that Russia could only be conquered by using particularist forces against the Muscovite core, overcoming it by means of alliance with the subjugated ethnic groups. No doubt Hitler, who ignored this thesis to his cost, got tired of hearing about it. He observed to Hermann Rauschning, 'Have you not noticed that Germans who have lived for a long time in Russia can never again be Germans? The huge spaces have fascinated them. After all, Rosenberg is rabid against the Russians only because they would not allow him to be a Russian.'[48] As Rosenberg travelled, Nilus' slow poison worked in him; three years later he wrote that, during his travels at this time he had personally observed that ninety per cent of all the Bolsheviks whom he saw were Jews – and carried copies of 'Pravda'.[49]

F. T. Hart maintained that Rosenberg returned to Reval in the hope that German troops would soon march in and he would be able to enlist. This is improbable; chaotic as the situation was, he still wished to secure his diploma as an architect and in January 1918 he went to Moscow for his final examination. There is irony in the fact that the design that he submitted for his diploma was for a crematorium. It must have appealed to the examining professor who not only passed Rosenberg but asked him to stay on in Moscow as his assistant. This was indeed a parting of the ways. Rosenberg in his memoir allows us to assume that his rejection of the offer was inspired by German patriotism. It may be so; in any case it must have been clear to him that Russia had lost the war, whoever else might be about to win it. Two weeks after he got back to Reval with his diploma the Germans at last arrived – a famous Hanoverian regiment – and he volunteered for service. His offer was, of course, rejected by the military authorities because he was not of German nationality.

At this crucial phase of his career we begin to have sources of information to corroborate what he later chose to reveal and his denials of what his calumniators alleged. When the Munich police in the time of the Weimar Republic were compiling a dossier on him, they obtained reports from German officials who at the relevant time had been with the occupation force in Estonia. These sources bear out his statement that from June to September 1918 he was employed as a teacher by the German administration.[50] He also tried to make some money by holding an exhibition of his drawings. Meanwhile Hilda's health had deteriorated and her family obtained permission for her to go to Badenweiler in the Black Forest; later she moved to Arosa in Switzerland. It was, in effect, the end of their marriage.

In November came the Armistice; Rosenberg wept when he heard the news. By the end of the month the German troops were in retreat from the most easterly of the Baltic provinces. The Reich was in agony, wrote Rosenberg later in his memoir; he decided to share its fate and not 'stand between two fronts. . . . I abandoned my home in order to acquire a Fatherland.'[51] He left Reval on the last day of November 1918, travelling in the same cattle truck as Pastor Hahn. He had burned his boats earlier that day (according to the police report) by addressing a public meeting on the Jewish question.[52] Other sources amplify the report by adding that the meeting took place at the Town Hall and that, when he spoke of the connection between Judaism and Bolshevism and the danger to Germany, the owner of a big Jewish warehouse staged a counter-demonstration by leading out of the hall all the Jews who were present. The son of this man is said to have been the first to hoist the Red Flag in Reval, when Russian troops marched in in 1940.[53] It was thus in Rosenberg's birthplace, which he was not to see again until May 1942, that he first gave public utterance to the supposed identification between Bolsheviks and Jews, which was to become his leitmotiv and to play so important a role in Nazi policies and ideology.

# 2 Rosenberg and the Birth of the NSDAP

Rosenberg's immediate destination was Berlin; but he stayed there only long enough to see the defeated troops marching along Unter den Linden on their way to demobilisation. 'It is a picture I have never forgotten,' he wrote in his memoir.[1] Why did he leave Berlin? Hart's laconic observation that conditions there were not suited to the political activity that he intended does not carry conviction. Rosenberg himself was more candid when he later admitted that up to this time he had no thought of taking up politics. He was thinking more about how to earn his living. He had written from Reval to the well-known architect, Peter Behrens, who lived in Berlin and trained some of those who later constituted the 'Bauhaus' movement.[2] Although Rosenberg received a friendly reply, he decided not to visit Behrens, but went on to Munich. In later years the Bauhaus was to become an object of his hostility as Nazi cultural expert. Munich drew him because of recollections of the holiday he had spent in Bavaria in 1911; moreover some of his Baltic friends had turned up there, notably one of his former teachers, Ernst Thode, and his fellow Rubonian, Kursell. If it also occurred to him that in South Germany he would be nearer to his sick wife, he did not say so.

Bavaria, where he arrived at the beginning of 1919, was having her share of the troubles besetting all the German states (soon under the Weimar Constitution to become Laender) in the aftermath of defeat and revolution. Traditional jealousy of Prussia had led Bavarians at the end of the war to blame Prussian leadership for impending defeat, and Crown Prince Rupprecht of Bavaria had been an advocate of a negotiated peace. Others, discreetly encouraged by France, believed that, if Bavaria asserted her independence, she would get off more lightly. Even before the

Armistice was signed, a short-lived alliance of peasants, Munich proletariat and returning soldiers and deserters had thrown out the ancient royal house of Wittelsbach, the first to go in all Germany. An Independent Social Democrat, named Kurt Eisner, proclaimed the Bavarian Republic, before the German Republic had been announced in Berlin.

Whilst Eisner played with separatist ideas and spoke freely of German war guilt, Roman Catholic, monarchist and conservative forces, which had been caught off balance, began to rally. One centre of this growing resistance was Army HQ in Munich, where Major-General Ritter v. Epp and Captain Ernst Roehm were determined that the rot should stop and nothing further occur to sully the honour of the Reich and Reichswehr. Roehm was a fighting man, not in any sense an idealist, but he needed a flag under which to fight and a clarion call to bring in the recruits. His spare time was often devoted to touring the beer cellars of Munich with his gang, starting up the national anthem and giving violent assistance to anyone who failed to spring immediately to his feet. The army kept him well supplied with toughs and with money.

The second local centre of counter-revolution was of a more exclusive and conspiratorial kind. The patriotic Germanic Order, which had been created in 1912, had a Bavarian 'Province' under Freiherr Rudolf v. Sebottendorff, which disguised itself under the name Thule Society. The name had overtones of a legendary centre of pure Nordic influence in the remote North; those who had Jewish blood were excluded from membership. Those who were accepted underwent an initiation ceremony, which featured prominently exhortations to 'Remember that you are a German!' and 'Keep your blood pure!'. Influential members of Munich society belonged and his association with it must have been a godsend to Rosenberg, a friendless, penniless refugee in a country that had not yet accepted him as a citizen. Rosenberg in his memoir held to the 'cover story'; the Society was 'a club, which concerned itself with Germanic prehistory and rejected Judaism, but without being politically active'.[3] In fact, the Society was not only active, but had made a shrewd diagnosis of what the political situation required; it needed a new movement, which would attract the working class away from the pernicious doctrines of Karl Marx. The traditional recipe for this in Germany, since the time of Court

1. *Reval (Tallinn) at the turn of the century: 'German soldiers thought they must be in Luebeck, not in Russia'*

2. *The student in Russia*

3. *The editor of*
Voelkischer Beobachter:
*Rosenberg in Munich, 1923*

Chaplain Adolf Stoecker in the late nineteenth century, had been a limited amount of State Socialism, heavily diluted with anti-semitism. But how was a movement of this kind to be started?

Roehm and Sebottendorff independently became interested at about the same time in the 'Free Committee for a German Workers' Peace', which had been set up by a locksmith, Anton Drexler, under the influence of the patriotic Fatherland Front. In January 1919 Karl Harrer of the Thule Society moved in as Chairman and rechristened the group the 'German Workers' Party' (DAP). The young party, which was never as small and destitute as Hitler later made out, soon acquired an economic expert in the person of Gottfried Feder, whose views were anti-capitalist, but not dangerously so. Prescribed anti-semitic reading included Sebottendorff's *Muenchener* (later *Voelkischer*) *Beobachter* and *In Good German* (*Auf Gut Deutsch*), edited by Dietrich Eckart, who specialised in attacking Jewish war profiteers.

Eckart's background, like Feder's, was bourgeois. His father had been a lawyer, but Dietrich had drifted into Bohemian life in Munich and Berlin. He had become addicted to morphia and at one period was confined to an asylum, where he had induced some of the inmates to join him in putting on a play. He may have been moved to do so by the madhouse scene in *Peer Gynt*, since he had a great admiration for Ibsen and had done a free translation of *Peer Gynt*. He was convinced that his lack of commercial success was due to the boycott of his plays by Jewish-owned theatres and newspapers. He brought to the accumulated political wisdom of the Thule Society the belief that the hour for a great charismatic leader had struck, an idea currently propagated in Berlin by Moeller van den Bruck and his circle. In 1919 he was fifty-one; good living, drugs and hard drinking had affected his health, but he still had the restless energy and sophistication to make an immediate and profound impression on such people as an immature Baltic emigré with a diploma in architecture, and a politically minded Austrian, who was about to be released from the German army with the rank of Corporal.

Since his arrival in Munich Rosenberg had been dependent on a Relief Committee, which arranged accommodation for refugees as well as a communal kitchen, to which they came daily bringing their own spoons. Another Committee was raising volunteers to

C

defend the Baltic States against the Red Army. This at last put Rosenberg in mind of his sick wife; the Committee agreed, in the light of his responsibilities, that he could not be expected to go. Instead he spent his days in art galleries and public libraries; he was reading not only Indian philosophy, but everything he could find about Jewish history and religious literature, such as the Talmud. Walking along the street one day, he saw a familiar name on a billboard: 'Edith v. Schrenck: Dancing'. She had worked with Hilda in the Dalcroze school in St Petersburg. He went to see her, mentioned that he would like to write about his experiences in Russia and was advised to see Eckart, whose newspaper was familiar to her. It proved to be the decisive contact of Rosenberg's life, because even before he met Hitler it started him on his career as a publicist in the cause of political extremism.

There was nothing in his life up to this point that had marked him out for such a career. He had had no experience as a journalist and no particular gifts as an orator; indeed he never became a very effective or inspiring speaker. His mind had hitherto inclined towards art and philosophy; at the end of his long political life, when he came to write his memoir, he admitted that all the time he had felt 'a quiet regret that he had not kept entirely to painting'.[4] Why then did he come to such a prompt and drastic decision? The answer is that he was in acute need and even, as we shall see shortly, in some danger. He was a refugee in a land which, for all his claims to German blood, was alien to him. He had to identify himself with some element in society that could protect him and foster his career, even if that element represented extreme political views. Moreover, to this element he had something to offer, namely his first-hand experience of the Russian revolution, which was anathema to them. The career that ended in a condemned cell in Nuremberg began with the decision to peddle the only wares he had for sale.

He afterwards related how his first words to Eckart were: 'Can you use a fighter against Jerusalem?' Eckart laughed: 'Certainly!'[5] But he took the precaution of asking whether Rosenberg had written anything. Not only had he done so, but he had brought it with him. It consisted of his impressions of the disastrous impact on Russia of the destructive forces of Judaism and Bolshevism and was published under the title *The Russian-Jewish Revolution*. This fitted in well with a series which Eckart was publishing concurrently in his paper under the general title, 'Jewry Within Us and Without', in which the Jews were charged with seeking to destroy the world by depriving it of its soul ('Entseelung der Welt').[6] During the next few months Rosenberg expanded his impressions and gave them an historical perspective to justify his title, *The Trace of the Jew through Changing Times*. He completed it in December 1919 and it was published early in the following year. All the essential features of his anti-semitism take shape in this crude little work. The Jew is described as the source of both anarchism and Communism, though a footnote indicates that Rosenberg was uneasily aware of a certain incompatibility between these two forms of political activity. The Jew is also the destructive force in cultural life, because he represents materialism: 'The Jew can do nothing with myth and symbol....'[7] This first book displays none of the Anglophilia that later animated Rosenberg; on the contrary, London is described as the centre of world Jewry as well as 'the land in which Freemasonry itself originated'.[8] Lord Northcliffe was included among leading English Jews, though in later years, after Lord Rothermere had shown his sympathy with Nazism, this reference was omitted when reprinting. More significant, however, for the development of Nazi ideology is the remarkable sentence, 'The Black, the Red and the Gold Internationals represent the dreams of Jewish philosophers from Ezra, Ezekiel and Nehemia to Marx, Rothschild and Trotsky.'[9] The Germanic victims of this ill-assorted group were priest-ridden, riven by anarchy and oppressed by 'finance-capital'.

This composite image of the ideological enemy as the Jew, both rich and poor, allied to the priest, eventually became a standard target for attack by Nazis; but at first it represented little more than the prejudices of Eckart and Rosenberg, for whom anti-Christian sentiment was almost as strong as anti-semitism. Rosenberg later recounted how, as soon as he arrived in Munich, he began to sense, in a way that native Bavarians were scarcely able to, the hostility of the Roman Catholic Church to the concept of a Greater Germany, which would embrace both Catholic Austria and most of Catholic Poland. 'I, as a stranger, felt this atmosphere, which emanated from the Nunciate...everything was in the service of completely temporal rulership.'[10] Bavaria was allowed by the Weimar Republic to maintain diplomatic relations with the Vatican; the Nuncio in Munich at that time was the future Cardinal Pacelli, who became Pope Pius XII. Rosenberg believed that it was the aim of the Vatican, working through the Roman Catholic Bavarian People's Party (BVP), to create an Austro-Bavarian South German State, free from the domination of Prussia. He wrote: 'Here in Munich I felt compelled to take decisive issue with the world of Rome.'[11] In 1920 he published in Eckart's paper a series of articles on Jesuitism, in which he claimed to have traced 'its inner and outer relationship to the Judaism of the Talmud'.[12]

In adopting this attitude at such an early date, Eckart and Rosenberg were a long way ahead of Hitler. This had nothing to do with the fact that Hitler was, at least nominally, a Roman Catholic; indeed nobody outside the Papal Curia at any time attached much importance to his ostensible adherence to the Church. He masked his cynicism about religion for political reasons. In *Mein Kampf* he analysed the failure of the Austrian Pan-German party of Georg v. Schoenerer to achieve its objectives and ascribed it in part to his having involved himself in religious controversy. 'The policy of the Pan-German leaders in deciding to carry through a difficult fight against the Catholic Church can be explained only by attributing it to an inadequate understanding of the spiritual character of the people.'[13] Hitler wished to avoid making the same mistake and over the next fifteen years we shall see signs of friction between him and Rosenberg on this issue. Hitler modified his tactics as his power grew and at the end of his life there was little, if anything, to distinguish his anti-religious views from those of his party ideologist, though the Fuehrer was always more reticent in public.

There can be little doubt that at this period Rosenberg received considerable help from Eckart. Hanfstaengl – admittedly a prejudiced source – maintained that even some years later Rosenberg, whom he detested, still could not write grammatical German.[14] In any case, Eckart was a literary figure with a style of his own. Their collaboration continued in *Russia's Gravedigger,** for which Rosenberg provided the introduction, again linking Judaism with Bolshevism, whilst his friend, Kursell, did the drawings and Eckart the polemical verse. It was not politics all

* *Der Totengraeber Russlands* (Munich, 1920).

the time. Rosenberg has recounted in his memoir how, on the second occasion they met, Eckart took him to lunch and talked to him about the character of Peer Gynt, whom Rosenberg later described as 'the mirror-reflection of his [Eckart's] soul'.[15] Rosenberg, in his turn, spoke of 'the essence of the Gothic'; it cannot have been a very lively luncheon.[16] Their collaboration also took active forms; Eckart composed a pamphlet, *To All Workingmen*, which he and Rosenberg distributed all over Munich from a taxi.

Munich was still in a state of intermittent uproar. In February a young officer, Count Arco-Valley, who had been rejected by the Thule Society because of Jewish blood, decided to vindicate himself by shooting Eisner, who was Jewish. The murdered man was followed in office by the Social Democrat, Johannes Hoffmann, but he failed to stabilise the situation and early in April was driven out of Munich by a People's Soviet, in which Jews, such as Eugen Levine, Tobias Axelrod, Ernst Toller and Max Levin, were prominent. The last-mentioned succeeded in escaping to USSR when the counter-revolution prevailed. This was organised by General Ritter v. Epp with the help of paramilitary groups known as Free Corps; one of these was the Oberland League, which was subsidised by the ubiquitous Thule Society. As the Free Corps neared Munich at the end of April, supporters of the Red regime got out of hand and seven members of the seditious Society were killed, including the Prinz v. Thurn und Taxis, Baron v. Seydlitz and Graefin v. Westarp. When Epp marched in on 1 May, vicious reprisals were taken; many members of the Soviet, including Levine, were shot and a group of over fifty Russian prisoners of war awaiting repatriation was also liquidated.

The time and place were highly unpropitious for all Russians, who ran the risk of being shot at by one side or the other. Rosenberg had taken his stand on the evening of the day on which the People's Soviet was proclaimed. In the turmoil he climbed on to a parapet near the Rathaus in the centre of Munich and denounced to all and sundry the madness of Red revolution. It would be the height of folly, he told his impromptu audience, to set up in Germany 'an all-destroying dictatorship'.[17] Alarmed by his own temerity, he did not return to his lodgings, but sought out Eckart who, scenting trouble, took him to a hide-out in the Isar valley, where they weathered the storm. After it was all over,

Rosenberg, as an impecunious Russian refugee, had difficulty in securing permission to remain in Munich; but the respected and reactionary publisher, J. F. Lehmann, who was a member of the Thule Society, vouched for him. Even as an alien, however, he was allowed to join the Einwohnerwehr, or Home Guard, set up by the right wing, who were determined not to be caught napping again by the forces of the left. Bavaria increasingly became a citadel of reaction, as Free Corps units from all over Germany found it a haven for their anti-Left and anti-Entente activities.

Some understanding of these events is necessary, if the success of propaganda arising from Rosenberg's identification of Jews with Bolsheviks is to be fully comprehensible. Even allowing for the desperation and irrationality prevailing at the time, it still seems strange that men of some education should have persuaded themselves, and a substantial number of others with less power of discrimination, that a man's race determined his political beliefs and that Jews in Germany, constituting less than one per cent of the population,* many of them residents of long standing, were a threat to the stability of the country. It is true that Germany had a larger Jewish population than any other highly industrialised country. Moreover, the first two decades of this century had seen a considerable influx of Jews from the Russian and Austrian Empires who were opprobriously referred to as Eastern Jews (Ostjuden). A majority of them settled in cities, where Jews already constituted a larger proportion of the population than in the Reich as a whole; indeed in Berlin and Frankfurt the Jews formed over four per cent of the population.[18] This factor, together with the predominance of Jews in certain professions (of which more later), contributed to the impression that the Reich was becoming overrun by Jews. The identification of this supposed threat with that of Bolshevism, which was Rosenberg's main thesis, was made more plausible by ocular evidence of the leading part played by certain prominent Jews in revolutionary activity. This was not only the case in Munich; the short-lived Soviet Republic in Hungary was also dominated by the Jewish leaders Bela Kun and Szamuely.

* According to the 1925 census, the number of those practising the Jewish faith was 0.9 per cent of the population; this percentage does not include Jews who had become Christian.

During the latter part of May 1919, whilst Eckart and Rosenberg were getting *In Good German* back onto the printing press, they received a visit from Drexler and accepted his invitation to address the German Workers' Party (DAP) on Bolshevism and the Jewish question. At this meeting, held in a small public house, Rosenberg, as he later claimed, first heard Hitler's name mentioned; but he did not see him until he subsequently heard him speak at the inn 'Zum Deutschen Reich' to some forty or fifty people.[19] While it is very probable that Rosenberg did indeed attend this latter meeting, it was not the first time that he saw Hitler, nor is it at all likely that he could have heard of him at any meeting before 12 September 1919, when Hitler – at that time unknown outside Reichswehr circles – first went to a meeting of the German Workers' Party. Why Rosenberg later gave out this account, which was followed by his official biographer, is unclear. It may have been meant to conceal the extent to which the DAP was already a going concern when Hitler came on the scene. When all was over and Rosenberg was a prisoner of the Allies, he wrote that he met Hitler when the latter came to see Eckart.[20] This version was confirmed by Hitler in a letter which he wrote to Rosenberg on the occasion of the latter's fiftieth birthday: 'I still remember the day we got to know one another in Dietrich Eckart's home.'[21] We learn from Rosenberg that at this first meeting the two men discussed the disintegrating effect of Bolshevism, which undermined the state in the same way that Christianity had corroded the Roman Empire. This was one of the themes running at that time in Eckart's paper.

Many pages might at this point be devoted to speculation about the extent to which Eckart exerted a formative influence upon Hitler and Rosenberg, as well as about the influence of the two younger men upon one another. Since these speculations would not be susceptible of proof, we shall confine ourselves at this stage to a few specific remarks about the relationship between the three men. At the end of *Mein Kampf* Hitler praised Eckart for having 'devoted his life to reawakening his and our people'.[22] But apart from an appreciative mention of Feder's economic theories, Hitler did not admit that his own contemporaries in Munich had influenced him at all; to have done so would have detracted from his claim to be the political philosopher, as well as the political leader, of the NSDAP. His insistence that 'In Vienna I acquired the foundations of a Weltanschauung'[23] has led one later commentator to conclude that it was virtually complete by the time he came to Munich in 1913. This is not a tenable view. In June 1919, when the Reichswehr in Bavaria put Hitler through a course of political indoctrination, he was a man of thirty, he had left school at sixteen, after studying in a very desultory way, and had then drifted along the fringe of the underworld of Vienna before joining the German Army, in which he attained the rank of Corporal. To ask us to believe that such a man, however gifted, already had 'a view of life and a definite outlook on the world', to which he afterwards added 'very little',[24] is to ask us to believe an absurdity. Admittedly Hitler's anti-semitic and anti-Marxist prejudices may have been fully formed; but these, as we shall hope to show, did not constitute the whole of Nazi ideology. It is more plausible to assume that after 1919 Hitler and Rosenberg, like any other young men, continued to absorb certain influences from those with whom they associated and from each other. That these influences acted in the direction of intensifying their prejudices and making them more systematic will become apparent when we come to discuss the ideology itself.

Rosenberg naturally had less reason to be coy about the influence exerted on him by his Fuehrer, though he could never bring himself to praise *Mein Kampf*. Kurt Luedecke who knew both men described Rosenberg as being 'no great admirer of the Hitler intellect. I recall his condescending appraisal of Hitler's *Mein Kampf*: "A freshly written book".'[25] In public and on the record, however, Rosenberg added his own paeans of adulation for his Fuehrer; this was his account, written in 1934, of the impact on himself of the meeting at which he first heard Hitler speak: 'Here I saw a German front-line soldier embarking on this struggle in a manner as clear as it was convincing, counting on himself alone with the courage of a free man. It was that that after the first fifteen minutes already drew me to Adolf Hitler. . . .'[26] It was a bond which, sometimes taut, sometimes slack, was to endure for over twenty-five years. After it had been broken by death, Rosenberg could still write, 'Getting to know him determined my own fate and merged it in the fate of the whole German nation.'[27]

Towards the end of 1919 Rosenberg became a member of the German Workers' Party with the membership number 623.* Eckart had gone to live at Nymphenburg on the outskirts of Munich and Rosenberg followed him there. He had settled down as hack writer and researcher for the party. In Hitler's first report on his activities to Army HQ he had written, 'Anti-semitism as a political movement cannot, and should not, be determined by moments of emotion, but by knowledge of the facts.'[28] It became a large part of Rosenberg's work to supply the required facts and stitch them together into short books, articles and pamphlets. He was writing not only for Eckart's paper, but for two other periodicals, J. F. Lehmann's *Deutschlands Erneuerung* and R. J. Gorsleben's *Deutsche Republik*. Another right-wing publisher, Dr. E. Boepple, who had issued his first book, also published in 1920 his *Immortality in the Talmud*.† In the same year he translated a book by the French anti-semitic writer Gougenot de Mousseaux.‡ He claimed no share in drafting the programme of the party, which was announced by Hitler at the meeting in February 1920 at which the NSDAP acquired its name.

The next major step was the acquisition of a newspaper. It appeared only twice a week and each issue sold on average only 8,000 copies, but it was a beginning. The *Munich Observer* (Muenchener Beobachter) had been owned by the old-established publisher Franz Eher, who died in June 1918. In July 1918 it was acquired by Sebottendorff and one year later changed its name to *Voelkischer Beobachter (VB)* or 'Racist Observer'. In mid-December 1920 a grant of army funds enabled the NSDAP to acquire a controlling interest in the paper, using Eckart as intermediary. By this time Sebottendorff had left Bavaria and the importance of the Thule Society under other direction had declined.[29] In 1921, when Hitler became undisputed master of the NSDAP, he put in his former Sergeant, Max Amann, to manage the publishing company, which was in financial difficulties; friction soon developed with the editorial staff, who laboured under the economies imposed on them. Eckart had become chief editor and had made Rosenberg his assistant; but Rosenberg's responsibilities increased, as Eckart,

---

* Numbers started at 500. Hitler was No. 555. See *Fruehgeschichte*, p.106.
† *Unmoral im Talmud*, A. Rosenberg (Munich, 1920).
‡ *Le Juif, le Judaisme et la Judaisation des Peuples Chrétiens* (Paris, 1869).

burdened by matrimonial problems and ill-health, grew less and less regular in attendance. Rosenberg was soon sharing the office of chief editor, but was by no means master in the house; Hitler and Amann brought in as leader writer another young ex-soldier, Hermann Esser, with whom Rosenberg was soon at loggerheads. Esser was a loud-mouthed anti-intellectual, who modelled his oratorical style on that of Hitler; one can imagine his comments on leading articles by Rosenberg such as two appearing in the summer of 1921, which quoted from Lagarde and Spengler.

There was one field, however, in which Rosenberg could claim precedence; he spoke Russian and knew Russia; he had no difficulty in becoming the party's expert on the East. It was a time of confused fighting on Germany's eastern frontiers, which had not been finally determined by the Treaty of Versailles. Munich was full of White Russian refugees, still hoping that with the help of the Free Corps, or even of a reactionary German government, if one came to power in Berlin, the Bolshevik regime might be overthrown. Some of these groups had money and money was one of the crying needs of the young NSDAP. Moreover, now that the party had a newspaper, it was more necessary for it to take up a consistent attitude towards Germany's eastern neighbours. Rosenberg's supposed expertise in this field added to his standing in the group around Hitler. He was from the first strongly opposed to the so-called 'National Bolshevists' in Germany, who believed that Soviet Russia would prove a better ally than any of the capitalist powers, with which the Reich had so recently been at war. Rosenberg's close connection with the *VB* enabled him to oppose this trend. In January 1921 Rosenberg had a leader in the *VB*, which set a target for Nazi policy that, through many vicissitudes, was never really abandoned. 'And when the time comes and the storm is brewing over the eastern marches of Germany, it will be a case of collecting 100,000 men who are prepared to sacrifice their lives there.... Even if Lenin occupies Poland, there will still be time to liberate Poland. What is certain is that the Russian Army will be driven back across its frontiers after a second Tannenberg.'[30] In this field Rosenberg was quite prepared to cross swords with Hitler. In his attacks on the Treaty of Versailles, Hitler had made a speciality of explaining and defending the Treaty of Brest-Litovsk, imposed in 1918 by

Germany on Russia; but in May 1921 Rosenberg wrote condemning Brest-Litovsk for 'recognising Bolshevism', when the Germans
ought to have been helping to form 'a strong national Russian
government to combat it'.[31]

There were disagreements, too, about Russian refugee groups.
There were several such groups, but the two main ones were
represented by General Biskupski, who was for restoring a unitary
Russian monarchy, and the 'Hetman', Paul Skoropadski, who had
been a German puppet in the Ukraine in 1918. It was to the latter
groups that Rosenberg became attracted, because he was antagonistic to the centralising tradition of Great Russia. In the editorial
quoted above he had described how 'the German army, when it
occupied the Ukraine, was greeted as a liberator by the great mass
of the population'.[32] It was a preview of what was to recur nearly
a quarter of a century later. Although the Communist revolution
under Lenin's influence had begun by favouring the autonomy of
ethnic groups, the old Tsarist trend towards dominating them
from Moscow soon reasserted itself under Stalin. Moreover by
1922 patriotic German interests, with which Rosenberg had
now completely identified himself, could no longer count on the
imminent collapse of the USSR. He began increasingly to adopt
an attitude displeasing to Tsarist refugees; Biskupski objected to
what he called Rosenberg's plan for breaking up Russia into its
component ethnic groups. In November 1932, when the accession
of the NSDAP to power was imminent, Biskupski asked Hitler to
appoint a liaison officer to keep in touch with his group; Rosenberg
he added, would only be acceptable in this capacity if he had
dropped his plan for Russia.[33] This he never did.

Hitler was unconvinced of the merits of backing refugee groups,
though in the early days of the NSDAP he was very willing to take
the money of those that had any. Many years later, when he was
at war with Russia, he recounted to Field Marshal Keitel an argument he had had with Rosenberg in 1921. He had asked the latter
what hopes he had of 'the Ukrainian Hetman'. Rosenberg replied
that he was organising revolution. Hitler was not satisfied. 'For
that he must be inside Russia.' When Rosenberg cited Lenin,
Hitler argued that it was Kerensky who had made revolution
first.[34] But in many areas there was agreement. Kurt Luedecke, a
new recruit of the NSDAP in the summer of 1922, recalled Hitler's

telling him, that he must get to know Rosenberg: 'Get on good terms with him. He is the only man I always listen to. He is a thinker. His large conception of foreign policy will interest you.'[35]

Rosenberg and Luedecke did indeed strike up a friendship; but there was another recruit later in the same year who abhorred both Rosenberg and his policies – Ernst Hanfstaengl. Because of his personal animosity, Hanfstaengl can hardly be suspected of having exaggerated the influence exerted by Rosenberg at this time. This is what he has recorded about Hitler: 'I soon found that he was deeply under the spell of Rosenberg.... He was the anti-semitic, anti-Bolshevist, anti-religious trouble-maker, and Hitler seemed to have a very high opinion of his abilities as a philosopher and writer.... I warned Hitler of the dangers of Rosenberg's racial and religious diatribes.'[36] Hanfstaengl was a useful recruit, partly because he had connections in Munich society, some of whom might be induced to contribute to party funds, and partly because his family's business of selling art reproductions, both at home and abroad, put foreign currency in his pockets at a time when galloping inflation in Germany gave it unprecedented value. It was in large measure a contribution by Hanfstaengl of $1,000 that enabled Amann to make the *VB* into a daily in February 1923, though in later years Hitler gave credit to a wheat merchant named Richard Frank.[37] By the time of its suppression in November 1923 sales of the *VB* had reached 30,000 daily.

The increased pressure on the editorial staff of the *VB*, to which all party members were now obliged to subscribe, had an effect which neither Hanfstaengl nor Eckart had foreseen or desired: in March 1923 the latter was replaced as chief editor by Rosenberg. Rosenberg was reticent about this episode, claiming that he merely acted on Hitler's instructions. There is no doubt that his old mentor was offended by the way in which the change was made and he and Rosenberg were never on the old terms during the remaining months of Eckart's life. As recently as January 1923 in Munich at the first in a long line of NSDAP rallies, he had been beside Hitler on the stand as contingents of the Nazi Sturm Abteilung (SA) filed past with their new standards, which Hitler had designed. Rosenberg was thanked for having organised the rally; but it was Eckart whom Hitler had thanked for the progress recorded by the *VB*.[38]

For Rosenberg his promotion was a welcome sign of the confidence of the man who was already being called 'the Fuehrer'. At the end of his life he could still recall accompanying Hitler on a shopping expedition to buy a new desk and office furniture for the expanding *VB*. Neither was used to having money to spend. But editing the newspaper of an extremist party in the Weimar Republic had its drawbacks; such inflammatory attacks were made on the so-called 'traitors' of the November revolution that severe penalties were imposed on responsible editors. Rosenberg suffered both fines and imprisonment on this account, which made him particularly resentful of attempts of Esser to turn the *VB* into a scandal sheet on the lines of Julius Streicher's *Der Stuermer*, which in 1923 began publication in Nuremberg. Rosenberg treated its crude anti-semitic pornography with contempt and earned the enmity of its editor-publisher. Hitler, on the other hand, read *Der Stuermer* with avidity. He was also grateful to Streicher for having merged his small German Socialist Party in the NSDAP in 1922, so opening up Franconia to the Nazis.

In October of the same year the NSDAP had an opportunity to put on a demonstration in the neighbouring Land of Thuringia, where a left-wing government lived uneasily alongside the reactionary Grand Duke of Coburg, who was married to a relative of the late Tsar. Contact with the Grand Duchess Alexandra was maintained through Max v. Scheubener-Richter, who had been born in Livonia and spent part of his life in the Baltic provinces of Russia and had known Rosenberg in Riga. After the collapse of the Tsarist regime he had worked with counter-revolutionary forces and at one time had been German Consul in Erzerum. The Grand Duke of Coburg invited Hitler to attend a patriotic rally, or German Day, with some of his companions. Hitler jumped at the chance to try to wrest control of the streets of Coburg from the Communists and appeared with a train-load of 800 SA-men. He himself shared a carriage with Eckart, Amann, Rosenberg, Esser and Luedecke. A warm reception awaited them. Hitler and many others had prudently equipped themselves with stout cudgels, since firearms would have provoked the intervention of the otherwise sympathetic police. Rosenberg, who always carried a pistol at this time, had no other weapon; however the ranks of the SA included plenty of bully-boys and the whole contingent, albeit with a few broken heads, reached the Hof-braeuhaus where the meeting was held.

Luedecke has related how, 'Hitler's appearance in the meeting hall that evening was greeted with undisguised curiosity by the genteel committee, who looked at him askance.... I sat at a table with Eckart and Rosenberg. Again it was almost startling to see with what devotion and personal affection Hitler's immediate group regarded him in those days. Even Rosenberg, supposed to be a man without emotions, cold as the tip of a dog's nose, betrayed the warmth he felt in his heart for Hitler.'[39] After a night sleeping on straw, they marched next day round the citadel, perched high above the town, before returning through cowed opposition to the railway station. It was a famous victory and those who took part later became recipients of a Coburg medal only less prized than that awarded for participation in the abortive Putsch of 1923.

Scheubener-Richter had another contact more important than a Grand Duchess: General Erich Ludendorff, the great Quarter-Master-General, who had been the driving force behind Hindenburg's victory over the Russians at Tannenberg and later had made himself the virtual dictator of Germany. He had never reconciled himself to the Weimar Republic, which represented everything that he abhorred. In the summer of 1920, after having associated himself too closely with the abortive Kapp Putsch in Berlin in the spring, he had settled in Munich. There his political judgment, which had at no time been equal to his military talents, suffered further derangement through reading the books of an egregious blue-stocking, Dr Mathilda Kemnitz, whom he later met and married. Mathilda Kemnitz had written a work in three parts on the Folk Soul of Germany, in which, as Rosenberg later wrote, she 'made world history into an affair of mere secret conspiracies'.[40] Such a criticism, coming from such a master of the conspiratorial theory of history as Rosenberg, could scarcely have been more damning. But by this time the Nazi party itself was busy hatching a conspiracy that was a great deal more than theoretical. Ludendorff's role in it was to be primarily that of figurehead; the planning was largely in the hands of Scheubener-Richter, whom Otto Strasser dubbed 'the intellectual leader of the whole Munich group of conspirators'.[41]

# 3 The Munich Putsch and After

The year 1923 dawned auspiciously for conspirators. In January the Reparations Commission, Britain dissenting, declared Germany in default and French and Belgian troops occupied the Ruhr, where there was passive resistance. The Reich produced more paper money and tried to tide over the non-productive workers, thus greatly aggravating the already severe inflation. By August the situation was desperate and Gustav Stresemann became head of a coalition of four parties with the task of saving the Republic. Within the next hundred days he was faced with an attempted Putsch by illegal Reichswehr reserves in East Prussia, 'Popular Front' governments in Saxony and Thuringia, a Communist rising in Hamburg and – most serious of all – a resurgence of separatism in Bavaria, where the inclusion of Social Democrats in Stresemann's cabinet was resented. In spite of Entente protests, the Free Corps continued to flourish in Bavaria and boasted of having more military equipment than the Reichswehr; they devoutly believed that the best use for it would be to put down the Socialist-Communist governments in Leipzig and Weimar.

All the summer relations were strained between Hitler, who now claimed to be the 'uncrowned king' of Munich, and the Bavarian government of Eugen v. Knilling. When the usual left-wing processions took place on May Day, the police protected them against the SA, which was led by the portly and popular flying 'ace', Hermann Goering, and now numbered 15,000 men. In July a mass meeting organised by the NSDAP was forbidden and the vituperant *VB* was silenced for one week. At the beginning of September, 'German Days', celebrating the battles of Sedan and Tannenberg, took place at Nuremberg, where Ludendorff made an inflammatory speech. Two of the Free Corps, the Oberland

League and the Reichsflagge, joined themselves to the SA to form the Patriotic Combat League (*Vaterlaendischer Kampfbund*) which chose Hitler as its political leader. Rosenberg was so enthusiastic about this development that he wrote in the *VB*, 'The national myth, this new myth of the present has come alive. . . .'[1] It was in this sense that he was later to use the word 'myth' in the title of his best-known book.

The situation in the Reich as a whole continued to deteriorate, as the French tried to light fires of separatism all along the Rhine, including the Bavarian Palatinate, and Stresemann decreed the abandonment of passive resistance. Stresemann was a Freemason, which provided fuel for Rosenberg's prejudices; he was denounced all over Bavaria as a traitor. Knilling delivered a speech, in which he declared: 'In Germany two Weltanschauungen oppose one another irreconcilably. One side nationalist, Germanic, Christian; the other internationalist, Marxist, materialist.' Not much there to which Bavarian Nazis could object, though Ludendorff and Rosenberg would no doubt have preferred to leave out the word 'Christian'. The Combat League's demands for action grew daily louder. At the end of September Stresemann declared martial law and his Minister of Defence delegated his powers to the head of the Reichswehr, General Hans v. Seeckt; this move correspondingly increased the authority of the Reichswehr Commander in Bavaria, General Otto v. Lossow. Knilling resigned as Minister-President and his responsibilities were taken over by a right-wing civil servant, Gustav v. Kahr, with the designation General State Commissioner.

This move encouraged the Nazis, especially as Kahr made a pro-Nazi, Ernst Poehner, Police President of Munich; but the similarity of their common objectives was more apparent than real. Kahr and Lossow were monarchists at heart and supporters of the House of Wittelsbach; they were quite prepared to use the Combat League to suppress the left-wing government in the neighbouring Land of Thuringia, but to march on to Berlin and eject Stresemann was not in their programme. On the other hand, Hitler and Ludendorff had no intention of allowing themselves to be exploited for the purpose of putting Prince Rupprecht on the throne of an independent Bavaria. As far back as April Rosenberg had put the Nazi aim very clearly in a leading article: 'Not free

*4. The Coburg Expedition, October 1922. Rosenberg is standing in the middle row, second from left*

5. *Before the Munich Putsch, November 1923. Rosenberg behind Hitler, right*

from the Reich and from Berlin, but on to Berlin, back to the German Reich!'[2] This was the purpose for which the Nazis hoped to use the hesitant disloyalty of Kahr and Lossow.

The aggressive tone of the *VB* helped to bring matters to a head. An article abusing the Reich President, Chancellor, Minister of Defence and Seeckt himself led the latter to demand that Lossow should exercise his authority in Munich to suppress the paper. After consulting Kahr, Lossow refused to do so and thus found himself ipso facto in revolt against the Reich. Shortly afterwards the Reichswehr, acting on Seeckt's orders, threw out the governments of Saxony and Thuringia, thus depriving the Bavarian Free Corps of their immediate objective and also making it unnecessary for Lossow to take action outside the Land borders.

The question facing Hitler was how Kahr and Lossow could be forced to march on Berlin without declaring Bavarian independence. Rosenberg claimed to have devised the basic strategy of taking hostage those whose cooperation was required.[3] Others, more plausibly, have ascribed this plan jointly to Rosenberg and Scheubner-Richter.[4] Hanfstaengl's version, which does not differ in substance from Heiden's, is that Rosenberg 'had concocted a crazy plan for capturing Prince Rupprecht and his staff, together with the whole government, at the unveiling ceremony of the monument to the Unknown Soldier. . . . Ludendorff and Scheubener-Richter had also been behind the plan. . . .'[5] On the day in question, however, Rosenberg reconnoitred the ground and saw that the authorities had placed powerful police contingents in such a way that the coup de main had to be abandoned. The basic concept was retained for the next suitable opportunity.

It was not long before Kahr provided another opening by calling a mass meeting to be held in the Buergerbraeu Keller on the evening of 8 November. Since the cancellation of the previous plan, the Nazi leadership had been in constant session; the Combat League was growing impatient. Ten years later Rosenberg recalled a meeting at Scheubener-Richter's house, at which Hitler, Goering and Roehm were also present. Roehm recounted how on the previous day he had been cleaning his revolver when it had gone off; the bullet had lodged in the back of a copy of Rosenberg's book, *Die Spur des Juden*.[6] To Rosenberg it seemed a doubtful augury. Hanfstaengl has recorded how on the morning of

D

8 November he was sitting with Rosenberg in the white-washed office of the *VB*. In spite of the tension, Hanfstaengl was distracted by observing that Rosenberg 'was wearing a violet shirt with a scarlet tie, with a brown waistcoat and blue suit'. On his desk was 'the pistol he always kept prominently displayed. We could hear Hitler stomping up and down in the corridor. . . .' Before midday Hitler went into the office and said to Rosenberg, 'It's all set for this evening! Do you want to come along?'[7] Nobody had warned Ludendorff, but Scheubener-Richter was detailed off to bring him to the meeting when he was needed.

Shortly before 8 o'clock Hitler, travelling in his red Benz with Rosenberg, Amann and Ulrich Graf, arrived at the Hall. Luedecke has described how he saw Hitler standing near the entrance with Rosenberg, 'looking not at Kahr (who was speaking), but at a watch in his hands'. The Nazis had convinced themselves that Kahr's intention was to proclaim the restoration of the Wittelsbachs, but nothing of the sort had been said; nor was Prince Rupprecht on the platform. Kahr was flanked by Lossow and the Land chief of police, Colonel Seisser. Hitler had graced the occasion by putting on an ill-fitting morning-coat and Luedecke, who had friends in society, overheard an Admiral refer to him as 'that wretched little waiter'.[8] About 8.30 Goering burst in with his heavily armed SA-men and Hitler, Rosenberg and Graf pushed their way up to the podium, having released the safety-catches of their revolvers. Tumult had broken out and Hitler had to fire a shot into the ceiling in order to get a hearing.

The rest of the story is well-known: how Hitler forced the platform party to accompany him to another room, where Ludendorff later joined them, and persuaded them – or so he thought – to cooperate with him in a national government, in which, under his direction, Ludendorff would become Commander-in-Chief, Lossow War Minister and Seisser Minister for the Police, leaving Kahr as 'Regent' in Bavaria with Poehner as his Minister-President. The hall resounded to the national anthem. At this point Hitler unwisely left to settle a dispute that had broken out elsewhere between the Combat League and the army, and Ludendorff, equally unwisely, decided to accept Lossow's word, as a fellow officer, and let him go. He was followed by Kahr and Seisser. The release of the hostages, who were also members of the new governments, was the ruination of the coup.

Rosenberg hurried back to the office of the *VB*, where he composed for next day's edition a violent 'Call to the German People', who were exhorted to deliver President Ebert and a selection of other Social-Democrats associated with the founding of the Republic 'dead or alive to the People's National Government'.[9] Beneath this bombast, however, doubts were growing. Late that night Eckart said to Rosenberg, 'We are betrayed.'[10] This was also Rosenberg's view when Hanfstaengl came to his office in the morning: 'Rosenberg was under no illusions. "It is no good, the whole thing has failed," he said despairingly.'[11] Nonetheless in the middle of the morning he went to the Buergerbraeu Keller, which had become the HQ of the revolt, accompanied by Eckart, who had recovered his mystic faith in Hitler's destiny. 'Let it happen as it will and must, but I believe in Hitler; above him there hovers a star.'[12]

Hitler's star was not in evidence in the cold light of the morning of 9 November; the venture was clearly hopeless. Yet, if he did nothing, his stature would dwindle to that of just another ranting orator. He acquiesced in Ludendorff's project to march into the centre of the city; there was always hope that the citizens would rise and that the Reichswehr would refuse to fire on the prestigious figure of the great General. So ranks were formed with the leaders in front. Among those in the first rank were Ludendorff, Hitler, Goering and Scheubener-Richter, whose last words to Rosenberg were, 'Things look ugly!'[13] Rosenberg was in the second rank with Schickedanz on his right and a middle-aged merchant, named Oskar Koerner, on his left. It was as the leading column was approaching the Feldherrn Halle that the firing began. Ludendorff marched on, as if nothing had happened, and came through unscathed. Goering fell wounded. Scheubener-Richter was killed outright and dragged Hitler down with him – or so it was afterwards said. Of the sixteen Nazi dead he earned the finest epitaph from his surviving Fuehrer: 'All are replaceable, but for one: Scheubener-Richter.'[14]

Rosenberg followed his leader's example and found himself lying on the ground with a more zealous, or better armed, comrade firing over his body. 'Don't shoot!' shouted Rosenberg and as soon as he could crawled to the side and made his way from the scene of carnage; Koerner, the man marching next to him, had been killed. He did not venture to go home, but found an elderly lady, who took him in; for some days he moved about Munich under cover of darkness, trying to find out what had happened to his comrades. Meanwhile Hitler had found refuge in Hanfstaengl's country villa by the Staffelsee, where the police were soon closing in on him. There he 'scribbled out a political testament on a piece of paper. Rosenberg was appointed leader of the party, with Amann as his deputy....'[15] Rosenberg recorded that the pencilled note simply read, 'Dear Rosenberg, Lead the movement from now on.'[16] The recipient was, as he himself said, astonished, since he had never previously been responsible for the organisation of the NSDAP, which in any case had now been banned. He was soon to regret the honour thrust upon him. It was certainly not one to boast about openly; the police wanted to interview him and he did not wish to attract attention to himself. In this he was successful, since in 1931 the Munich police were unable to confirm the statement that Rosenberg had led the illegal NSDAP whilst Hitler was in prison.[17]

It has sometimes been assumed that Hitler made this appointment in the expectation that Rosenberg's irresolution as man of action would debar him, or any more dangerous man, from becoming a rival for leadership of the party. One flaw in this argument is that, when Hitler took his decision, he had no grounds for hoping that he would be out of prison in little over a year; he had every reason to suppose that he would get a stiff sentence for treason, or be deported to his native Austria, as was indeed recommended by the police. It was after he had turned his trial, which began at the end of February 1924, into a triumph that he first had reason to hope that his sentence of fortress confinement for five years would allow his release within a year. The other factors working in favour of his earlier release, such as the stabilisation of conditions in the Reich and the return of parliamentary government in Bavaria, were outside his control. In November 1923 it would have been excessively optimistic to have assumed that he would be leading the NSDAP again within the near future.

In the second place, there is no obvious answer to the question

who else might have been appointed. Within the NSDAP Hitler
always insisted on the primacy of political over military decision-
making; he would have been most unlikely to appoint Roehm or
Goering, even if we assume he was unaware that the former had
been arrested and the latter had fled the country. He was not
going to hand back the party to Drexler, who had disapproved of
the whole conspiracy. Scheubener-Richter was dead and Eckart,
who had not taken part in the march, was in failing health. He
was detained after the Putsch and died at the end of December, a
few days after his release. His divorced widow was left in her
poverty by the Nazis, though, after they came to power, Rosenberg
edited a book devoted to Eckart's memory* and in December 1933
presided over a ceremony commemorating him and his work.

The third defect in the argument that Rosenberg was appointed
because of his incapacity is that in 1923 he had given no evidence
of incapacity. On the contrary, he had organised the first major
party rally in January, had been placed in charge of the only party
newspaper, the circulation of which had sharply increased, and,
as we have seen, had taken a full part in planning the coup. His
reputation for incapacity began with his unsuccessful leadership
of the party. If we are to avoid reading history backwards, we
cannot make the assumption that Hitler appointed him in order
that the NSDAP should languish in his charge. What is certainly
true is that Hitler, for whose euphoria after showing his ascendancy over his judges there is ample evidence, was jealous of
any challenge to his authority and exploited the tolerance of his
gaolers to give audience to all and sundry and promote rivalry
between different factions.

As he turned at last to the work of political exegesis, about
which he had been talking for so long, he relished his celebrity
and began to think of himself as a man of destiny. After 1925
there are no more of the flashes of modesty that occasionally
marked his earlier behaviour. There can be no doubt that he later
regretted having conferred on Rosenberg a post of such importance
and refused to allow any prominence to be given to the episode.
In this he was certainly seconded by Goering, who subsequently
showed his hostility to Rosenberg on many occasions. If Hanfstaengl is correct in saying that at this period Rosenberg 'had

* D. Eckart: *Ein Vermaechtnis*, op.cit.

Goering struck from the roster of the party', this would provide an additional explanation.[18] The fact remains that Rosenberg's leadership is mentioned neither in Hart's biography, nor in the official directory of Nazi notables (Das deutsche Fuehrerlexikon). Such omissions can only have been made on orders from above.

The NSDAP had not grown to the importance that it achieved in the autumn of 1923 without feeling the need for a more solid body of doctrine than was provided by the twenty-five points in the programme of 1920. In particular the acquisition of the VB had shown the leadership how necessary it was to codify their thinking in such a way that the NSDAP could take a coherent attitude towards the problems of the day, domestic and foreign, as these came up. For example, in what sense was the NSDAP a Socialist party, as its name stated? With Horthy in power in Budapest and Mussolini victorious in Rome, should the NSDAP claim to be part of a Fascist wave in Europe, or was it a German commodity that was not for export? How, if at all, could the gulf be bridged between Ludendorff's belief in Wotan and the honest Roman Catholicism of many Bavarian members of the party? To these and many other questions there were nearly as many answers as there were National-Socialists. It was in an effort to put bounds to this confusion of thought that in 1922 Rosenberg had written a commentary on the 1920 programme, which was published in the following year. That it had originally been Hitler's intention to undertake this is apparent from the preface, in which Rosenberg justified his own effort on the ground that 'Adolf Hitler's work... has not yet progressed so far that one can expect it to be printed in the near future'.[19]

When Hitler finally sat down in Landsberg to repair this omission, there was one point on which he was no longer in doubt; he was not a mere 'front man', but the political philosopher of a new movement. In 1922 he had said to Moeller van den Bruck in Berlin, 'You have everything I lack. You create the spiritual framework for Germany's reconstruction. I am a drummer and assembler. Let us work together.'[20] By the time he came to write *Mein Kampf* he had convinced himself that he was not only a practical politician, but a political philosopher as well. It was a rare combination of talents; no wonder the established authorities had done all they could to thwart him. 'Within long spans of human progress it may occasionally happen that the practical politician and political philosopher are one. The more intimate this union is, the greater will be the obstacles which the activity of the politician will have to encounter.'[21] At the time when Hitler was writing this sentence there was only one man in the NSDAP still living who could claim, to the exclusion of Hitler, to be its political philosopher – Rosenberg.

Since the end of the war certain historians have tended to assume that, because his influence in the NSDAP dwindled away to nothing, he could never have been influential; again, history read backwards. Such was never the opinion of German observers who lived in Germany between the wars. Karl Heiden wrote, 'Eckart and Rosenberg were his [Hitler's] teachers. Hitler was little more than their mouthpiece for some years to come.'[22] Otto Strasser, who was personally antagonistic to Rosenberg, confirmed this: 'Hitler was for years known as "the mouthpiece of Rosenberg".'[23] Rauschning commented, 'Rosenberg was the driving power behind the scenes....'[24] The Communist, Willi Muenzenberg, quoted from another contemporary author, 'Hitler commands what Rosenberg wills!'[25] It may be that the judgments cited above contain a good deal of exaggeration; but they do establish that Rosenberg had a contemporary reputation as party philosopher and *eminence grise*. This must have been peculiarly galling to Hitler in the light of his own pretensions and may explain his petulant remarks about his loyal follower in the intimate circle from which, after 1925, Rosenberg increasingly found himself excluded. If this feeling was growing in Hitler's mind whilst in Landsberg he was labouring to set down his own political philosophy, this would explain the way in which he pulled the rug from under the feet of the man whom he had nominated to act for him.

Esser, Hanfstaengl and Luedecke had foregathered in Salzburg after the disastrous Putsch and were shortly joined there by Streicher and Amann; none of them, except Luedecke, had any liking or respect for Rosenberg and the frustration of the hour was easily translated into antagonism towards the temporary leader. Luedecke has recorded how they tried to get into touch with Rosenberg, who 'was in hiding, changing his quarters almost every night because the police were searching for him. He could do

little to direct us.'[26] Rumours of splits in the residue of the
NSDAP, which were current in Austria, led Rosenberg to slip
across the frontier at night. He reached Salzburg in the small hours
of the morning and spent most of the day discussing future
cooperation with Albrecht v. Graefe, leader of the Deutsch-
Voelkische Freedom Party, a North German group, which was
close to Ludendorff and strongly anti-clerical. To become too
much tied to it would tend to detach the NSDAP from its base in
Bavaria; on the other hand, Ludendorff was now the only prominent
adherent still at liberty in Germany; an inconclusive argument
developed, with Graefe claiming that a merger of the two parties
had been agreed and Rosenberg denying it. Later, after a brush
with Austrian authorities at the frontier, Rosenberg returned to
Munich. When he had gone, the pot of venom boiled over. Esser,
Streicher and Amann, according to Luedecke, 'spoke of him with
hatred and contempt. One could see all their resentment of his
intellectuality, his reserve, his cold unfellowship, boiling to the
surface. . . . Calling him a traitor, they claimed that he was partly
Jewish, and that as a Balt of un-German origin he had spied for
France during the war.'[27]

Back in Munich Rosenberg began to gather up the threads. The
bluff Bavarian, Gregor Strasser, who had owned a chemist's shop in
Landshut, was anxious to collaborate. He and his younger brother,
Otto, stood a great deal further to the Left, but the elder at least
was a man with whom Rosenberg could work amicably. The pusil-
lanimous Bavarian court had freed Ludendorff, who assumed that
Hitler's former followers would now transfer their allegiance to him.
Graefe was fully prepared to cooperate with Ludendorff on a basis
of equality; this would have meant running the combined party as
a duumvirate, leaving Rosenberg and a large section of the Bavarian
NSDAP out in the cold. The Strassers agreed with Rosenberg that
this was unacceptable. Matters were brought to a head by the
imminence of elections to the Reichstag, in which Graefe's party
was already represented. Should the various splinter groups take
part, in spite of Hitler's pre-Putsch insistence that the NSDAP was
not a parliamentary political party? If so, who should run the combined party and what should it be called? It could not in any case
use the name NSDAP, since the ban on it was still in force in May
1924, when the election took place.

Rosenberg, while continuing to resist a merger, favoured joint participation in the election; otherwise the party, already wracked by dissension, would disintegrate. As regards the merger, Hitler failed to give any clear, forthright answer, thus leaving the field free for all contenders for leadership and influence.[28] But he came out firmly against contesting the election; he was only gradually reconciling himself to the unpalatable conclusion that the NSDAP, if it was ever to come to power, would have to follow the long, hard road of legality. Under pressure he finally conceeded that Rosenberg must decide; but he privately encouraged the opposition of Streicher and Esser, whose reputations were such that they had no chance of figuring in any list of candidates. Rosenberg decided not to be a candidate himself, but that the NSDAP, while retaining its administrative independence, should compete in the election as the Voelkischer Block. He then appealed to Hitler to approve expulsion from the party of his open enemies, but the Fuehrer evaded the issue. As Luedecke put it, 'Conferences which followed between Hitler, Rosenberg, myself and others did not move the leader to make a decision which would end the impossible hostility among his followers.'[29]

The outcome of the election must have further irritated Hitler; the Block won thirty-two Reichstag mandates, twice as many as the Bavarian People's Party (BVP), and also became the second largest party in the Bavarian parliament. This success led at once to the claim by Graefe and Ludendorff that leadership now resided in the Reichstag group, which they dominated. Faced with this situation, Hitler notified his baffled followers that he had not authorised the merger announced by Graefe and Ludendorff; that he was withdrawing from involvement in political life until he regained his freedom; and that henceforth 'nobody has the right any longer to act in my name, to claim my backing or to issue statements in my name.'[30] This meant the end of Rosenberg's nominal leadership, which in any case had never been generally respected. According to his own account, he himself asked Hitler to withdraw his mandate and recommended Gregor Strasser.[31] Hitler, however, issued no further instructions.

The problem of the leadership remained. In mid-July 1924 a conference was held in Weimar under Strasser's chairmanship in an attempt to put an end to feuding. The opening was highly inauspicious; Ludendorff was late and Esser filled the interval with remarks calculated to intensify antagonisms. When Ludendorff finally appeared, Strasser called upon Rosenberg to speak. After an appeal for rededication to the aims for which Hitler had called the movement into existence, he gave an account of the tortuous negotiation with Graefe, which showed the latter in an unfavourable light and provoked a barrage of offensive comment by Esser and Streicher, who demanded that the party close ranks behind Ludendorff.[32] The meeting thus proved inconclusive; in practice the affairs of the Block were conducted by a triumvirate of Graefe, Ludendorff and Strasser. Rosenberg occupied himself with editing a newspaper, the *Voelkischer Kurier*, as a substitute for the banned *VB*. He also founded at this time an anti-semitic monthly, *Weltkampf* (World Struggle).

Meanwhile improved conditions in the Reich, especially the stabilisation of the currency, were proving unpropitious for political extremism. When further elections were held in December 1924, the Block polled less than one million votes and won only fourteen mandates. Shortly before Christmas Hitler was released on parole and, on giving assurance of his intention to abandon revolutionary activity, was permitted to reorganise the NSDAP and resume publication of the *VB*. Rosenberg's hopes that Hitler, on emerging from prison, would take cognizance of the true course of events and vindicate his deputy's stewardship were rudely disappointed. On the contrary, Hitler continued to be sharply critical of the decision to contest the May 1924 election. This indeed appears to have been Hitler's pretext for venting on Rosenberg one of his legendary displays of rage. That Rosenberg was exposed to this ordeal early in 1925 has been recorded by Hanfstaengl. 'Early in the year I had enjoyed the temporary satisfaction of hearing Hitler give Rosenberg the most tremendous tongue-lashing, accusing him of disloyalty, incompetence and all the crimes in the calendar.'[33] Even at the end of his life Rosenberg could not bring himself to describe what occurred; he wrote only that he had twice in his life been exposed to Hitler's rage, once in 1933 for an error in the *VB*.[34] He passed over the earlier occasion, admitting only that Hitler resented his decision to take part in the 1924 election.

One interesting feature of Hitler's histrionics is that these obscured the fact that he was himself intending to pursue the course Rosenberg had marked out. As a result of the abortive Putsch, he had reluctantly reached the conclusion that, if the NSDAP was to have a future, it would have to be as a parliamentary party within the hated Weimar 'system'. This painful decision was made no easier for him by the fact that Rosenberg had been before him in arriving at this conclusion. It also complicated his relations with Roehm, who had been trying to revive the SA as a paramilitary organisation under another name. Roehm was not interested in Hitler's new plans and went off to Bolivia in pursuance of his career as a soldier of fortune. In mid-February those holding provisional office resigned, in order to give Hitler a free hand, and at the end of the month all the leaders were summoned to a meeting of reconciliation at the Buergerbraeu Keller. On the day of the meeting the *VB* reappeared; it carried a leading article by Hitler, in which he rapped both Ludendorff and Rosenberg over the knuckles. Ludendorff was sharply told not 'to bring religious disputes into the movement'. Rosenberg was informed that it was not 'the task of a political leader to attempt to improve upon, or even to fuse together, the human material lying ready to his hand'.[35]

Ludendorff, Roehm, Rosenberg and the Strasser brothers all stayed away from the meeting. As Rosenberg said to Luedecke, 'I know the sort of brother-kissing Hitler intends to call for.'[36] Ludendorff never made his peace with Hitler, who encouraged him to stand for President in March 1925, when he failed to prove a vote winner. After the leading candidates had been deadlocked on the first round of voting, Hindenburg, the venerable Field Marshal, emerged as champion of the Right wing and most Nazis transferred their votes to him. He duly succeeded the dead Social-Democrat, Friedrich Ebert, as President of the Reich.

In mid-March the Strasser brothers went north to organise the reborn NSDAP in areas where criticism of 'the Munich gang' was loudest. They recruited in the Ruhr a young man with a club foot and a venomous tongue named Josef Goebbels. Like Rosenberg, he was one of the very few Nazis who had completed his university studies and was entitled to be addressed as Doctor. He was soon put to work as speaker and editor of 'National-Socialist Letters', intended to provide guidance for officials of the party. Although no immediate clash occurred between him and Rosenberg, he was destined to eclipse the latter in the two fields of culture and the press, which he had hoped to make his own. For the next twenty years their relationship was marked by constant friction and Rosenberg at the end of his life described Goebbels as 'the Mephisto of our once so upright movement'.[37]

Although most of those who had played leading roles during the inter-regnum had now left Munich, peace had not yet been restored. Rosenberg, faced with Hitler's refusal to vindicate him in the eyes of his chief traducers, decided to take legal action against two of them, Esser and Hanfstaengl. This was the last thing Hitler wanted and he seems to have confronted Rosenberg with the alternative of dropping his law suits or abandoning his connection with the refounded *VB*. Rosenberg reluctantly accepted this deal, though it was February 1926 before his name reappeared as that of chief editor. He said at this time to Luedecke: 'But what can I do? I have to accept the measly salary, I'm married; it's too late to discover a new career for myself outside the party. Besides, the work is my life, I cannot give up the cause.'[38] He did, however, extract from Hitler, as part of the transaction, a letter dated 2 April 1925, which the latter – hating, as he did, to petition and explain – can have had no pleasure in writing.

'In connection with your assumption of the post of editor,' Hitler began, 'I find myself obliged to address a personal request to you. As I learn, there is still some litigation in the air, in which you are the plaintiff. Little as it is my wish to intervene in the personal relationships of others ... I must depart from my normal practice in this case out of love for our movement, as well as out of anxiety for those involved, whether as plaintiff or defendant.' Hitler went on to observe that, 'The period after November 1923 was so confused and could so readily give occasion and cause for every kind of rumour that, in my view, it is difficult to discover where right and truth are to be found among men of whom it is my conviction that all, without exception, suffered alike and were animated by the same feeling for our movement.' After dwelling on the particular problems and sensibilities of those who, for his sake, had had to fly the country or had endured imprisonment, he commented, 'When the heart is full, the mouth overflows. I therefore find it humanly comprehensible that this mood and atmosphere should have brought forth some remarks which in themselves must be regarded as insulting. If today I do all I can to ward off litigation, the deeper origin of which is to be found in the general tension of that time, I believe I am thereby serving not only the movement but all concerned. I know you, Herr Rosenberg, and regard you not only as one of the most valuable collaborators with our movement, chief editor of my former *VB*, to whom was due the main share in developing the paper, so far as content was concerned, but also as a man of whose integrity of personal intention I am absolutely convinced. In the difficult period in which, quite unexpectedly and without explanation, you took over leadership of the movement, you tried to advance the cause as much as possible – with me this conviction goes without saying; in the process mistakes may have crept in, as can happen with you, as with everyone else. But it is not my object to give an opinion on mistakes, but solely on intention and good will. For this I must give you the highest credit in everything.'[39]

The contorted phrasing of the letter and the last-minute altera-tions bear witness to the effort which it cost Hitler to write. It was not the vindication for which Rosenberg had hoped, but it was an *amende honorable*. If, however, he deluded himself with the belief that all would now be as before, he was due for a disappointment; the friendly relationship of the early days was never resumed. Indeed as late as September 1925 a member of the anti-Munich group in Lower Saxony described the relation-ship between Hitler and Rosenberg as being one of 'open con-flict, the cause of which is to be found in the prominent posi-tions occupied by Esser, Amann and Streicher in the party'.[40] Hitler rarely came to the *VB* offices and backed Amann on the numerous occasions when the latter's administrative decisions exasperated Rosenberg. Till January 1927, when Wilhelm Weiss joined the staff, the whole newspaper was being run with only three or four sub-editors under Rosenberg.[41] It was not until 1928 that he was able to insist with Amann that his old enemy Esser should be kept off the *VB* premises and that nothing he wrote should in future be published.[42] It is a sign of his subordination that he was treated in this way despite the vital part played by the *VB* in the years up to 1927–28, when Hitler was banned from speaking in the larger Laender and had to rely in great measure on the printed word for dissemination of his views. Rosenberg's relative subservience during this period must have been all the more galling to him because, as chief editor, he was the target for charges of defamation and incitement brought against the *VB* under the Law for the Protection of the Republic, which had been enacted in 1922 in the shock of horror at the cold-blooded murder of Walter Rathenau, the Foreign Minister, who was Jewish. Rosenberg had hardly resumed the chief editorship before, in March 1926, he was sentenced to one month's imprisonment; he found himself in the cell that had housed Eckart just before his final illness.[43] Rosenberg was again in court in June 1927, but on that occasion got away with a fine.

Hitler's first extravagance on leaving Landsberg had been to buy a supercharged Mercedes, in which he delighted to drive about the country. In addition to his driver, he was usually accompanied on these expeditions by Amann, Esser, Heinrich Hoffmann, his photographer, and others whom he found congenial. Rosenberg did not fit into this court circle, but resented his exclusion. Many years later he recalled how he had once asked Hitler if he could come on one of his expeditions; they did indeed go together to Berlin, taking with them one of Richard Wagner's grand-daughters, but the experiment was not repeated. When it was all over and Hitler was dead, Rosenberg recorded of him with evident chagrin, 'He valued me very much, but he did not like me.'[44] Yet he had been too long in the Fuehrer's magnetic field ever to escape.

Meanwhile Rosenberg had at last begun to create a home life for himself. In July 1923 he had obtained a divorce from Hilda, appearing himself as the guilty party.[45] One day, walking from the *VB* office, he saw entering a Greek restaurant 'a beautiful, slim lady in a dark costume and a large black hat with a tartan band. ... I was suddenly interested.'[46] He followed her into the restaurant and struck up a conversation, which was continued in the Englischer Garten. Her name was Hedwig Kramer and on 3 January 1925 he married her. Long after he recalled that their first excursion as a married couple was to the old castle at Heidlberg, where they heard Beethoven's ninth symphony. They had a son, who died in infancy, and a daughter, Irene, born in

1930. His memoir is almost as reticent about Hedwig as it is about Hilda; since his death Hedwig has been equally reticent about him.

Whether as a result of his marriage or of settling down to a more regular schedule of work on the *VB* and the manuscript of the *Mythus*, Rosenberg from this time seems more and more to have reverted to his bourgeois background, abandoning the habits of Schwabing, the 'Bohemian' quarter of Munich. Hanfstaengl – admittedly a prejudiced source – has referred to Rosenberg's 'unsavoury love-life' and adds that in later years he became 'the intimate friend of Steffi Bernhard, who was the daughter of the editor of the *Vossische Zeitung*'.[47] Whatever the truth of this may be, Rosenberg was discreet about his later liaisons. If Hanfstaengl's supposition is correct, discretion would in any case have been essential, since Georg Bernhard was a Jew and the famous liberal-minded newspaper, which he edited until 1930, was particularly detested by the Nazis. It is possible, however, that Hanfstaengl was either repeating ill-intentioned gossip or confusing Steffi Bernhard with another pretty Jewess, Lisette Kohlrausch, whose relationship with Rosenberg rests on better testimony.* Accusations of Jewish ancestry or other connection with Jews were part of the common language of insult among Nazi leaders. The final breach between Goebbels and the Strassers came about because he alleged that their mother had Jewish blood. Rosenberg was strongly critical of Goebbels over this episode.

In 1925, however, Goebbels and Gregor Strasser were still actively cooperating in the organisation of their Working Group of Northern and Western Districts (Gaue) of the NSDAP. Among those who had joined them were several who came to prominence later, such as Bernhard Rust and Hans Kerrl, who in due course became Ministers, and Erich Koch and Heinrich Lohse, who soon became the Gauleiters of East Prussia and Schleswig-Holstein respectively. These men at that time stood well to the left of Hitler and, indeed, Rosenberg on most of the current issues; they believed that the estates of the former German kings and princes should be expropriated and that there should be fundamental changes in the structure of society. In foreign affairs most

* See Chapter 8, pp. 172–3.

of them had more sympathy with the USSR than with Britain and France.

While Rosenberg's political views were very far from those of the Left wing, he seems to have been reluctant to alienate them, so identifying himself with those whom Goebbels alluded to in October 1925 as 'Esser and his gang'.[48] Goebbels had actually been offered employment with the VB and in mid-November Rosenberg agreed to publish his article on 'National-Socialism and Bolshevism' together with a commentary which, according to Goebbels, would be 'partly pro, partly contra'. It proved to be wholly contra.[49] When on 22 November Strasser called a meeting of his followers at Hanover, Goebbels disparagingly referred to Hitler as 'petty bourgois' and demanded that his delegate at the meeting, Feder, be ejected. Hitler countered the break-away movement by calling another meeting in mid-February 1926 in Bamberg, where Strasser and Goebbels found themselves face to face with the Munich battalions. Hitler's opening speech, in which he enunciated the foreign policy which Rosenberg had always advocated, was not at all to Goebbels' liking and he wrote in his diary: 'Russian question: altogether beside the point. Italy and Britain the natural allies. Horrible!'[50] But later in the meeting Hitler succeeded in detaching Goebbels from Strasser and from that time antagonism grew up between the latter two.

Outward harmony was restored in time for a general rally of the NSDAP and SA to be held in July 1926 in Weimar; it was one in the long line of similar rallies which took place in Nuremberg, but in 1926 Hitler was still banned from speaking in Bavaria and had to accept the hospitality of Thuringia. On this occasion Goebbels spoke on propaganda and Rosenberg on the press. Since Goebbels in his diary described the latter's report as 'brilliant',[51] it may be assumed that the major rift between them had not yet come about. Rosenberg in his memoir ascribed it to his rejection of contributions from Goebbels, which in his view were too egotistical and artificial. If these were the ones in which he tried to glorify his success in Berlin, to which Heiden has referred,[52] the break cannot have come before November 1926, when Goebbels became Gauleiter there. Goebbels got his own back by setting up in July 1927 his weekly paper, *Angriff*, which some three years later became a daily. The *VB* had an office in Berlin and Rosenberg installed there his old friend Schicke-danz; but as long as the *VB* was printed in Munich, the delay in getting it to Berlin virtually left the field open to Goebbels. In October 1931, when *Angriff* was over-extended financially, Rosenberg suggested to Hitler and Amman that, as an economy, he should take over both papers; but by that time Goebbels was already in the ascendant and nothing came of the proposition.[53]

Rosenberg, challenged in the field of press and propaganda, attempted to win new territory for himself in cultural affairs. It was natural that he should turn in this direction, since he believed that the Aryan rebirth of the German people, to which the NSDAP was dedicated, would manifest itself not only in political revolution but also in the production of great works of art and letters. This belief was shared by Hitler, who always looked upon himself as a man of culture, unlike some of his paladins, and was prone to demonstrate this in his speeches. In a speech in Munich in April 1929, after denouncing Max Reinhardt, the great Viennese theatrical producer, he declaimed: 'We mean to create, out of our ideology and our political will to power, documents of stone and bronze, in order to imprint again upon every German mind that it is a proud thing to be a German.'[54]

The Nazis resented the fact that Jews, partly because of natural gifts and partly because of exclusion from leading position in the army and the state, had become disproportionately prominent in other professions, especially finance, medicine, science and certain branches of academic life. But it was upon the role of Jews in journalism, artistic life and the entertainment media that popular attention was chiefly concentrated. Rosenberg, often speaking in the name of Christian morality, was loud in condemning Jewish influence in theatre and cinema. 'Today,' he wrote, 'a cinema industry has been spawned from the movie art and overwhelmingly this industry is found to be in the hands of Jews. For this reason, the film has become a means of infecting the Volk – through lascivious images; and, just as clearly as in the Jewish press, there are revealed here plans for the glorification of crime.'[55] Propaganda of this kind was not without effect in conservative quarters, opposed to modernism in all its forms.

Rosenberg must have hoped that, by carrying the fight into the field of culture, he would win new adherents to the party and so

E

strengthen his own position. At the first of the great Nuremberg rallies, which took place in August 1927, it was decided to set up a National-Socialist Society for Culture and Learning, which two months later was placed under Rosenberg. In 1929 it was renamed the Combat League for German Culture (Kampfbund fuer deutsche Kultur – KFDK). He aimed to use it to create for himself an apparat with branches in the Gaue, but his organisational talents were unequal to the task. Moreover, the attempts of his supporters to drive out manifestations of 'degenerate' Jewish art were carried to absurd lengths; unapproved painters after 1933 were actually deprived of brushes and paints and efforts were made to eradicate cadenzas, which Jewish violinists were believed to have insinuated into Beethoven's violin concerto. In a passage in the *Mythus* on Jewish painters Rosenberg rashly alluded to the painter Schwalbach, 'who already has dared to represent Jesus as flat-footed and bow-legged'.[56] Schwalbach retorted in a letter to Rosenberg that he was not Jewish, but did not pursue the discussion of the Saviour's legs.[57] It might be thought that in these by-ways Goebbels' rivalry would not pursue him; but after 1933, when Goebbels became Minister for Propaganda and Popular Enlightenment, he acquired primacy in this area also by allying himself with Robert Ley, who had replaced Strasser as organisational leader of the NSDAP, and was developing the recreational 'Strength through Joy' movement.

The common hostility of Strasser and Rosenberg towards Goebbels should have made them allies again, as they had been in 1924; but doctrinal disputes held them apart. Rosenberg adhered to the line adopted in his commentary of 1923 on the NSDAP programme; Socialist thought, he had then written, originated long before Marx, who had indeed falsified the spirit of the community as a whole (Gemeinschaftsgeist) by his theory of class war. The NSDAP was Socialist in so far as it believed that the state had a duty towards all who worked together to sustain it; a national pensions system was demanded as fulfilment of the sense of community of the people (Volksgemeinschaft). On the other hand, 'National-Socialism refuses to regard a large concern as in itself harmful'.[58] What was harmful was that 'whole states find themselves in the hands of a few hundred bankers, to whom the populations have to pay tribute.'[59] Later he referred again to the bankers as 'the three hundred, of whom each knows the other'.[60] It will be seen that the attack is similar to that launched by the Left in France some years later, directed against 'les deux cents familles', by whom French industry was allegedly controlled. In 1923 the Nazis were still demanding that banks be nationalised; later this was modified to a demand that they be placed under increased state control.

Strasser persisted in his view that, whatever the 1920 programme might have said and however immutable Hitler might proclaim its twenty-five points to be, the NSDAP was nonetheless moving Right. He wished to concentrate on setting up NS trade unions. This was opposed by Rosenberg in an article of 1 February 1927, which provoked Strasser to counter-attack.[61] Rosenberg then wrote to him to explain his own position. Quoting H. S. Chamberlain and Werner Sombart, he affirmed 'that capitalism would never have come to dominate in its existing form if it had not been for the Jews'. He himself was only against capitalism in so far as it represented the predominance of the Jew and so was contrary to 'the higher racial values of the Volk'.[62] These differences of opinion carried over into the field of foreign policy, since the Strasser brothers objected to Rosenberg's anti-Soviet attitude and rejected his wish to align Germany with British imperialism. In the latter's view, the evil genius of Gregor Strasser was his brother Otto, whom Rosenberg described as a 'parlour Bolshevik' (Salonbolschevist).

Hitler's attitude towards socialism was close to Rosenberg's, though in the interests of party unity he at first expressed it more cautiously; it was not until 1930 that he finally decided that Otto Strasser was too much of a liability and forced him out of the NSDAP. For Hitler the only acceptable form of socialism was what was then called 'front-line socialism' (Frontsozialismus), defined as follows by Rosenberg: 'Out of the battlefield the men in gray brought back something new: a feeling for the social and national cohesiveness of the different classes.'[63] The abolition of distinctions between classes was never part of orthodox Nazism, any more than the levelling of incomes; egalitarianism in all its aspects was anathema. On the other hand, Hitler had to pay lip service to socialism, especially in the early years, in order to hold the Left wing of the NSDAP. He found the requisite formula in Feder's differentiation between capital productively employed and 'stock-exchange capital'; it was this distinction that he praised in *Mein Kampf* as 'a truth of transcendental importance for the future of the German people'.[64] Since by means of the familiar Nazi syllogism the stock-exchange had already been identified with Jews and Freemasons, the way was open to abandon economic theory, which in any case did not interest Hitler, in favour of racial theory.

This line was increasingly adopted by Hitler as his pursuit of power by legal means obliged him to make his peace with men of property. Particular embarrassment was caused by point 17 of the 1920 programme, which declared that the needs of the community justified expropriation of land without payment of compensation; this was highly objectionable to the big land-owners East of the Elbe, where natural allies for the NSDAP might otherwise be found. In 1923 Rosenberg's commentary had tried to limit application of point 17 to land needed for roads, railways and canals; he had also adopted Feder's distinction between land exploited for productive purposes and land bought and sold speculatively. But the objectionable principle remained. In April 1928 Hitler, faced with an election in the coming month, overcame his dislike of tampering with the programme sufficiently to issue an 'elucidation' of point 17, asserting the belief of the NSDAP in private property and designating the Jewish land speculator as the real enemy. This was, of course, a further set-back for the Strasser wing.

Most Nazis, like Hitler himself, had little or no patience with theories of national economy; what they throve on was economic disaster. In October 1929 the world slump, which began in New York and rapidly spread eastward, exceeded their most ardent hopes. By September 1930, when another election was held, there were three million unemployed; two years later this figure had doubled. In such circumstances the success of the NSDAP was more a sensation than a surprise. In 1930 the tally of Nazi members rose at one bound to 107 and they became the second largest party in the Reichstag. The only other party to register a substantial gain was the Communist party (KPD); it was the beginning of the growth of the extremes at the expense of the middle, which led to the collapse of democracy even before Hitler became Chancellor. Bad news for Germany had been good news for Hitler ever since October 1921, when the Entente, as he had prophesied, awarded to Poland a substantial part of industrial Silesia. Now the prophet of doom, who had repeatedly said that the post-1925 prosperity could not last, had again been proved right. So had Rosenberg's peculiar brand of economics. At the Nuremberg rally of 1927 he had cried out that German national aims were being suppressed by international financial interests. He had depicted the world's money markets as ruled by Paul Warburg and Bernie Baruch in New York and by the Strauss and Samuel families in London. Now everybody knew that the collapse of the fragile German economy had been precipitated by withdrawal of British and, above all, American short-term loans. The villains were the Jews in Wall Street and Threadneedle Street, just as the Nazis had said.

There was, however, another reason for the success of the NSDAP, which deserves more serious consideration. In 1930 some 4,600,000 young people voted for the first time. They had been under five when the war had broken out; some of them had known no father, or had known him as a cripple. Most of them had left school in 1923, the year in which the fortunes of post-war Germany touched their nadir. Now it was going to happen all over again. None of them had experienced the solid world of their fathers and grandfathers, in which incomes and classes remained comparatively stable and the right to rule and own property was conferred by birth. They had been born into a jungle in which it seemed that only the very strong and the very lucky would survive. They had seen no evidence that any account of their needs would be taken either by the stratified form of authoritarian government traditional in the Reich, or by the parliamentary system imported into Germany in the baggage of the Entente powers. Why not try something new, something that derided both the other systems? What had they got to lose? Melita Maschmann has written, 'No catchword has ever fascinated one quite as much as that of the "National Community" (Volksgemeinschaft).'[65]

The foregoing offers some explanation of why a great mass of voters, especially the young, rejected the parties of liberalism as well as the Social-Democrats, who were Marxist only in theory; what it fails to elucidate is why, at the peak of Communist strength in November 1932, their vote was still barely fifty per cent of the Nazi vote. Although Hitler skilfully exploited the supposed threat of a Communist take-over, there was never the faintest likelihood of it after 1919. To seek to explain why, as extremist views began to prevail, the KPD failed to become a serious contender for power would be outside the scope of this book. It is, however, our purpose to outline the ideological tenets, which the Nazis opposed to those of Marxism, and to indicate why these should have offered such compelling attractions. For it is a remarkable phenomenon that a party refounded as recently as 1925 should within eight years have achieved power without embarking on extra-constitutional action, even though others stretched the constitution in its favour. Yet such men as Hindenburg, Hugenberg, Papen and Schleicher helped the NSDAP at various times in 1932–33 only because of its massive popular support. That this support was in great measure due to the impressive oratory of Hitler and the skilful propaganda of Goebbels and others is not in dispute; nor that the times were evil and demanded desperate remedies; but a party which in the free election of July 1932 could attract 13,745,000 votes was a party which had convinced the electorate that it stood for something. The successful propaganda of an opposition party over a period of years must rest on some ideological foundation. It is to the discussion of this foundation that we must now turn.

# 4 The Germanic Ideology: The Jewish World Conspiracy

If we begin with a definition of ideology, we can well adopt that formulated by Z. K. Brzezinski: 'Ideology . . . the link between theory and action . . . combines action . . . with a consciousness of purpose and of the general thrust of history. It gives its adherents a sense of consistency and certainty that is too often absent among those . . . brought up in the tradition of short-range pragmatism.'[1] What then is Weltanschauung, the term more often used by Hitler and Rosenberg at a time when the word 'ideology' was less commonly employed than is the case today? Unlike ideology, which is usually applied to views held collectively, Weltanschauung, in its primitive sense, need mean no more than the outlook of an individual on the world around him. That Hitler and Rosenberg tend to use the latter word when they mean the former, need not surprise us; they were seeking to impose their view on those around them, undeterred by the fact that it was a view of the world which was both subjective and in some aspects highly unreal. But the measure of success that attended these efforts, with the result that eventually their views were held collectively in many circles in Germany, does not, in itself, bring them within our definition of an ideology; they must also give their adherents 'a sense of consistency and certainty'. In other words, the views must form a coherent whole; provided that this whole is communicated effectively to the adherents of the ideology, the question of its relation to reality need not concern the historian, though it may remain a problem for the philosopher.

The trained minds of political scientists and philosophers may look at the world in a way that reflects the existence of a coherent system of political, economic and social ideas; if so, the distinction between Weltanschauung and ideology will vanish for them, as it did for the untrained minds of Hitler and Rosenberg. But most men and, in particular, the bulk of the adherents of political parties in the Western world, do not see the world in this way at all. They retain the right to hold mutually inconsistent views, to let their passing moods colour their judgment and to take 'snap' decisions or, as they might prefer to claim, to decide each case on its merits. A democratic system is content to work with this fluid political substance, of which the 'floating voter' provides the classic instance; but it is a very insecure basis for totalitarianism, which demands the whole man and his unswerving obedience. It was thus necessary for the Nazis to unify, at least to some extent, the disparate Weltanschauungen of their followers. They never succeeded in doing so, any more than they succeeded in creating a fully totalitarian state; but that they aimed to do both can scarcely be in dispute.

Nobody understood the connection between these two aims more clearly than Hitler who, in addition to moulding his own party, was throwing it into the front line against the Marxist parties, which themselves had a well defined ideological tradition behind them. 'Force,' said Lenin, 'is the midwife of history.' Hitler, too, knew that he would require force for his purpose and at an early stage of his leadership of the NSDAP he built up the SA, just as, after he had come to power, he built up the Wehrmacht and later the military wing of the SS. But he also knew that he could not succeed by force alone, especially during the years in the wilderness, when the NSDAP was trying to win adherents and impress publicists and financial backers. As Hitler put it in *Mein Kampf*, 'Ideas and philosophical systems as well as movements grounded on a definite spiritual foundation, whether true or not, can never be broken by the use of force after a certain stage, except on one condition: namely, that this use of force is in the service of a new idea or Weltanschauung which burns with a new flame.'[2]

To show that Hitler understood the need for an ideology is not the same as to establish that a Nazi ideology actually existed; the latter thesis has been denied directly by some, indirectly by others in the sense that they have largely ignored it in their work. Most Marxists, for example, treat Nazism as an extreme case of the aberrations of 'monopoly-capitalism' and, if they sometimes refer to it as National Fascism, this is primarily a term of abuse. In the West there is a school, derived mainly from Rauschning, which holds that Nazism was little more than a nihilistic striving to win and then exploit power, led by a fanatical opportunist in the person of Hitler. This interpretation becomes more plausible if one concentrates – as many Anglo-Saxon historians have in fact done – on the period shortly before Hitler achieved power, on his apparent reconciliation with the Prussian tradition, which immediately followed, and on the shifts and expedients by which he brought his foreign policy to fruition, culminating in the essentially opportunist pact with Stalin, which so much pained the party ideologist, Rosenberg. During the war British propaganda never quite succeeded in making up its mind whether it was fighting the First World War against Prussia all over again; it never achieved the assurance with which Burke declared, 'It is with an armed doctrine that we are at war'.[3] Some of the ambivalence has persisted.

Yet what was the war against Russia, if not an ideological war? In the summer of 1941 Hitler had Europe at his feet. Stalin was showing almost craven anxiety to avoid conflict and Germany was drawing from and through Russia more in essential raw materials than she was ever able to extract after Hitler's invasion. Britain, it is true, was holding out, but without America's open intervention was powerless. Even after the Americans, through no initiative of their own, were plunged into war, another two and a half years elapsed before the Allies felt strong enough to open a second front across the Channel. If Hitler was no ideologist, what led him to stake all that he had won on an invasion of the USSR? Why did he introduce his hated euthanasia campaign in Germany in 1939, when he needed maximum solidarity of opinion on the home front? And what induced him late in 1941, when he needed to concentrate every effort to overcome Russian resistance, to order Himmler to embark on the liquidation of the Jews, which meant building extermination camps and transporting truck-loads of 'undesirables' across Europe? These irrational decisions were not those of a fanatical opportunist, but of a fanatic of a very different kind. Finally, when Hitler sat in the last bunker in Berlin, confronting his end and the ruination of his hopes, what, if not passionate ideological conviction, could have led him to enjoin on the German people in his testament that they must 'above all else uphold the racial laws in all their severity, and mercilessly resist the universal poisoner of all nations, international Jewry.'[4]

We shall get a better perspective on Hitler as ideologist, however, if we turn back from the final phase, when he was trying to put his ideological concepts into practice, and examine how these originated and how he tried to impose them, at least in rough outline, on his followers. Rosenberg's role will emerge as we do so. To follow the progressive evolution of Nazism is, moreover, well suited to its own dynamics; it never achieved fulfilment; it was always, in a Nietzschean phrase, in the process of becoming. The NSDAP did not come into being in 1921, 1925 or 1930 as a fully fledged totalitarian movement; it went on its way increasing from year to year its ideological consistency and discarding those who would not conform. Similarly, the Nazi state did not become fully totalitarian in 1934 or even in 1939 on the outbreak of war; it can indeed be argued (though this is not the place to do so) that it never did become totalitarian in a Stalinist sense. The Third Reich was always just around the corner.

Two provisos must be made at the outset. The first is that, while the ideology gradually acquired greater consistency, it was never intended to mean the same thing to everyone, whatever his rank and degree of initiation. There was nothing egalitarian about Nazism at any level; even the propaganda, although the words had to be the same, took on rather different connotations to those who knew what lay behind them. The investigator resembles Peer Gynt peeling his onion; as each layer comes off, the inner face represents another ideological aspect and the outer face, which is the propaganda, also acquires another look. Let us take a rather oversimplified illustration. The average German citizen (Volksgenosse) was meant to see himself as a member of a privileged race, encircled by a hostile world, which had denied him his natural, or strategic frontiers. But to the NSDAP these frontiers (the frontiers of Versailles) were already largely irrelevant, except for propaganda purposes. The party member (Parteigenosse) knew that he was heir to immense living space, which would be conquered for him by the mass of Volksgenossen, serving as cannon fodder. But for the inner core of leadership within the

NSDAP the party itself was a convenient tool, through which the domination of the elite was maintained; the loyal bond between leadership and followers (Gefolgschaft) was no more than a slogan, good for a round of applause at a party rally. It appears to have been Rosenberg's misfortune to have taken some of these slogans seriously; this alone would in due course have ensured his exclusion from the innermost circle, quite apart from personal factors mentioned in previous chapters.

The second proviso is that, even within the leadership, acceptance of the ideology was never uniform. Himmler, Bormann and Rosenberg, all of whom cordially disliked one another, nevertheless all took the ideology seriously. Others, like Goering and Speer, only paid lip service if it was necessary; like the Renaissance Pontiff, who regarded Christianity as a profitable superstition for Popes, they found National-Socialism a profitable superstition for National-Socialist leaders. After the war, when Weltanschauung had become a bad word, Baldur v. Schirach expressed it as follows: 'Of the leading men of the party ... every one interpreted the party programme differently – Gregor Strasser in a Socialist sense, Rosenberg in a mythical sense, Goering and some others even up to a point in a Christian sense. ... Thus practically every leading National-Socialist had his own National-Socialism.'[5] There were, of course, certain fundamentals which were accepted without question by all the leaders. The first was allegiance to the Fuehrer around whom they revolved; they were all heliocentrists. Secondly, they were all nationalists and racialists in the sense that they believed in the dominant racial community of the German people. Thirdly – as a corollary, as they had come to believe – they were all anti-semitic.

It would, of course, be impossible within these pages to trace all the individual variations that existed outside and within these three broad categories of belief. Our aim is, rather, to give an account of the life and thought of Rosenberg and examine the inter-action between him and Hitler. In the process it will be possible to deduce certain general conclusions about Nazi ideology as a whole, in the light of Hitler's appointment of Rosenberg in January 1934 to be his Delegate for the Supervision of the whole intellectual and ideological Indoctrination and Education of the

National-Socialist Movement.* This appointment (which we shall abbreviate to 'Delegate for Indoctrination') did not mean, of course, that Rosenberg was expected to try to impose ideological uniformity on the NSDAP. It would have been impossible to do so and it does not seem that Rosenberg – to do him justice – would have wished to do so. What he did aim to do was to see that divergencies of belief did not become too strong, or at least were not too strongly expressed. His hope, like that of any Archbishop of Canterbury since Laud, was to keep heresy within reasonable limits.

There were several reasons why variants of belief were bound to persist and why it would have been useless to try to eliminate them entirely. In the first place, Nazism never claimed to be a rational system of thought; it was the faith of men who prided themselves, like their Fuehrer, on being intuitive men of action. As Rosenberg put it, 'National-Socialism is an attitude.'[6] As we shall see,† even the most deeply held Nazi tenets about race were not susceptible of scientific, or even practical, definition. Although Himmler set up a Race and Settlement Main Office within the SS, nothing could dissuade him from picking out future SS-men by studying their photographs. For Hitler, proof that the Czechs had Mongol blood was to be found in the way in which their moustaches dropped, when they let them grow. The pure doctrine of Germanism itself suffered transformation in the ideological mind of Himmler. In the last years of the war, when the need for manpower was desperate and a European crusade against Bolshevism had been declared, the SS, which had originated as a racially pure elite, admitted to its brotherhood an armed riff-raff from all over Europe.

In the second place, the Nazis lacked a holy book; they could not lay claim to a cohesive body of doctrine, such as Marxists could boast of. There was, of course, *Mein Kampf* and loyal attempts were made to extract guidance from it; but there were many areas that the Fuehrer had overlooked, or dealt with inadequately. For example, Hitler's account of prejudices acquired by him at school in Austria was applied, as far as was possible,

* Der Beauftragte des Fuehrers fuer die Ueberwachung der gesamten geistigen und weltanschaulichen Schulung und Erziehung der NS Bewegung.
† See, in particular, Chapter 9, pp. 198–9.

to the educational system; but it was impossible to carry through comprehensive reform on this fragile basis. There were also immense lacunae in such important areas as the corporate organisation of the state and the relationship of party and state to the Churches. Even the vital question of choosing a Fuehrer was very inadequately covered. Rosenberg's *Mythus,* as we shall see when we come to discuss it, only partially supplied the deficiencies. In any case, it was never made an official publication of the NSDAP in the same category as *Mein Kampf* and the 1920 programme.

In the third place, the Nazis' claim to be heirs to all that was finest in the Nordic-Aryan tradition led them to enroll a remarkable range of incompatible historical figures as proto-Nazis. Even after these had been subjected to the process of ruthless distortion and assimilation, of which Rosenberg was a master, the calendar of saints made very odd reading. It was difficult to draw a straight line linking Homer, Plato, Odin, Zarathustra, Widukind, Henry the Lion, Frederick II Hohenstaufen, Meister Eckhart, Copernicus, Rembrandt, Luther, Frederick the Great, Schopenhauer, Wagner, Nietzsche, and Bismark. Under Rosenberg's hand, Hitler's line of spiritual descent looked more like the perambulation of a spider with ink on its legs. It was only in an anti-intellectual milieu that the Delegate for Indoctrination could pass as an intellectual.

There was, however, an ideological tradition of a more recent and intelligible kind, which all the Nazi leaders had in common, namely the nexus of ideas and prejudices which Fritz Stern has designated 'the Germanic ideology' and analysed in connection with Paul de Lagarde, Julius Langbehn and Moeller van den Bruck, all born in the nineteenth century. Lagarde (1827–91) was very generally accepted by the Nazis, and by Rosenberg was regarded with much the same filial respect as he always showed towards Houston Stewart Chamberlain. Langbehn was scarcely mentioned by Rosenberg, perhaps because towards the end of his life he had been converted to Roman Catholicism; but a whole generation was influenced by Langbehn's book, *Rembrandt as Educator* (*1891*), and Rosenberg, with his concern for art, could hardly have escaped. It was Moeller v.d. Bruck (1876–1925) who brought into common parlance the term Third Reich, which Hitler later tried to discard. He also developed the Fuehrer cult before anyone had heard of Hitler; yet he was the only one of the trio whom the Nazis refused to treat as a forerunner. This could be accounted for simply by the fact that Moeller v.d. Bruck had been unimpressed by Hitler when they met; in addition he was objectionable to Rosenberg, who regarded him as standing too close to the so-called National Bolsheviks, who flourished briefly in the early days of Weimar. In any case one should not seek to define with exactness what Fritz Stern describes as 'the effect of confused ideas on irrational men and movements'.[7] The Germanic ideology is chiefly useful in order to sketch in the discontents and aspirations of a substantial section of the pre-1914 generation.

The malcontents of the second half of the nineteenth century, represented by Fritz Stern's trio, were disgusted by liberalism in all its manifestations. The enlightenment of the eighteenth century and the revolution of 'Liberty, Equality and Fraternity', which had largely destroyed it, were both equally anathema to them. They rejected, too, modernity as expressed in the industrialisation and urban civilisation of Western Europe. They looked back with nostalgia, some to the First Reich of the Middle Ages, others to a more primitive Germanic (Urdeutsch) past, which existed mainly in their imaginations. There the idealised Volk still felt in its blood the tribal ties binding it together in a deep, instinctive manner, transcending artificial distinctions of wealth, class and creed. Modernism and materialism, which had corrupted this rude paradise, were associated in their minds with the Jews. They were also hostile to the Christian Churches, which had ceased to exercise the function of 'binding', originally associated with religion, and had become divisive forces within the community. Moreover, as Lagarde put it, Christianity was 'doomed to extinction because of the Jewish elements which it has absorbed'.[8] To react by becoming atheists, however, would have brought them too close to the revolutionaries of 1789 and contemporary Social-Democrats; they passionately demanded a faith, but could find nothing worthy of belief, except a tissue of illusions about the past and hopes for the future, both linked to German blood and the place of Germany in history.

Although the ideology was so deeply imbued with Germanic ideas, there were elements in it up to this point which, with national variations, might have been found in other European countries. Its primarily Germanic character derived partly from exaggerated German nationalism and partly from a peculiarly perverse adaptation of Social Darwinism. Men like Lagarde and Moeller v.d. Bruck, who had even less claim to scientific knowledge than H. S. Chamberlain, had applied to human beings the hypothesis of the survival of the fittest, in its crude physical sense, and gone on from there, by analogy, to regard nations and races as subject to the same inexorable law. Where Nietzsche had rejected this perversion of Darwin's original theory, these shallow minds extended it beyond all reason by dividing nations arbitrarily into those which were still young, vigorous and destined to survive, and those which were old, sated and condemned to decline. The geopolitical writer Karl Haushofer, whom Hess admired, was deeply infected by this virus. Needless to add that Germany was put into the former category; Britain and France into the latter. Russia's status varied; Moeller v.d. Bruck and Haushofer bracketed her with Germany; Rosenberg regarded Russia as in decline, because of Judaeo-Bolshevist influences.

This categorisation was purely subjective and therefore could not be refuted. Where relevant statistical evidence existed, it was ignored. For example, rising birth-rate was regarded as one sign of a young, vigorous people; but although the birth-rate in Germany ceased to rise after the 1880s this inconvenient fact was not allowed to damp down the demand for overseas colonies or Lebensraum in the East for Germany's supposedly cramped and expanding masses. The agitation to which such a body as the Pan-German League devoted itself had an emotional basis; it was readily translated into a moral right to absorb new territory, if necessary by making war, in order to provide for the Volk. Justification for this arbitrary and aggressive attitude was supplied by H. S. Chamberlain, who wrote in *The Foundations of the Nineteenth Century* that 'The Germanic peoples belong to that group of most gifted people which we are accustomed to designate as Aryans'.[9] This was a clear warning to less gifted Slavs and decadent French to make way. In Chamberlain's eyes, Germany had a duty to save Europe from the degenerate admixture of races, which he designated 'chaos of peoples'.

The religion of race, the myth of the blood. . . . How very Teutonic, we are tempted to say. But a word of caution is appropriate; it would be possible to disinter remarks made at the turn of the century in England and North America about the destiny of Anglo-Saxons which are scarcely less disturbing. British and American racialists and imperialists in the late nineteenth century were able to work off their *furor britannicus* at the expense of non-Europeans and thus, through application of the double standard, were largely exempt from the moralising of those who have always believed that inhuman means can never be justified in terms of theoretical ends, whether these take the form of claiming to be a racial Superman or merely a bearer of the White Man's Burden. As soon as imperial ambition involved Britain in a colonial war against white Boers she learnt, through being virtually ostracised in Europe, that such behaviour was not to be tolerated.

Unfortunately German ambition and sense of historic mission blended with the heady brew of national myth. There was the German King Henry I, whose stalwart figure, as he drove back the Slavs, so impressed Heinrich Himmler that some thought he had come to regard himself as a reincarnation of the tenth-century hero.[10] There were the Teutonic Knights, so beloved of Rosenberg and other North Germans, who had brought Christianity and ordered government to the benighted, heathen tribes along the shores of the Baltic. The appeal of these Volk heroes was bound up with the fact that German national unity had come so late in the nineteenth century and, when through Bismarck it finally came, it remained incomplete. Critics of Bismarck, like Lagarde, pointed to several million Germans living outside the frontiers of the Second Reich. What better way of proving Germany's unique fitness to survive than to bring these scattered communities of oppressed Volksdeutsche 'home to the Reich' – not by repatriating them, but by extending the Reich? There grew up a mystical faith in Germany's destiny. As Fritz Stern puts it, 'Lagarde's conception of the nation was a mystical corollary to his Germanic religion. A people can become a nation only through the collective acceptance of its divinely ordained mission.'[11] God, who had been a Habsburg in the sixteenth century, a Bourbon in the seventeenth and an Englishman ever since, was in the twentieth century to be a German.

Upon these exaggerated pretensions the defeat and revolution of November 1918 clanged to with the heavy metallic sound of a prison door. The surviving apostles of the Germanic ideology, like Moeller v.d. Bruck, found themselves trapped in the Weimar Republic, a shadowland, faintly imaging the hated parliamentary system of the victorious Entente powers. There seemed no way of escape, except with the wings of Superman. Some of the members of the post-1919 Juni-Klub in Berlin took refuge in the myth of a Messianic Fuehrer, who would fulfil all prophecies and lead the Volk out of bondage. In the figure of the coming Fuehrer the Germanic ideology found its final and most alarming expression.

Such, then, was the climate of opinion common to those who grew to manhood in Germany shortly before, and during, the First World War, those who provided the raw material with which the Nazis worked. We can now ask ourselves what new ingredients, if any, were added to this death potion by the Nazis in general and, in particular, by Hitler, Rosenberg and Eckart, whom we discussed in the two preceding chapters. The question can be briefly answered; what they added was a new virulence of anti-semitism and new hatred of Marxism, both identified since the October Revolution with Communist Russia. Lagarde had been only a moderate anti-semite; Moeller v.d. Bruck wrote only one anti-semitic book – his last (*Das Dritte Reich*, 1923). He numbered the USSR among the 'young' nations, which would dominate the future. He was not himself a serious political thinker, but he would have regarded Rosenberg's automatic identification of the Jew with the Communist as an absurdity. Before we examine this identification, however, we must again turn back to the nineteenth century and observe how anti-semitism had changed its form.

Anti-semitism, which is at least as old as Christianity, took a new and sinister turn in the nineteenth century. While the old hostility on religious grounds continued, a new and more terrible hostility on racial grounds developed; more terrible because it had earlier been possible for a Jew to avoid discrimination by abandoning his religion, especially if he also became rich. This escape hatch was now closed. Indeed, in the eyes of the new racialists the attempt of the Jew to become assimilated made it even more necessary to isolate him, since it would otherwise become more difficult to detect and prevent the admixture of

F

Jewish with Aryan blood. Exaggeration of Germanic virtues and Jewish vices created a distorted picture of the two races as representing irreconcilable and contrasting cultures, the concept of the Gegenrasse, already explicit in the title of Wilhelm Marr's book, *The Victory of Jewry over Teutonism (Germanentum)*, which appeared in 1873. This concept, in turn, was coloured by Social Darwinism; if the two protagonists of opposing racial characteristics could not coexist, one of them was destined to destroy the other. The ultimate conclusion was that drawn by Himmler in a speech at Posen in 1943: 'We had the moral right to wipe out this people bent on wiping us out....'[12]

The antagonism, already grave enough, was exacerbated towards the end of the nineteenth century by the application to it of the dogma that every ethnic group ought to constitute a nation-state within frontiers of its own. Eugen Duehring advocated herding the Jewish people together in a Jewish state.[13] At about the same time a section of Jewry rejected the concept of assimilation and began to demand a national home for their persecuted race. This movement culminated in 1897 in the Zionist conference at Basle, which provided the peg on which the Tsarist secret police hung their famous forgery, *The Protocols of the Wise Men of Zion*. The origins of this forgery have not been in doubt among scholars and historians of good will since 1920, when Philip Graves, the *Times* correspondent in Constantinople, unearthed there a copy connecting the Protocols with a satire on the ambitions of Napoleon III, which had been published anonymously in 1867. This was transformed by the Cheka into an anti-semitic 'horror-comic', which appeared in Russia in 1905 in a version ascribed to Sergei Nilus, a pious extremist of the Orthodox Church. It purported to be the record of a secret meeting, at which the leader of world Jewry explained to a circle of trusted followers how the ruin of the Gentiles was to be accomplished. 'If any state dares to resist us; if its neighbours make common cause against us, we shall unleash a world war.'[14]

It was this terrible prophecy that so impressed the ignorant and ill-intentioned all over Central Europe in the aftermath of the most destructive war the world had yet seen. Copies were brought to Germany in the baggage of refugees fleeing from Bolshevism and a translation into German appeared in 1919. The theme that the war had been due to the machination of Jews and that they had been the sole beneficiaries was developed by Rosenberg in all his early articles and booklets. In the immediate post-war period, when Britain was prolonging the blockade to ensure signature of the Treaty of Versailles, she was at least as much the enemy as Bolshevism. Rosenberg therefore expanded his composite picture of international Jewry by identifying it also with Freemasonry, which, as he claimed in *Die Spur des Juden* (1920), had originated in Britain. Its symbol was Edward VII, who was regarded in Germany as the chief instigator of the Entente and the encirclement of the Reich. Rosenberg spiced the broth by describing as Freemasons the assassins of the Archduke Franz Ferdinand.

The concept of the Freemasons as authors of a vast underground conspiracy was not a new one; the credit (if that is the word) belonged to a French Jesuit, Abbé Barruel, who early in the nineteenth century had saddled the Masons with responsibility for the French Revolution and attendant disorders.* The fact that the Masons used Hebraic symbols and did not disbar Jews from membership was enough to give a spurious plausibility to Rosenberg's theory, which conveniently ascribed to the same Jewish instigators both the French and Bolshevik Revolutions. As we shall see shortly, it also explained how the same agency of international destruction could express itself both through wealthy bourgeois groups and dispossessed anarchists and Communists.

In 1922 Rosenberg devoted a booklet† to the study of Jewish penetration of British political life and the pressure exerted by the Zionists to bring about the issue of the Balfour Declaration, by which the principle of the national home was at last conceded. In the introduction to his commentary on *The Protocols*, which was published in the following year, he began by citing a recent speech in which Lord Robert Cecil (later Viscount Chelwood) had said that the establishment of the League of Nations and of the Jewish home in Palestine were the only notable results of the Great War. For Rosenberg and, it must be added, many of his readers, this was sufficient proof that it was the Jews who had brought about the war in order to achieve their sinister ends. By

---

* *Mémoires pour Servir à l'histoire du Jacobinisme* (Paris, 1806).
† *Der Staatsfeindliche Zionismus* (Hamburg, 1922).

1923 the issue of war debts due to America and their bearing on payment of reparations by Germany had come to the fore and Rosenberg concluded in the same booklet that the centre of gravity of world Jewry had moved to the USA.

It was not enough to allege that the Jews had motives for promoting strife among Gentile nations; for the Nazis' polemical purposes it was also necessary to point to the enemy within the gates. Rosenberg in his first book had stressed that Jews indiscriminately sowed the seeds of anarchy or Communism as best suited their aim in a particular country. Class war was the subtle instrument devised by Marx with this end in view and the toiling masses were systematically provoked by 'the bondage of interest'.[15] In *Immorality in the Talmud*, Rosenberg's second book, he continued this campaign of vilification. The Talmud is a miscellaneous collection of traditions of Jewish elders going back to remote biblical times. The traditions were compiled by many hands and relate to cultures and epochs very different from our own. It was not difficult, therefore, for an unscrupulous polemicist to select random passages, which in loose translation and out of context could be made to present primitive Jewish society in a disagreeable light. Indeed, Luther himself had quoted from the Talmud with precisely this object in view. Rosenberg's aim was to show that 'the Jews' road to power has lain through lies, deceit, treachery and assassination from Father Abraham to the present day'. Their hatred of Christianity 'has reached its summit in the systematic persecution of Christians by the Jewish Bolshevik rulers in Russia'.[16] The same theme was pursued in his book *Plague in Russia* in which he cited Bolshevik attempts to destroy the Russian intelligentsia and root out pockets of good German blood in the Volga basin, where Germanic communities had survived for centuries.

While Rosenberg spattered the map of contemporary Europe with charges of conspiracy and terror, he had also from the outset projected backwards into history the picture of the Jews as destroyers of civilisation. The motive for undertaking this research may have been to make the bald accusations more plausible by adding a wealth of historical data. It may also have been intended, by quoting anti-Christian passages from the Bible, to rouse up the anti-semitism of Bavarian Roman Catholics. This use of a pseudo-historical method to reinforce one's prejudices had been adopted by H. S. Chamberlain, who was the inspirer of both Rosenberg and Eckart. We have already noted that, when the two latter met in 1919, Eckart was running in his paper an anti-semitic series of articles; in one of these he demonstrated to his own satisfaction that Judaism, acting through Christianity, had given the death blow to the Roman Empire. In the following year Rosenberg cited the Book of Esther to show how Mordecai secured authority in ancient Persia,[17] and in his commentary on *The Protocols* he had an allusion to Isaiah (Ch. XIX, v.2) which soon became a warm favourite with anti-semites everywhere: 'And I will set the Egyptians against the Egyptian: and they shall fight everyone against his brother, and everyone against his neighbour; city against city, and kingdom against kingdom.'

Ernst Nolte has pointed out with reference to Conservatism, Liberalism and Socialism that, 'Every significant ideology of the nineteenth century had its own brand of anti-semitism'.[18] This dispersion of prejudice, however, did not help the Jewish people; it merely exposed them to attack on more than one front. Defenders of the established order identified Jews with radicalism, while some radical groups tended to regard them as spearheads of capitalism. These contrasting points of view were not as arbitrary as might appear. The nineteenth-century relaxation of discrimination against Jews in Germany had attracted poor ghetto Jews from further East. On the other hand, both Habsburgs and Hohenzollerns, in their efforts to promote industrialisation, for which their land-owning aristocracies were disinclined, had granted privileges to rich Jews. As Hitler put it, 'Every Court had its "Court Jew", as this plague was called ... while at the same time the Jew provided the means which the princes squandered on their own pleasures.'[19] Families like the Rothschilds came to symbolise a financial conspiracy, which was alleged to be destroying the harmonious relations which had existed between landowners and peasant cultivators; instead the flight from the land was creating an urban proletariat divorced from the good earth in which alone virtue could flourish. In this aspect, anti-semitism thus voiced the demand that, instead of the class struggle, there should be a return to the former sense of community of the people. But under-privileged Jews upheld the struggle to change society and reduce the power of a governing class, which in their view represented only the diminishing economic interest of land.

The infant NSDAP, as it sought to frame its policies, or at least to direct its propaganda, was faced with a difficult alternative. Its National Bolshevik wing, supported by some Free Corps groups, would have been content to regard the Jew as a monopoly-capitalist, while rejecting the identification of Jews with Communists. Conservative anti-semitism, on the other hand, was associated with such bodies as the Pan-German League, which represented the old-fashioned discrimination on religious grounds and had not debarred Jews from membership before 1918. As we have seen, both the reactionary Thule Society and the Reichswehr would have been glad to use the young party for their own ends; but in their grip it would have had difficulty in establishing an identity of its own. Adopting opportunist tactics, the Nazis decided to play both sides of the street. In a leading article in May 1921 Rosenberg quoted Lagarde: 'Nationalisation of the Banks – provided the government is in German hands – is the first voelkisch demand after the expulsion of all Jewish officials.'[20]

The success of this tactic is illustrated by the fact that there were soon complaints both from the Communist party and the right-wing German National People's party (DNVP) that their members were defecting to the NSDAP. Himmler was one of those whose early sympathies lay with the DNVP.[21] In an editorial in August 1921 Rosenberg commented on this trend in terms calculated to encourage it: 'In the two above-mentioned parties are to be found the most active and self-sacrificing section of our people. In both there are fighters.'[22] A party that could hold, even for a few years, both Ludendorff and Otto Strasser was indeed performing a balancing act requiring considerable political skill. The safety net beneath the tight-rope was provided by the great, if imaginary, web of international conspiracy – Red, Gold and Black, like the flag of the Weimar Republic. Nothing was lost, except contact with the ground – reality.

If Rosenberg was accused of dealing in contradictions, when he maintained that Communists from the ghettos and rich bankers from the City were part of the same conspiracy, he had an answer: the bankers, if not themselves Jews, were as often as not Free-masons. The Red International was sapping below the ground, while the Gold International was openly manipulating world financial markets, thus fatally exacerbating the defects of the capitalist system. 'Here, in the Stock Exchange, all the threads come together and lead out again into the world to create unrest, confusion, chaos and – to profit from it.'[23] This thesis, implausible as it must now seem, gained a certain cogency from the circumstances of the 1920s.

In general, it was a period in which financiers could find no remedy for the evils arising largely from the maldistribution of purchasing power and thus of the goods that men had learnt to produce. They clung crassly to a 'hard money' policy, regarded the gold standard as a life-boat in the storm and watched helplessly while wind and water swept away the unemployed hunger marchers. It was much the same in all countries; but in Germany it was easiest to devise, and believe in, a theory of victimisation. It was possible for a rational economist to show that inflation had begun in Germany at least as early as the voting of the first war credits in 1914; but it was a great deal more convenient to believe that what had ruined the currency was the French occupation of the Ruhr. It was possible to demonstrate that the Federal government suffered from inadequate revenue and an antiquated tax system; but it was easier for a politician to persuade himself, and the public, that the financial problems of the Reich were solely due to payment of reparations. When eventually the USA stepped in and the Dawes Plan was negotiated, in order to provide Germany with enough capital both to earn her living and to begin to pay the Entente, the Nazis and other nationalists observed only that an alien Commissioner sat in the Reichsbank and that the dollar loans were secured on the revenues of the state railways. It was, in Rosenberg's terms, a classic case of the domination of international high finance.

To what extent did the German people really believe in the existence of an international conspiracy? We have already noted that Jews were prominent in revolutionary activity in Central and Eastern Europe in the years 1917–19; but this was a relatively short-lived phenomenon. In the Reich itself in the 1920s there was only one Minister of Jewish origin (Rudolf Hilferding: 1928–29) subsequent to the murder of Rathenau in 1922. Nor were Jews conspicuous in other fields in which political power was exercised. As Werner Mosse sums it up: 'Among officers on the active list, in top Civil Service posts and in the direction of heavy industry, in brief, in the ruling classes, there were scarcely any Jews by faith, any more than there were in the landed property-owning class.'[24] The reason for this lay primarily in the disabilities under which Jews had for so long suffered; even after emancipation, prejudice against them had continued to operate. This was not, of course, admitted by anti-semites. Rosenberg countered the argument as follows: 'The great lie which we have been constantly spoon-fed is that the Jews, through dispersion and prejudicial laws, were shut off from all activities other than trade and were thus compelled to become money-lenders.'[25]

In so far as Germans did believe the conspiracy theory, it must be stressed that this was not their first step away from the firm ground of political reality. The first step had been their insistence that the war itself had been forced upon them; that the Entente powers had encircled them. For most Germans, it was not merely a question of rejecting the exclusive war guilt, which the victorious Entente had unwisely linked to the reparations clauses of the Versailles treaty; they rejected all responsibility for the outbreak of war. The second step had been the refusal to admit military defeat; according to the 'stab in the back' legend, which the Nazis and others so ardently promoted, the collapse of 1918 had been due solely to the activities of traitors and weaklings on the home front. It was only a short further step to claim that these elements had been under the influence of international, hostile forces. The German High Command knew well that such forces could act with extraordinary speed and effectiveness; it had itself consigned Lenin to Russia in a sealed train and watched the dramatic disintegration of Russian resistance. All that was needed, in the eyes of patriotic and frustrated Germans, who wished to accept the conspiracy theory, was some visible symbol of the sinister forces linking the external with the internal enemy – the Jew. As Hannah Arendt has written, 'The most efficient fiction of Nazi propaganda was the story of a Jewish world conspiracy.'[26]

If we assume, as we must, that most Nazis accepted, in one of its various forms, that the conspiracy actually existed, the question remains whether the leaders themselves believed the extreme version embodied in *The Protocols of the Wise Men of Zion*.

We have already briefly examined the evidence that Rosenberg at first gave credence to it, but later became more sceptical. In 1923, when he published a commentary on *The Protocols*, he cited only relatively short extracts, embedded in factual and explanatory matter designed to make them more digestible. Even so, he was obliged to admit that there are 'some apparently crazy passages'. These, he explained, were to be understood in the light of the exaggerated hate of Gentiles felt by Jews, who were thus led at times into absurdity. Making a pretence of objectivity, he concluded, 'As matters stand today, it is impossible to adduce juridically conclusive proof either for their absolute authenticity or for their fabrication.'[27]

Hitler was less prudent; in *Mein Kampf* he asserted that *The Protocols* were genuine, though he adduced no evidence of this, other than that the Jewish-owned *Frankfurter Zeitung* maintained the contrary. H. S. Chamberlain in his last published work observed, 'I do not know whether there is really a secret league of Jews, which has set itself the conscious aim of bringing about the physical, spiritual and moral destruction of the Indo-Europeans.' He concluded, however, with a quotation from Wagner to show that such a process had over the centuries been taking place 'from mere instinct'.[28] Even if allowance is made for the credulousness of Chamberlain, whose book was published in his declining years, there was no excuse for Rosenberg, who in 1943 permitted his commentary to be reissued. For in the years 1934–37 a case had been fought out in the Swiss courts, which could have left no doubt at all in the mind of a serious enquirer that *The Protocols* were fraudulent.

Before we leave behind us the theme of Jewish conspiracy, mention must be made of another booklet, which throws light on the influence exerted upon one another by Hitler, Eckart and Rosenberg. In March 1924, when Eckart was dead and Hitler was undergoing trial, a subsidiary of the firm publishing the *VB* put out a remarkable book attributed to Eckart, bearing the title, *Bolshevism from Moses to Lenin: a Dialogue between Adolf Hitler and Myself.** A note by the publisher explained that Eckart had been unable to complete the booklet and expressed

* *Der Bolshevismus von Moses bis Lenin: Zwiegespraech zwischen Adolf Hitler und mir*, D. Eckart (Hoheneichen Verlag, Munich, 1924).

the hope that Hitler might in due course be willing to do so. Not only did Hitler never do so, but on coming to power he went to considerable lengths to withdraw copies available in public libraries and prevent any further circulation. If this action had arisen from displeasure at misinterpretation of his views on the part of Eckart, one might have expected to see this reflected in some modification of the tribute paid to Eckart in *Mein Kampf*. Since this did not occur, one is entitled to conclude that Eckart's booklet was suppressed not because it inaccurately expressed Hitler's views, but because it expressed them with a clarity that was embarrassing to a man who had meanwhile become Chancellor of the Reich. We know that it made a marked impression on the youthful mind of Himmler.[29]

The dialogue, which was presumably a composite version of several conversations, is based upon the axiom that the Jewish conspiracy has existed not just since 1897, but throughout history. But how is proof of this to be supplied? Neither alludes to the fact that this was precisely the task upon which Rosenberg had been engaged since his arrival in Munich. There are, however, striking parallels between the pseudo-historical proofs cited in the Hitler–Eckart conversation and those given in the five works attacking Jewry and Freemasonry, which Rosenberg had published in the preceding four years. In the Hitler–Eckart conversation the two men indulge in long tirades, designed to show how deeply they have researched into the sinister effect of Jewish influence through the ages; but all they succeeded in demonstrating is how attentively they have read the works of Alfred Rosenberg. It can scarcely be a coincidence that the following ill-assorted names are common both to the latter's early anti-semitic tracts and to the conversation in question: Pontius Pilate, Trajan, John Chrysostomos, Giordano Bruno and, coming to more recent times, Kant, Goethe, Schopenhauer, Werner Sombart, Bela Kun, Trotsky and Zinoviev. Two biblical episodes are common to both, namely those from Esther and Isaiah, of which mention has already been made. As Hitler and Eckart gloat over alleged ritual murders by Jews, they cite an obscure nineteenth century work by Gougenot de Mousseaux, which had recently been translated from the French by Rosenberg.*

* *Le Juif, le Judaisme, et la Judaisation des Peuples Chrétiens* (Paris, 1869).

It would be possible, though tedious, to extend these parallels; enough has been set down already to indicate that Rosenberg was earning his keep by providing ammunition for the bigger guns of anti-semitism. It would not seem justifiable to make the further deduction that Rosenberg was responsible for influencing the general character of Hitler's profound hatred of the Jewish people. Indeed influence was probably exerted in the reverse direction. At Nuremberg after the end of the war Rosenberg, like most of the other surviving Nazi leaders, maintained that he had never interpreted literally Hitler's threats against the Jews. In 1933, he maintained, 'Nobody thought of concentration camps on a large scale, not to speak of gas chambers.' A sinister connotation could be put on all that was said, in the light of 'the order Hitler is apparently proved to have given for the mass destruction of the Jewish people'.[30] Rather than admit his part in genocide, Rosenberg went to his grave maintaining that there was no necessary connection between what he had said and written and what Hitler had later ordered to be done.

We may claim thus far to have demonstrated that Hitler understood the necessity for a revolutionary political movement to rest upon an ideological foundation and that, like Rosenberg, he was himself strongly inclined to ideological motivation. We have further indicated a congruence of ideas between the two men, who shared a common attitude towards the supposed Jewish world conspiracy and the need to incorporate in the programme of the NSDAP a limited amount of non-Marxist social doctrine, mainly in the form of stressing the community of the people as a whole and the need for state intervention in the economic process. Before completing our survey of the ideology, we must examine two areas in which divergences emerged at various periods between the views of Hitler and Rosenberg. One of these relates to foreign policy;* the other to religion. It is to the latter theme that we shall now turn.

* See Chapter 8.

# 5 Rosenberg and Religion: The Myth of the Twentieth Century

The first significant point to note about Rosenberg's *Mythus,* which appeared in 1930, is that it is at least as much an attack on Christian Churches as it is upon Jewry. He may already have been anti-semitic when he came to Germany, but it was his stay of eleven years in Munich that turned him against the Churches, or against Christianity, as his opponents in the Churches alleged. His contemporaries were used to Nazi attacks upon Jews; they were much less familiar with Nazis attacking religion. It was therefore this latter aspect of the book that chiefly attracted attention; this naturally increased after 1934, when the Vatican placed the book on the Index. Indeed, Hitler accused the Roman Catholic hierarchy of having promoted sales by their assaults upon Rosenberg.

Before investigating the question to what extent the *Mythus* is, indeed, anti-Christian, as well as being directed against Church theology and institutions, we shall briefly summarise the book's structure. Rosenberg himself admitted that he had been unsystematic, though he always refused to undertake any revision of substance. No summary can fail to invest the book with greater coherence and lucidity than it actually possesses. It is not merely that the underlying thesis of eternal Aryan virtues and Judaeo-Christian depravity is fanciful and extravagant, but even the exposition of it is rambling and inconsequent. Moreover, the verbiage seems almost wilfully obscure in some places; a contemporary admirer – for there were admirers – tried to help less perceptive readers by publishing in Munich a glossary of 850 difficult words and expressions to be found in the book. A German theologian, who by 1936 had become a refugee from the Reich, observed frankly, 'Rosenberg's outlook on life is stark dementia'; but he added the sinister prophecy: 'the folly is certainly spreading and may lead to an access of frenzy which will set Europe aflame.'[1] It is the fact that this prophecy came true that justifies a closer look at the characteristics of this persuasive dementia.

The 1938 edition of the *Mythus* comprises just over 700 pages sub-divided into six main sections. Section one is mainly historical, though it must be borne in mind that history to Rosenberg simply consists of illustrating implausible and unprovable theses. Section two is an analysis of the distinctive features of Germanic art and creative achievement. These two sections comprise between them nearly two-thirds of the book. The next longest section is the third, entitled 'The Coming Reich'; it is noteworthy that after 1933, although numerous editions followed, Rosenberg neither amended this title nor significantly revised the content of this section. As far as he was concerned, National-Socialism, or his vision of it, was never realised. Section four deals with what the Nazis called race hygiene and may be said in some respects to have foreshadowed the Nuremberg Laws of 1935. Section five treats rather perfunctorily, in a mere thirty-seven pages, the responsibilities of 'The Coming Reich' in the spheres of religion and education. The final section concerns international affairs and, within the pattern of the present volume, will be discussed in Chapter 8.

Rosenberg wrote at the end of his life, 'In the centre of the spiritual and intellectual conflict stands Christianity, the forms it takes and its relationship to the peoples and problems of our epoch.'[2] As we have already noted in Chapters 1 and 2, he left an account of particular causes leading to his antagonism to the Christian Churches; it is a good deal harder to penetrate the barrage that he sets up when it comes to examining his attitude towards fundamental Christian beliefs. Even the meaning that he attaches to religion itself is shrouded in Nordic mist. In as much as he repeatedly declared that the cult of Wotan was dead, he was not a pagan in the traditional sense in which one might apply the term to Ludendorff. He more than once attacked the growth of astrology and other superstitions in Nazi Germany, and he opposed Rudolf Steiner's Anthroposophists, who were thought by Nazis to be organised on a similar basis to that of Masonic

Lodges. He certainly did not regard himself as an atheist; his attitude was reflected in a circular issued by Hess to the NSDAP in June 1937: 'National-Socialist Weltanschauung presupposes a religious attitude; it goes without saying that a religious attitude does not mean being bound by the creed of a Church.'[3]

It should be emphasised that, while the Nazis persecuted the Churches and martyred individual priests and pastors, they always claimed to be doing so because of the political activities of the institutions and individuals concerned. Since the war abundant evidence of their ultimate intention to destroy the Churches has become available; but until the Third Reich finally disappeared it maintained the fiction that everyone was free to believe what he wished and would only suffer for it if his beliefs, like those of the Jehovah's Witnesses, who rejected military service, led him into collision with the state. But the latter-day hard core of anti-Christians round Hitler, including the otherwise barely compatible figures of Bormann, Goebbels, Himmler and Rosenberg, all believed that the Christian ethic was fundamentally opposed to Nazi ideology. It was their hope that the German people could be brought to share their views; but they knew that it would take time. Meanwhile concessions had to be made to popular belief, in order to maintain morale, especially in wartime. Goebbels issued a circular about the need to avoid controversial questions and in November 1941 Bormann reminded Rosenberg that public discussion of religious matters was not desirable.[4]

If we accept that the basic Christian beliefs are that Jesus Christ was God, that through His death and resurrection man is redeemed from original sin and that the soul survives the death of the physical body, it is clear that Rosenberg was no Christian. He wrote respectfully of Christ as an heroic, historical figure; but he also wrote approvingly of the Arian heresy, denying Christ's divinity, which was widespread among the early Lombards and Goths. A suspicion indeed arises that there was some confusion in Rosenberg's mind between the Aryan race and Bishop Arius, from whom the heresy derived its name. Rosenberg, like Himmler, delighted in all historical expression of religious heresy. He followed H. S. Chamberlain in recognising in Christ, as man, 'the probability of His non-Jewish descent'.[5] Unfortunately for humanity, Christ's message had at once been perverted by the

Jew, St Paul, who had laid all the emphasis on the negative side of His mission, namely on His suffering and death. 'Jesus is the hero; not the bruised one. . . .'[6] Worse still, Paul had made Christianity into a universal religion by ignoring the importance of ideas of aristocracy and race. Rosenberg quotes with disapproval the famous passage in the Epistle to the Galatians: 'here is neither Jew nor Greek, neither bond nor free. . . .'

Rosenberg passionately rejected the doctrine of original sin – at least as applied to Germans. As regards the after-life, he rejected 'dismal pictures of the pains of hell' and other 'unhealthy imaginings about the world after death'.[7] He did not take up a dogmatic position, however, and in April 1942, when Bormann consulted him on the question whether the concept of immortality was compatible with the Nazi ideology, he replied that this lay within the freedom of conscience of each National-Socialist.[8] He made his own attitude plain in the memoir written in Nuremberg gaol: 'Man's existence is perpetuated only in his children or his work.'[9] He refused the consolations of religion before his execution.

Rosenberg affected to deplore the decline of Christianity, which he ascribed to absorption of Jewish elements, because a people without a faith was exposed to Jewish influence of another kind, namely to materialism and Marxism. He based his substitute faith upon one of Lagarde's aphorisms: 'Races are God's thoughts.'[10] From this he derived what he called 'the religion of the blood'; each race evolved its own religion and had its own race-soul. 'Soul signifies race seen from within. And conversely race is the external form of soul.'[11] The individual soul had significance only in so far as, through its racial purity, it was linked to the collective race-soul; only through the survival of the race itself did the individual soul survive the death of the physical body that had housed it. The nearest Rosenberg got to defining this shadowy concept was in a speech delivered to school-teachers after the Nazis had come to power: 'The new Weltanschauung . . . does not take as its point of departure either the individual ego or the abstract idea of humanity; it derives from an experience that we cannot always carry home with us in black and white, but which we can approximately render by the notion of race-soul. And it is from this secret core that there develops what we call racial characteristic (Volkstum) and race-culture. . . .'[12] Elsewhere he commented on the error of failing to seek religion 'in the ground of a man's being' (auf dem Gebiete des Seins), an error that necessarily led to materialism.[13]

Pseudo-mysticism of this kind was not at that period confined to Germany. The following quotation from D. H. Lawrence contains something comparable in a more literary and less racialist form: 'My soul knows that I am part of the human race, my soul is an organic part of the great human soul, as my spirit is part of my nation. In my own very self, I am part of my family. There is nothing of me that is alone and absolute except my mind, and we shall find that the mind has no existence by itself; it is only the glitter of the sun on the surface of the waters. So that my individualism is really an illusion. . . . What we want is to destroy our false, inorganic connections, especially those related to money, and re-establish the living organic connections with the cosmos, the sun and earth, with mankind and nation and family.'[14] Lawrence, too, was in revolt against the atomisation of traditional communities under the impact of urbanism and industrialisation.

It seems to have been this strain of mystic pantheism that Rosenberg thought he had discovered in the works of the medieval Dominican known as Meister Eckhart, who in 1327 had been obliged to appear before the Pope and Curia to answer accusations of heresy. Rosenberg read a translation of Eckhart's Latin works in the version of a German student of Plotinus, H. Buettner, who is alleged by a modern commentator to have mistranslated the Dominican in the interest of establishing his thesis that 'the true religion taught by Eckhart consists in reuniting our being with the "ground" that is one and eternal'.[15] Rosenberg was thus able to identify Eckhart with his favourite biblical text 'The Kingdom of Heaven is within you'. But in order to annex Eckhart for his purposes, Rosenberg had in some way to identify him with the German race-soul. This he did to his own satisfaction by making the assumption that, because Eckhart had had difficulties with Pope and Curia, he was defending Germanic freedom of conscience against arid scholasticism and priestly tyranny. 'In the German mystic the new, reborn German man makes his first conscious appearance. Not in the time of the so-called Renaissance, not in the so-called Reformation did the spiritual birth of our culture come about. . . . No, in the thirteenth and fourteenth centuries the idea of spiritual personality, the dominant idea of our history, becomes for the first time a religion and way of life.'[16] In 1934 Rosenberg extracted from the *Mythus* a short book on *The Religion of Meister Eckhart;** it deservedly proved to be the least popular of his books. Whatever the Dominican may have suffered at the hands of the Avignon Pope John XXII, he suffered far worse indignities in the pages of his admirer, Alfred Rosenberg.

This strange aberration on the part of the Nazi ideologist may become more intelligible if examined in relation to the thinking of another object of his veneration, H. S. Chamberlain, whom he hailed as 'the apostle and founder of a German future'. Chamberlain, the friend of Kaiser Wilhelm and sage of Bayreuth, was more of an 'establishment' figure than was Lagarde (the other forerunner acknowledged by Rosenberg), who had left the Protestant Church and had been a severe critic of Bismarck. Chamberlain was no revolutionary; he believed that Christianity, like society, could be reformed and saved. But he was only interested in the salvation of Germans and this made him the spiritual father of the German Christians, of whom we shall have more to say shortly. 'I see the greatest danger for the future of the Germans in the lack of a true religion, which corresponds to our nature and derives from it. . . .'[17] The great need, as he saw it, was for a new Luther, who would again rescue Christianity from Roman and 'universal' tendencies and give it back to the German people. Luther, for Chamberlain, was 'the greatest man in world history'.[18]

This went too far for Rosenberg. He was prepared to pay lip-service to Luther as a heroic, anti-Roman figure; but whole-hearted admiration would have conflicted with the revolutionary direction in which he wished Nazism to move. To have attempted to reinterpret Luther for the twentieth century would have brought him into competition with Lutheran theologians with the whole weight of the Church behind them. This was a battle which he could not hope to win; Luther had been a revolutionary figure in the sixteenth century, but he could not answer this purpose 300 years later. In any case, Nazi historiography, whilst it honoured Luther's stand against Rome, recognised that his action

* *Die Religion des Meisters Eckhart*, A. Rosenberg (Munich, 1934).

G

had led ultimately to the Thirty Years War, the greatest disaster in German history before the First World War. Moreover the defeat of 1918 had had its roots not only in the opposing world conspiracy, but also in defects in the Second Reich, which had been predominantly Lutheran – the Holy Evangelical Reich of the German Nation, as Court Pastor Stoecker had called it. The Third Reich needed a different religious basis and a different apostle. The Nazis never found either, but in the meantime it was useful to have a relatively obscure one, unacknowledged by either of the leading Churches, whose prophet Rosenberg could become. Useful, because Eckhart's beliefs, as interpreted by Buettner and Rosenberg, would act as a dissolvent of all existing Churches, by making religion once more a matter between each German believer and his Germanic God. Each would understand God in his own way; but those who were of the blood would all come to understand Him in a broadly similar way.

At this point the religion of the blood again found Chamberlain an unsatisfactory Church Father. In his youth he had studied biology and he knew that the Aryan race was not a scientific concept, however convenient it might be as a political concept. He must have known that 'Aryan' could properly be applied only to language and had nothing to do with anatomy. To overcome this obstacle he had evolved purely subjective criteria for determining whether a man was Aryan; the decisive factor was 'the possession of race in the consciousness of the human being himself. He who avowedly belongs to a race experiences this every day.'[19] In other words, a man who acted as an Aryan was, by this fact, recognisable as an Aryan. Rosenberg readily accepted this as a partial definition, since it enabled him to claim for the Aryan race many historical figures who were no longer able to produce their credentials for Himmler's Race and Settlement Main Office. As his official biographer explained, 'In every human achievement, be it in the form of philosophy, politics or art, a race-soul finds its expression with as true a resemblance as does the physical form of the individual.'[20]

On the other hand, Rosenberg was enough of a practical politician to know that a definition that might satisfy a philosopher would be inadequate to permit a politician to divide Aryan sheep from non-Aryan goats. He therefore readily accepted more recent

research, notably that of the Nazis' chief academic racialist, Professor H. F. K. Guenther, who claimed to have established on a
scientific basis the racial characteristics of Nordic-Aryan man.
Rosenberg noted that in Chamberlain's last book, *Man and God*,
the ancient inhabitants of India, Greece and Germany were
described as belonging to the same race and concluded that the
sage had seen the light in his declining years.[21]

In the last analysis, Rosenberg took refuge in upholding
mystical experience as the true religion to escape a dilemma of
his own making. He was resolved to reject religions bound up
with what he called the abstractions of universalism, humanism
and individualism and to found the 'religion of the blood' upon
experience; but human experience, as usually understood and
recorded in the pages of history, would have meant, in his terms,
following the Churches in their descent into materialism, by which
he understood their creeds, ritual, organisation and historical existence. To all this he opposed the claim that 'For Aryan man, the
true religious experience, however, has always been outside space
and time and non-causal, that is, non-materialist, non-historical
and non-rational. . . .'[22] He followed Chamberlain in holding that
it was the failure of the Churches to keep their distance from
the material world that had led them into dogmatic statements
about its nature and so into collision with scientific thought.

It was impossible, however, to remain at this exalted level,
partly because Rosenberg, as a politician, wanted Nazi ideology
on all planes, including the religious, to be an effective force, and
partly because he was determined to link it with race. The
dilemma arose because the Aryan race was itself an abstraction and
could only be rescued from this undesirable category by being
defined, however subjectively, in terms of human characteristics.
The ones chosen by Rosenberg, under Chamberlain's influence,
were the unique Aryan capacities to found states and produce
great art. Armed with these preconceived ideas, he therefore
plunged back into history, in order to demonstrate who were
the Aryans and what their historic, indeed divine, mission had
been in the past and would be in the future.

For Rosenberg, 'the history of the religion of the blood is . . .
the great world story of the rise and fall of peoples, their heroes
and thinkers, their inventors and artists.'[23] This mad Valkyrie

ride through the pages of history is recorded in the long first section of the *Mythus*. In it, as Helga Grebing has pointed out, he uses indiscriminately the terms Aryan, Nordic and Germanic to describe manifestations which earn his approbation. 'He speaks of "Aryan India" of "Aryan Persia" of "Nordic Hellas", of "Nordic Latinness" (Latinertum), of the Nordic creation of Russia, of the Nordic Germans, with whom everything representing true worth and creative culture originated. ...'[24] Like others before and since, he found it easier and more rewarding to interpret history in terms of his prejudices, rather than trace throughout history how these prejudices originated.

There is an entry in Rosenberg's diary which must concern the genesis of the second section; after recording the fact that the Fuehrer, unlike himself, did not like Gothic art, he refers to a passage in the *Mythus*, explaining why it was no longer possible to build in the Gothic style. 'This passage,' he adds, 'was written in about 1917–18.'[25] He had then begun to set down thoughts about forms of artistic expression, as well as about prehistory and race. His *magnum opus* had not started as a political polemic at all; but as a cultural tract. He did not develop it in a systematic way, however, and it soon began to take political colour from the activities in which he became immersed on arrival in Munich. 'The *Mythus* does not bear the mark of a rounded, thought-out, academic study, but rather bears many signs of having been written in a time of struggle. ... I wrote it in the intervals of my editorial work and on Sunday mornings. ...'[26] As the struggle of the NSDAP for political victory became hotter, the heroes of German culture, Rembrandt, Herder, Wagner and the others, began to give way before the great fighters, Henry the Lion, Frederick the Great and Moltke. By 1925 the book was 'complete in its essential features'.[27]

By these arbitrary and haphazard methods Rosenberg produced a work designed to fulfil the function of a philosophy of history, to root the NSDAP firmly in the Germanic past and indicate its future direction. For this purpose, the title of the book, which so much irritated Hitler, was apt. Whatever Rosenberg's pretensions to being an artist, he never claimed to be a biologist or anthropologist; he was content to leave the scientific basis of racialism – if indeed there was one – to others. He may even have shared in secret some of the doubts of his mentor, H. S. Chamberlain, who had written: 'Even if it were proved that in the past there never was an Aryan race, we want there to be one in the future.'[28] The function of a myth is not to record history, but to create it by first evoking belief. C. D. Darlington has written of the origins of Christianity: 'It was not history; but, as a whole, through being believed, it became history.'[29] Such is, indeed, the aim of myth-makers. Rosenberg, at least, was specific on this point: 'the new *Mythus* and the new power to create a type cannot in any way be refuted. They will establish themselves and they will create facts.'[30]

In Rosenberg's philosophy of history the twin forces of disintegration, namely universalism and individualism, are in perpetual conflict with the Germanic concept of race, the only sure foundation on which to base the state. It would be tedious and unrewarding to follow him in his attempt to make the history of ancient India, Persia and Greece conform to a pattern in which observance or neglect of doctrines of race and caste determine the rise or fall of nations, empires and their cultures. He expends special care on the decline of 'the Roman world system', because this enables him to illustrate the fatal influence of Christianity, exploiting both the universalism already present in the imperial system and the individualism present in the Christian doctrine of the soul and its salvation. If all Christians have souls, all Christians are at least potentially equal; but to the Nazis equality in all its aspects was detestable. 'Everything still imbued with the Roman character sought to defend itself against the rise of Christianity, all the more because Christianity, alongside its religious teaching, represented a completely proletarian-nihilistic political trend.'[31] The religion of love and the politics of equality were both poison to the state; the pacifism of early Christians had undermined Rome in the same way that defeatists had handicapped the Reich in the Great War.

Once the 'Roman world system' has been captured by Christianity, its anti-racial, universal tenets make it the implacable foe of the best interests of the German Volk. Although the Roman Church may appear to be opposed to Judaism, it is, in fact, the main channel through which Jewish ideas infect the healthy corpus of Germanic thought. For example, the Germanic ideal of living in conformity with nature and esteeming fine physique and manly beauty has been undermined by Christian antagonism to 'the flesh' and by sentimental ideas about preserving the lives of defective children and allowing criminals and those with hereditary illness to propagate their defects. Impurity of race 'produces fragmentation of character, loss of the sense of direction in thought and action, inner uncertainty ...'. This has been aggravated by the Christian doctrine of original sin, which 'would have been incomprehensible to a Volk of unbroken racial character... Homer's heroes know no "sin"; no more than did the ancient Indians and the Germans of Tacitus....'[32] At the Nuremberg party rally in 1937 Rosenberg assured his hearers, 'The German people is not born in sin, but born in nobility' (Nicht erbsuendig, sondern erbadlig).

The more feeble nations became, through absorbing Christian doctrines of individualism and love of humanity, the more easily they could be dominated by Rome, using the priesthood as its main instrument. In the sixteenth century this domination had been checked by Luther, but the Counter-Reformation had enabled Rome to reassert her power in the Thirty Years War with disastrous results for Germany. Later, a new weapon was developed in Freemasonry, which made its headquarters in England, France and Italy and fomented revolutions which 'undermined the foundations of Germanic being.... This atomistic Weltanschauung was and is the precondition for the political doctrine of democracy.'[33] It was no coincidence that the resurgence of this newly formulated doctrine of human and racial equality occurred at a time when Frederick the Great, by his courage and insistence on the military virtues, had regained for Germany the concept of honour. During the first World War the continuing hostility of the Papacy is illustrated by quotations from Pope Benedict xv and by the treasonable behaviour of his puppet, the last Habsburg Emperor, in suing for a separate peace. After the war, Germany is kept prostrate by an unholy alliance between Social Democracy and the Catholic Centre party in Prussia, while in Bavaria political Catholicism plays the separatist game.

The Popes of Rome are not, of course, alone in their onslaught on the German people; they have been joined in their sinister work by the Jews and Marxists. The proletariat falls a ready victim to the doctrine of class war, because industrialisation has destroyed the relatively stable social structure. Rosenberg has no use for what he describes as 'the individualism of economic man'; this is a figment of the Jewish mind to lure men to their doom. Their only salvation is in a new faith – the religion of the blood. Within the bond of race man can escape 'the throttling of individual life under the materialist pressure of the age.'[34] Without this faith he is condemned to frustration and despair.

This was the clarion call of Nazism, as of other forms of Fascism: to stand together, to feel strong, to act heroically, in accordance with one's new-found strength. But for those already impregnated with racialism German Nazism was even more attractive than Italian Fascism, because its adherents were able to believe themselves to be potential heroes simply by virtue of being born Germans; they were predestined to greatness and anyone opposing them was flying in the face of the laws of Nature and of Fate. Rosenberg was described by his Nazi colleague, Schwerin v. Krosigk as 'the father of this teaching ... everyday people now had it in black and white: each was a "Superman".'[35] In 1934 a student wrote to Rosenberg to tell him which was the passage in the Mythus that had most impressed him. It was: 'Today there awakes a new faith; the myth of the blood, the faith to defend with one's blood the divine essence within the human being'.[36] There can be no denying the shimmer of idealism masking the harsh realities of the Nazi programme; indeed the distinguished German historian, Hans Rothfels, has himself referred to the 'illusionary and soon deceived idealism' that accompanied the Nazi revolution, and to 'the power of attraction of the ideology of Volkstum.'[37] Melita Maschmann has written, 'But for this racial mystique, the scientific orientation of National-Socialism would certainly not have impressed me.'[38]

It is not hard to understand the powerful appeal of this doctrine to a once proud nation, now ground down by frustration and humiliation. The political atmosphere in Germany from 1919 to 1923 was oppressive with doom, almost eschatological; a rational, intellectually satisfying ideology was the last thing people were looking for. The contradictions and historical errors to be found in the Mythus were not going to offend anyone who had been initially attracted to Nazism. Those who bought copies –

and by January 1937 500,000 had been disposed of – were seeking to regain confidence in themselves, to recapture – against all the evidence – the belief that they were a people of destiny. 'I believe because it is impossible,' Tertullian had affirmed of his faith. As a substitute faith for Christianity, Nazism was doomed; there was a hollow, if resounding, emptiness at the heart of it. This only became widely understood in the Reich, however, when the god of war was seen to have turned against Hitler; up to a point the Nazi 'Ersatz' creed had been devised with some ingenuity. Marxists preached the struggle against the exploiting class; the Nazis substituted the struggle against the Jew. Marxism identified labour as the source of all value; Nazism replaced it by blood. This latter substitution was particularly useful, because it enabled Rosenberg and the anti-Christian faction to move towards a further substitution: the blood of Christ in the sacrament was to be replaced by the blood of the German war dead, who must not be thought to have died in vain.

It will be recalled that the Nazis had from the first seized avidly on the legend of 'the stab in the back', which served the dual purpose of exculpating the ex-serviceman from any share in the débâcle of 1918, while pillorying the 'November traitors'. Scarcely less bitter than defeat itself were the disarmament clauses of the Treaty of Versailles; restrictions on bearing arms were insulting to German military honour. This was a key factor in the success of the para-military Free Corps, including the SA, in the immediate post-war period. As the Nazis began to build up their movement and their propaganda on the need for struggle and self-sacrifice, they increasingly invoked the recent war dead in the role of sacrificial victims. In November 1925 we find in the anti-semitic monthly, *Weltkampf*, which Rosenberg had started in the previous year, an article in which he addressed himself to the question, among others, why the First World War had produced no great war poet. This was because, as he explained, 'no one knew in his innermost self that he was fighting and dying for a new myth. Today millions of all peoples think about the grave of "the unknown soldier" . . . Soon they will realise that these twelve million men of the white race are martyrs; that they are all victims of a crumbling epoch and at the same time the heralds of a new one. These men, who today lie dead ... are the noblest witnesses to the immortality of the ideas of race and people. ... Out of this myth a new culture and a new art will someday arise.'[39]

This formulation, however, was of too general a character; it was not long before Rosenberg abandoned the twelve million European dead in favour of the two million German dead, who had entered into the Valhalla of the race-soul. By posing as their heirs, the Nazis were able to exploit recollections of the feelings of comradeship and solidarity that had animated the front-line soldiers. Because they were the party of the 'outsiders', they had a greater appeal to the young than did the more staid veterans' organisation, the Stahlhelm, which was associated with the traditional conservatives of the German National People's Party (DNVP).

Passages in the *Mythus* in which Rosenberg pays tribute to the fallen heroes of 1914–18 were popular; this is clear from the fact that his biographer, F. T. Hart, selected so many of them for reproduction. 'The field-grey German People's Army was proof of the readiness for sacrifice which creates myth. Today's movement of rebirth is the sign that countless men and women begin to understand what it is that two million dead heroes represent: martyrs of a new myth of life, indeed of a new faith. ...'[40] Rosenberg's use of the words, 'martyr' and 'faith' represented in his mind more than an analogy; his 'religion of the blood' required religious symbolism. He was not daunted by the fact that so much of it was borrowed from Christianity; in the early days of the Christian faith, he claimed, the Church borrowed from heathendom in much the same way. But certain Christian symbols must be rejected; the crucifix, representing Christ's suffering and symbolising the religion of love, was to be replaced in every village as its spiritual core by 'the two million German heroes who are really alive. ... The men of the coming age will transform the heroes' war memorials and glades of remembrance into the places of pilgrimage of a new religion; there the hearts of Germans will be constantly shaped afresh in pursuit of a new myth.'[41] If the German invasion of Russia had succeeded, and Nazism had consolidated its hold, we can picture non-Christian memorials to the heroic dead arising all along the new eastern frontiers, where Aryan blood had been so abundantly shed.

In addition to battening upon war dead, the Nazi myth sought to link itself to a remoter past. The Third Reich needed a tradition, if only in order to differentiate itself from the parvenu Republic of Weimar; but the tradition of the Second Reich, with its dynasties, its strict social hierarchy and its final ignominious collapse, was unserviceable. To this extent the myth was a substitute tradition: it was to provide for the new state what the cult of the Fuehrer and his charisma had done for Hitler. Everything heroic, Germanic, pre-Christian was grist to Rosenberg's mill. He sought out the burial place of Widukind the Saxon and with Himmler made a pilgrimage to the supposed grave of the Saxon King Henry I in Quedlinburg. At Verden, where Charlemagne had defeated heathendom, Rosenberg called for a memorial of 4,500 stones, one for each Saxon slain. In May 1934, in cooperation with Himmler, Darré and Roever, the Gauleiter of Oldenburg, where the Roman Catholics were strong, he organised a solemn commemoration of the 700th anniversary of the battle of Altenesch, in which a whole community, condemned as heretics by the Medieval Archbishop of Bremen, had been put to death. Before a crowd comprising, as he claimed, 40,000 farmers and peasants, he asserted to great applause, 'The Holy Land for Germans is not Palestine.... Our holy places are certain castles on the Rhine, the good earth of Lower Saxony and the Prussian fortress of Marienburg.'[42]

The attempt, expressed in the *Mythus,* to create a national, racial cult was parallel to the efforts to build up a cult within the NSDAP itself. This proved more difficult, if only because the NSDAP had had so short a history. Yet even this unpromising fact could be pressed into service to bolster the cult of the Fuehrer. In 1936 Goering – perhaps the leader least touched by ideology – exclaimed, 'And then suddenly, comrades, the turning point came. In later time the historians will not know how to depict it. For the first time in world history the historians will conclude: that did not happen by the normal process.'[43] There is little doubt that many Nazis believed this. In May 1941, when Rosenberg addressed a memorandum to Bormann, drawing attention to the need to curb the growth of astrology and other superstitions, he attributed it in great measure to Hitler's sensational rise to power. 'The achievements of National-Socialism, the singular emergence of the Fuehrer have no parallel in German history. . . . Soon after the assumption of power they [i.e. many Germans] were depicting the Fuehrer as a Messiah and ascribing the great outcome of the struggle to supernatural powers.'[44]

Fanatical loyalty to the Fuehrer was the first ingredient, but it was not enough. It needed to be supplemented by an emotional feeling of comradeship and collective loyalty within the movement. The Nazi 'religion of the blood' needed a cult of its own dead. After an early SA-man, Leo Schlageter, had been shot by the French during the occupation of the Ruhr in 1923, the Nazis claimed him as a martyr. The sixteen who fell before the Feldherrn Halle in Munich on 9 November 1923 were added to the roll of honour and a swastika flag, said to be stained with their blood, was named the 'blood flag' and used in ceremonies, beginning at the Nuremberg rally in 1929, to dedicate other flags. In 1935 the coffins of the dead Putschists were removed from consecrated ground, without any attempt to obtain the permission of relatives, and placed in a so-called 'Temple of Honour', constructed in the Koenigplatz in Munich. Hitler called out the name as each coffin was brought in and a detachment of the HJ replied, 'Here!'

This was an embellishment of a practice adopted by Italian Fascists and praised by Rosenberg in an editorial in the *VB* in honour of the interment of the best known and least savoury of all the Nazi heroes, Horst Wessel. Rosenberg in his editorial described how the Fascists, after one of their comrades had been killed by Communists, reinscribed his name in their muster roll and answered to it at roll call. 'Like the other martyrs, Horst Wessel, too, is not dead. Combat group (Sturm) 5, which he led and expanded tenfold, already bears his name ... unseen and yet perceptible, the souls of the "dead" struggle together with us for a new life.'[45] From this time on Nazi dead who, like ancient Vikings, died in battle, were referred to as 'summoned to Horst Wessel's standard'. In a speech in Berlin on 30 October 1933 Rosenberg praised the German Christian Bishop Joachim Hossenfelder, who at the burial service of a Nazi named Maikowski had declaimed in the Church, 'Our comrade Maikowski has been mustered to Horst Wessel's combat group.'[46]

The fact that these cults were being openly practised within the NSDAP makes the complacent attitude of the Christian

Churches towards Nazism particularly hard to comprehend. Here distinctions must be made both between the Roman Catholic and Protestant Churches, and between the periods before and after Hitler came to power. In the former period the NSDAP was treated in most Roman Catholic dioceses with marked hostility, although treatment even then was not uniform through the Reich. The Roman Church, partly because of its experience of having to resist Bismarck's attacks upon its ultramontane character, was more suspicious of nationalist extremism than the Protestants showed themselves to be. Until 1933 Nazis were refused the sacraments by Catholic priests and columns of uniformed Nazis with their swastika banners were excluded from their Churches. This robust attitude, as we shall see in the next chapter, largely vanished when Hitler came to power.

Within the Protestant Churches, especially among Lutherans, possibilities of coordinated resistance to the NSDAP had been largely destroyed even before 1933; indeed a substantial section of laity and clergy actively supported the party. A frank and comprehensive account of the sad decline of inner conviction and moral discrimination within the Evangelical Churches still awaits its historian; it is impossible to do full justice to the theme in these pages. Already in the nineteenth century these Churches had become so tainted with nationalism, anti-socialism and anti-semitism as to make it exceedingly difficult for them to oppose a political party that skilfully exploited these prejudices, all of which were aggravated by the creation of the Weimar Republic. The disappearance of the Kaiser meant that the Evangelical Churches lost their secular head and relapsed into a loose association of twenty-eight Land Churches. They saw themselves confronted, especially in Prussia, with a coalition between the Catholic Centre party and the SPD, which was highly repugnant to them.

This was not all; heresy was also rife. H. S. Chamberlain and Paul de Lagarde, himself a Protestant theologian, had both wished to reform Christianity by purging it of Jewish elements and giving it a distinctively Germanic character. Chamberlain combined this with that exaggerated sense of obedience to the state, to which Lutherans are doctrinally prone. These two men were among the precursors of various groups of 'German Christians', who found nothing repellent in the pretensions of the NSDAP. The 1920 programme of the party had been ambivalent; it claimed to uphold 'a positive Christianity' and envisaged 'liberty for all religious denominations in the state, so far as they are not a danger to it and do not militate against the morality and moral sense of the German race.'[47] It was no secret, of course, that his latter phrase contained an allusion to the anti-semitism of the NSDAP. Unfortunately this encountered no objection on the part of the German Christians; indeed two major groups, which combined in 1932 as 'The Faith Movement of German Christians' under Pastor (later Bishop) Hossenfelder, wished at first to be known as 'The National-Socialist Evangelical Church' and had to be prevented by Hitler from assuming this designation. In synodal elections in November 1932 this movement won one-third of the votes and in January 1933 held services of thanksgiving for Hitler's accession to the Chancellorship.

Karl Barth wrote of the Evangelical Church as a whole: 'It is notorious that the political change of the year 1933 meant for it above all a serious temptation. The Church had almost unanimously welcomed the Hitler regime with real confidence, indeed, with the highest hopes.'[48] Lutherans, who believed that God manifested himself in history, not once, in the person of Christ, but repeatedly, were painfully exposed to the euphoria of the hour. Cries of 'One Church, One Reich, One Fuehrer' were widespread and Church Councillor Leutheuser went so far as to claim, 'Christ has come to us through Adolf Hitler.'[49] Blasphemy could scarcely go further.

The German Christians had always been strong in Thuringia, where one of their leaders, Dr Artur Dinter, also became the first Nazi Gauleiter. Dinter aimed not only at founding a new German People's Church, but at becoming its new Luther; for this purpose he had enunciated 197 theses, which in his view completed the work of the Reformation.* Luther's work was imperfect, because he had accepted the Old Testament, the Synoptic Gospels and Paul's Epistles as the word of God. In Dinter's view, the only Gospel that could be accepted was that of John, and that only after radical 'retranslation'. For good measure, he threw in the theory of reincarnation. All this was a considerable embarrassment to Hitler who, as Rosenberg remarked in his memoir, 'set

* *197 Thesen zur Vollendung der Reformation*, A. Dinter (Leipzig 1926).

his face from the beginning against racial cultism'.[50] Thuringia was important to him, however, as from 1925 to 1928 he was banned from speaking in most of the other Laender; Dinter played quite a prominent role in the NSDAP rally which took place at Weimar (Thuringia) in July 1926. Hitler replaced him as Gauleiter by Fritz Sauckel as soon as he safely could and in 1929 drummed him out of the party.

Rosenberg was never in danger of becoming identified with this theological misadventure. In the first place, to have recognised one of his own contemporaries as a latter-day Luther would have destroyed his own claim to be the chief ideologist and philosopher of the party; his attitude towards the pretensions of Dinter was no more friendly than that which he adopted later towards Hans Kerrl's efforts to solve the problems of the Lutheran Church. He wrote in the *Mythus*: 'Nowhere in Germany has a religious genius arisen, who might have shown us a new religious type besides the existing ones.'[51] In the second place, he did not want an institutional church with a set of beliefs and an order of service. Religion was something between a man and his own soul, or, if he had the good fortune to be a German, between himself and the folk-soul. In an editorial in the *VB* he quoted Lagarde: 'The state cannot create a religion.'[52] This continued to the end to be his attitude. Moreover Hitler, before he came to power, was determined not to allow the build-up of the NSDAP to be handi-capped by religious controversy. He must surely have approved before publication Rosenberg's review of Volume II of *Mein Kampf* containing the following passage: 'Adolf Hitler . . . affirms the necessity that the NSDAP should guard against all disputes about Church problems, in order to concentrate all its forces against one enemy. . . .'[53]

It must have been exasperating to Hitler, who had just disposed of Dinter, to be confronted with a politico-theological problem of another kind. The MS of the *Mythus*, typed by Frau Rosenberg, had been completed before the end of 1929. 'Then I took it to Hitler in a fairly complete form and asked him to look it over.'[54] Six months elapsed before Rosenberg plucked up courage to enquire about the verdict on his book; the reply that he then received was: 'It is a very clever book; only I ask myself who today is likely to read and understand such a book.' Rosenberg asked whether, in the interests of the NSDAP, he should suppress it, or publish it anonymously; to this Hitler's answer was: 'Not at all; it is your intellectual property.' Finally, when Rosenberg enquired whether he should resign party office, he was told that Hitler had not even thought of it.[55] If, as Rosenberg later claimed, his MS was lodged in mid-June 1930 with the Hoheneichen publishing house, a subsidiary of the firm publishing the *VB*, this would be consistent with Hitler's having given his consent in the course of the conversation just cited. But the fact remains that Rosenberg did not sign a contract with the parent firm, Franz Eher successors, until 15 September 1930.[56] It can scarcely be a coincidence that this was the day following the sensational victory of the NSDAP at the polls, when it became overnight the second largest party in the Reichstag. It is difficult to resist the conclusion that Hitler and Amann continued to procrastinate until they felt that the NSDAP was strong enough to stand the loss of support, especially among Roman Catholics, that might be expected to follow publication.

How vigorous this public reaction, in fact, proved to be is a question to which we shall address ourselves in the next chapter. The question that immediately arises, however, is that of Hitler's real attitude to the book. That he must have had serious political misgivings is evident from his long delay in reaching a decision, as well as from his general views on religious controversy, to which reference has already been made. We have also suggested that Hitler had certain feelings of hostility towards Rosenberg's pretensions as a political philosopher, based on the Fuehrer's exclusive claim to this role, as far as the NSDAP was concerned. It may have been on his insistence (though Rosenberg does not say so) that only one explicit mention of the NSDAP occurs in the *Mythus*. Hitler himself is only referred to by name in three places, one of these a footnote. On the other hand, it would have been surprisingly naive of Hitler to have assumed that he and the NSDAP could dissociate themselves from a book written by such a prominent member of the party and published by a subsidiary of its own publishing house.

Presumably in order to explain this discrepancy Konrad Heiden made the assumption that Hitler never bothered to read the *Mythus;* most later historians have followed him in this view.

Substance is given to it by one of Hitler's wartime conversations, in the course of which he said that, like many Gauleiters, he himself had only read a small part of it, 'as in his view it was also written in a way that was too difficult to understand'.[57] While anyone who has taken up the book must agree with Hitler's verdict, it is not easy to give full credence to his remark. It is also necessary to recall that the record of these talks was edited by Bormann, who was hostile to Rosenberg. Hitler's view on the political damage wrought by religious dispute was on record in *Mein Kampf*; Rosenberg's attitude towards religion was a matter of common knowledge; it would have been inconsistent with what we know of the Fuehrer's tight control over the NSDAP in its early days for him to have allowed the book to be published without having read it. Hanfstaengl has quoted Oswald Spengler as condemning Hitler's intellectual capacity, because he 'swore by Rosenberg's *Mythus*'.[58] There is moreover the evidence of Otto Strasser, who in late May 1930 had the lengthy discussion with Hitler that led to his exclusion from the party. In the course of Strasser's published account, which Hitler never refuted, he was quoted as having said, 'All revolutions in world history – and I have studied them in detail – are nothing save racial struggles. If you would only read Rosenberg's new book – the most tremendous achievement of its kind even greater than Chamberlain's – then you would understand these things. . . .'[59] Otto Strasser was certainly no friend of Rosenberg; there would have been no object in his recording this comment unless Hitler had, in fact, made it.

There is, of course, evidence of Hitler's later distaste for the book and, indeed, for its author. Speer has recorded, 'The book was widely regarded by the public as the standard text of Party ideology, but Hitler characterised it summarily at these tea-time talks as "that thing that nobody can understand, written by a narrow-minded Balt, who thinks in a fearfully complicated way". He was astonished that such a book should go into so many editions.'[60] Against this evidence, however, must be set the public record of support: Rosenberg's party offices, the imposition of his book upon the educational syllabus, and the award to its author in 1937 of the first National Prize for Art and Learning. Knowing, as we now do, how closely Hitler's real views about the Churches and Christianity approximated to Rosenberg's, one can only reach the conclusion that the Fuehrer was glad that this ideological poison should be disseminated, while seeking to escape personal identification with it. He, as tribal chief, was the main beneficiary of the primitive cult, of which Rosenberg was witch-doctor; in the long term the hocus-pocus would be useful to him, whatever his private feelings about it may have been. After all, the ideology was not primarily intended for the inner elite; it was one of the instruments of their ascendancy over the party and thus over the Reich.

There is now no reliable means of assessing the influence exerted by the *Mythus*; it cannot be gauged by recording the massive figures of the book's circulation. Secondary schools and institutions of higher education were required to have copies in their libraries; but to what extent these were read cannot now be estimated. All that one can affirm with confidence is that apprehensions about the book's effect were soon aroused in religious circles. A Protestant Pastor, Heinrich Hueffmeier, who in 1935 published a refutation, described the *Mythus* as being 'read by all those who made even the least pretensions to intellectual development'.[61] A Roman Catholic priest, Father Neuss, whose counter-attack on the *Mythus* we shall consider in the next chapter, thought that it 'must have a very bad effect on a reader unable to form his own judgment, because of its self-assured tone'.[62]

Contemporary voices are the only ones to which it is now useful to listen, however remote may seem the epoch from which they come. When the Thousand-year Reich crumbled to ruin, nobody wished to be identified with its excesses and absurdities; none of the other prisoners at Nuremberg would admit to knowledge of the contents of the book. The rank and file wanted to forget the past; in 1942 over one million copies had been in circulation, but these quickly vanished. Nothing proved less durable than the ideology; cradled in the delusion of the 'stab in the back', brought to manhood by the military triumphs of 1938–42, it seemed in the aftermath of renewed defeat as if it had never existed. The gutted concentration camps remained, like survivals of some remote and scarcely explicable system of violence and superstition. The German people could not, or would not, reveal by

H

what terrible forces they had been driven; they sought refuge in such partial alibis as Hitler's demonic powers of mass hypnosis and the irresistible tyranny of the ss.

For Germans of a later generation the elements of contorted and misguided idealism embodied in the ideology have become opaque. For non-Germans they never had much appeal. Rosenberg himself maintained that the *Mythus* had been written for Germans and denied that he had wanted to see it translated into other languages, though there had been a Japanese version.[63] This denial certainly went too far; his publishers had, in fact, tried to place the book in England and America. In 1934 they informed him that four American firms had rejected it and, without an American edition, no British publisher would take it.[64] In the following year a Dutch Pastor wrote to Rosenberg offering to undertake a translation[65] and in 1942 a French version was sent to him for his approval.[66] He claimed in 1940 to have refused permission for renderings into Spanish and Italian.[67] When in 1944 there was a proposal for an Hungarian text, he commented that this was 'unnecessary'.[68] It was a verdict that, by that date, nobody was likely to dispute. Even if translation rights were insubstantial, sales in Germany were quite enough to keep him in comfort. After 1933 Nazi authors were generously treated by tax authorities and in 1943 all receipts from publications of the Eher publishing house were declared to be tax-free.[69] The *Mythus* was certainly a financial success, however adverse the verdict of history on it may be.

# 6 Delegate for Indoctrination

Felix Kersten, who from being Himmler's masseur became his confidant, once asked his master, 'Why have you at one and the same time made implacable enemies of the Jews and the Masons on the one side, and their professed enemy, the Roman Church, on the other...?'[1] Himmler evaded the question, remarking only that such matters were for the Fuehrer to decide. Hitler had not come to a final decision in 1930; but by permitting the *Mythus* to be published he encouraged the ideological wing of the NSDAP and set it on the road that it was to follow more and more openly as time went on. In the short term, however, Hitler must soon have begun to regret his decision to authorise publication. His success in the 1930 election had made him a serious contender for the office of Chancellor; but he could only hope to come to power legally, as he intended, by allying the NSDAP either with the DNVP or with the Catholic Centre party. The Centre under Monsignor v. Kaas had been moving to the Right since 1928 and since March 1930 its leader in the Reichstag, Heinrich Bruening, had been governing the country without a stable parliamentary majority on the strength of President Hindenburg's invocation of his emergency powers. This was a situation that the Nazis felt well able to exploit.

It was in this context that the author of the *Mythus* proved to be an embarrassment. He had taken his seat in the new Reichstag, wearing his brown shirt, like the other 106 representatives of the NSDAP; but he was more exposed than others, because he was a target for the missiles that could be quarried from the pages he had written. He had, for example, quoted with approval a statement by a certain Professor Wieth-Knudsen to the effect that German blood could not have fertilised Europe but for the practice of

polygamy during the Voelkerwanderung.[2] Rosenberg had commented that a future Reich could not allow surplus women of true German blood to pine away without a chance to do their racial duty by true German men, irrespective of whether the latter were single or married. This was indeed a gift to the other political parties, especially the Roman Catholics of the Centre. The fact that his doctrine was only later taken up by Himmler did nothing to mitigate the immediate awkwardness, especially as the Nazis posed as the party that was bent on cleaning up the moral iniquity of the Weimar Republic. Rosenberg was not the only obstacle to cooperation between the NSDAP and the Centre party, but he was certainly a hindrance. In March 1931 the Prussian Ministry of the Interior received a report from an agent in touch with Otto Strasser, who was now in open opposition to his former political associates. According to the report, 'The Centre and the BVP would only form a coalition with Hitler if he would drop Rosenberg. That he can in no circumstances do at present.'[3]

There was another reason, fully exploited by the Social-Democrats as well as the Centre, why Rosenberg was a liability in the Reichstag. The most damaging allegation that could be made about a fellow German between the two wars was that he was, or had been, in the pay of the French. Such an allegation had been made in the past against Rosenberg, as well as against his protégé, Kurt Luedecke, who had been put under arrest in Munich in January 1923 as a result of the gossip of brother Nazis. As we have seen, Rosenberg had been in Paris in the spring of 1914; it was an easy matter to shift the date to 1918 and insinuate that he had been working for the Deuxième Bureau. This was the version supplied by Hanfstaengl to Goering and relayed by the latter in the corridors of the Reichstag with the incriminating comment, 'The fellow should say at last what he was really doing in Paris during the war'.[4] It is interesting to note that the Prussian police, who in June 1931 consulted the Munich police about these suspicions and slanders, ascribed them to the envy of other party members 'on account of Rosenberg's influence over Hitler'.[5] In spite of consulting the French security service, neither police force could obtain confirmation of these stories. After the Nazis came to power the police assured Rosenberg privately that their enquiries in Paris had come to nothing;[6] but in 1930–32 the Prussian Minister of the Interior was a Social-Democrat, who naturally had no wish to end the dispute, more especially as Social-Democrat newspapers were having a field day at Rosenberg's expense. He was forced to take two cases before the Berlin courts, where damages were awarded in his favour.

Another charge levelled against him by political opponents was that he revealed in the pages of the *VB* information obtained by him as representative of the NSDAP in the Foreign Affairs Committee of the Reichstag. He mostly spoke in this capacity and on one occasion early in 1932, after he had attacked Bruening's conduct of foreign policy, the latter contemptuously described him as 'the so-called Balt, who at the moment that I was fighting to the last breath in the war had not yet discovered which his real Fatherland was'.[7] On the following day Rosenberg made his defence, speaking, as he claimed, on behalf of all Baltic Germans who had been denied the privilege of fighting for their true country; but he had to admit that the only overtly pro-German activity in which he had been able to indulge during the war had been to join with his student fraternity in singing German folk songs.

The other potential ally of the NSDAP, in its attempt to win power, was the DNVP, which since 1928 had also moved to the right under the leadership of Alfred Hugenberg, a former director of Krupps, who had later acquired important interests in newspapers, news agencies and films. This made him exactly the right man to fuel the Nazi propaganda machine, which Goebbels was busy reorganising. In 1929 when Germany was prostrated by the economic crisis, Hitler and Hugenberg had already formed a combined front against the Young Plan, by which German reparations payments were to be scaled down and phased out over a lengthy period. The crisis led to a moratorium on payments, but the fury of the two Right-wing parties continued unabated. Its connection with the DNVP gave to the NSDAP a cloak of respectability and industrialists showed themselves increasingly responsive to Hitler's demands for financial support. The need for these new contacts brought Goering further to the fore and through him Hitler came closer to Hjalmar Schacht, the former President of the Reichsbank. Schacht was a Freemason and thus an object of suspicion to Rosenberg. In any case ideologies were at a discount in the hard-headed world of business.

After the re-election of Hindenburg, and the fall of Bruening in the spring of 1932, the Nazis were only kept from power by the short-lived Chancellorships of Franz v. Papen and Major-General v. Schleicher. Faced with a decline in electoral support, one wing of the NSDAP, led by Gregor Strasser, favoured a coalition with Schleicher; but this would have meant a government without Hitler, who would settle for nothing short of the Chancellorship. In this he was backed to the hilt by Goebbels, whilst Rosenberg's inclinations lay more with Strasser, whose decisive break with Hitler occurred at this time. He resigned his offices and was replaced by the drunken braggart, Robert Ley. On 30 January 1933 Hitler at last became Chancellor through the complicity of Papen, Hugenberg and General v. Blomberg, who believed that, under the overriding authority of the senile President, they could use Hitler to maintain a working majority in the Reichstag, while charting a course back into the calmer waters of the Second Reich. It was to be a marriage between the new right-radicals and the old Conservatives and it was solemnised on 21 March 1933 in the Potsdam Garrison Church, where homage was paid at the tomb of Frederick the Great and Hitler, discarding his old trench coat for the traditional frock-coat, bowed low over the outstretched hand of Field-Marshal v. Hindenburg. In his speech the Chancellor announced, in addition to minatory references to making Germany safe from Communism, that 'The national government will allow and confirm to the Christian denominations the enjoyment of their due influence in schools and education.' If the Centre party noted the omission of these cautious words from the *VB* on the following day, they decided to ignore it. They voted in the Reichstag for dictatorial powers to be conferred on Hitler, and Monsignor v. Kaas hastened to Rome to begin negotiations for a Concordat with the Third Reich.

On 12 March 1933 Hitler, accompanied among others by Rosenberg, flew to Munich and laid on the memorial to the dead heroes of the 1923 Putsch a wreath bearing the words, 'And yet you conquered'.[8] The conquest of the Reich, however, meant different things to different Nazi leaders. To some, notably Goering and Goebbels, it was simply a question of securing a firm foothold in the state apparatus and exploiting the power that it provided. Goering, as Prussian Minister of the Interior, controlled the

Prussian state and political police (Gestapo). Goebbels in April 1933 was made Minister for Propaganda and Popular Enlightenment and soon began to dominate the field of cultural life, in which Rosenberg's KFDK was active. Goebbels, as Gauleiter, was strong in Berlin, where political activity was concentrated. Rosenberg had lingered too long in Munich, in spite of the entreaties of Schickedanz, and only installed himself in Berlin in January 1933, a few weeks before Hitler became Chancellor.

Quite apart from the predominance of Rosenberg's enemies, his usefulness, as ideologist of a party that had just come to power, was at a low point. In the years of struggle, possession of a body of doctrine, however superficial and irrational, had given substance to the claim of the NSDAP to be a serious political movement, transcending the factional strife of the despised Weimar 'system'. But the leaders, from Hitler down, had always been more hungry for power than for dogma; consistency in action meant no more to them than logic in doctrine. Although for the benefit of their followers they talked loudly of having seized power, they knew very well that they had come to it through political bargaining and were still heavily dependent on the cooperation, or at lowest the acquiescence, of Hindenburg and the Generals. In their compromise with the established forces of the state there was no room for an ideologist who believed that the state existed only to serve the party.

In this situation, with the established forces seeking to hold their own and party leaders contending for such spoils as could be prised loose, success depended upon the relationship of individual leaders to their Fuehrer. Until Hitler became Chancellor, most of the 'old fighters' had had reasonably free and easy relations with him. A British under-cover agent, William de Ropp, who was introduced to Hitler in 1931 by Rosenberg in the *VB* offices in Munich, has described the latter's almost casual attitude. 'There was no heel-clicking, no saluting. They met as equals.'[9] After Hitler became Chancellor, it seemed at first as if this state of affairs might continue; Rosenberg has recounted how, after Hitler had been sworn in, he rejoined his old comrades at the Hotel Kaiserhof and begged them to address him by name and not as 'Herr Reichskanzler'.[10] It did not last; most of the few (Rosenberg had never been among them) who had used the intimate

'Du' in speaking to Hitler had the privilege withdrawn. Rosenberg found himself kept at arm's length; not till the last day of March 1933 was he able to obtain a private interview. On that occasion, instead of being given a governmental post, he was fobbed off with authority to set up the Foreign Policy Office of the NSDAP (see Chapter 8). In June 1933 he was made a Reich Leader of the NSDAP, together with sixteen other leading party members, but he was no nearer securing a power base or apparat.

Rosenberg's failure to obtain a grip on the formulation of the foreign policy of the Reich was matched by neglect of his advice on how to conduct relations with the Churches. Hitler's accession to power had greatly modified his outward attitude towards both Confessions. He believed that he could exploit them in differing ways in order to consolidate his position and rally behind him those elements of the population that had not yet fallen under his spell. The wave of enthusiasm that had greeted him and, in particular, his spectacular reconciliation with the traditional authoritarian forces in the country had disconcerted the Roman Catholic hierarchy, who feared that, if they continued to oppose Nazism, they would be dubbed unpatriotic, as in the time of Bismarck's Kulturkampf, and would lose their hold on many of the faithful. Moreover leading prelates, both in Rome and in German dioceses, saw a chance to safeguard Church privileges, especially in the educational field, by concluding a Concordat. This had eluded them hitherto, because there had never been a majority forthcoming in the Reichstag; with that body in abeyance, new vistas opened up.

Hitler, for his part, welcomed the enhanced prestige that an agreement with the Vatican would bring to his regime, both at home and abroad. He was prepared to disown his ideologist for this short-term plan. His Vice-Chancellor, Papen, who was also a Catholic, has recorded, 'In our early conversations about Rosenberg and his new "myth", he [Hitler] used such expressions of ridicule that I could not believe these aberrations presented any danger.'[11] On 26 April 1933 the Bishop of Osnabrueck, who had previously called on Papen, had a conversation with Hitler, which reassured him, though this, in retrospect, may seem surprising. Hitler, after praising the hostility shown to the Jews by the Roman Catholic Church for 1,500 years, denied all intention of allowing anyone to found a new religion. 'That is why I opposed Ludendorff and broke with him, and why I reject Rosenberg's book. The book is written by a Protestant. It is not a Party book. The Protestants can dispute with him about it.'[12] The dissolution of the Centre party and signature of the Concordat in Rome, suggest that the Catholic Church accepted these bland assurances at face value.

In dealing with the Protestant Churches, Hitler was confronted with a different problem. Their drive towards unifying themselves was already in full flood; the question was whether he should let it take its course or himself seize the helm. Ignoring the precept of non-involvement, to which he had hitherto adhered, he plunged into the negotiations by appointing Ludwig Mueller, an Army chaplain, to represent him with a brief to the effect that the Evangelical Church could unify itself only on a basis to be approved by the state. The position was backed by the German Christians (GCs) who held a great rally in April 1933, at which Goering and Frick, the new Reich Minister of the Interior, were Presidents of Honour. In the following month, when a Reich Bishop was chosen who was not acceptable to Hitler, Mueller and the GCs demanded new Church elections. These took place in July and, after Hitler had broadcast on behalf of the GC candidates, the latter won handsomely. In September a National Synod at Wittenburg duly elevated Mueller to be Reich Bishop; his only contribution to theology was to produce in 1936 a Germanic version of the Sermon on the Mount, entitled *God's German Words*. The value of this work may be gauged from one example: 'Blessed are the peace-makers' becomes 'Happy are they who keep peace with their fellow countrymen'.[13]

Mueller's aim was to set up a state Church and so reverse the disestablishment decreed by the Weimar Constitution. Opposition to this plan came from two widely separated quarters: one within the Church itself; the other Rosenberg and the ideological wing of the NSDAP. Martin Niemoeller began to organise the Pastors' Emergency League, which later became the hard core of the Confessing Church (Bekennende Kirche). It was the first organised opposition to Hitler's known will. At first it was predominantly Calvinist, but it increasingly attracted Lutherans also, as Mueller's gross inadequacy became apparent; by the end of 1933 it numbered 5,500 pastors. Unlike the bulk of the Evangelical Church, it refused to adopt the so-called 'Aryan paragraph', which excluded pastors who were racial Jews from the Church.

Rosenberg's opposition to Mueller's pretensions came in a leading article in the *VB*, written after the success of the GCs in the elections, but before Mueller had become Reich Bishop. The recent Concordat, the article pointed out, had obliged the Roman Church to withdraw from politics and the 'confessionalising' of parties, which had begun long since with the Centre party, was thus at an end. But the same principle applied also to the Evangelical Church. The NSDAP was, of course, grateful to those who had supported it, but this did not mean that it must commit itself to political support for a particular religious group. The contrary was laid down in the 1920 programme. 'The restoration of a strong, self-aware nation-state goes hand in hand with genuine tolerance towards every true religious manifestation. Liberalism, which mixed up politics with religion, is at an end....'[14] Hess backed up Rosenberg and on 13 October 1933 issued a circular enjoining neutrality upon party officials.[15]

One month later the GCs held another great rally in Berlin, at which Dr Reinhold Krause, drawing some of his ammunition from the *Mythus*, denounced the Old Testament and 'Pauline' elements in the New, and demanded that the 'Aryan paragraph' be applied not only to pastors, but to all Church members. This was too much for many Lutherans, who had hitherto hesitated to line up with Niemoeller. The agitation grew so rapidly that Mueller felt himself obliged to remove Krause from Church office. This further provoked Rosenberg, who on the same day announced his withdrawal from the Evangelical Church; Mueller, he charged, by describing certain of Krause's remarks as heretical, had identified himself with the dogmatists of the Roman Church, who had once applied the same adjective to the Protestants.[16] From this time onwards Mueller and all who, with him or without him, sought to unify the Evangelical Church and associate it more closely with the state found an implacable opponent in Rosenberg. He began collecting material to illustrate their abuse of the principles of National-Socialism, which he regarded as incompatible with Christianity. As he said in a speech in Hanover in January 1934, 'When we put on our brownshirts, then we cease to be Catholics or Protestants, we are only Germans.'[17] He showed himself more sympathetic to the Confessing Church not because he preferred its beliefs, but because it was weak and he wished to promote schism; the greater the disorder and disagreement in the Church as a whole, the sooner it would collapse in ruin.

Hitler eventually came to share this view; but not until further attempts at unification had been made, persisting into the beginning of 1937. Meanwhile he made a surprising and apparently inconsistent move by appointing Rosenberg on 14 January 1934 to the high-sounding, if insubstantial, post of his delegate for the supervision of the entire ideological and intellectual indoctrination and education of the NSDAP. One month later in the Kroll Opera House Rosenberg addressed a specially invited audience, including Hess and most of the Reichsleiters and Gauleiters, on 'The Struggle for the Weltanschauung'. It was an elaboration of the theme enunciated some months before by the Fuehrer himself, namely the need for 'stamping the National-Socialist Weltanschauung on the German people'.[18] 'If today', said Rosenberg, 'we were to be content with only the power of the state, the National-Socialist movement would not have fulfilled its mission. . . . The political revolution in the state has indeed been completed, but the intellectual and spiritual recasting of men's minds is only just beginning.'[19]

Rosenberg's new appointment cannot be explained in terms of any tactical or strategic plan devised by the Fuehrer; it seems to have been a by-product of the political in-fighting that he allowed, or perhaps actually encouraged, among subordinate leaders. During the summer of 1933 a struggle had taken place between Goebbels, who aimed to control cultural life through his Reich Chamber of Culture, and Ley, leader of the Nazi Labour Front, who wished to use the confiscated funds of the Trade Unions to promote the recreational organisation that became 'Strength through Joy'. At the end of November the two rivals reached an uneasy agreement on demarcation of territory, which left Rosenberg's theatre organisation out in the cold. He was so incensed by his exclusion that on 1 December 1933 he wrote at great length to Hitler and concluded that, if the agreement between his competitors forced him to dissolve his Combat League for German Culture (KFDK), 'there would then be a compelling need for me to withdraw from the entire cultural activity of the NSDAP'.[20] Four days later he decided that this threat had been altogether too bold and wrote again to explain that he had only meant to indicate that his exclusion might be taken to imply that the Fuehrer did not require him to pursue his cultural activities; but it had not been his intention to contradict the maxim that 'we work wherever you find it right to direct us'.[21]

Rosenberg received no direct reply to these letters, though three weeks later Hitler sent to him, as well as to other senior party members, a cordial letter, thanking him for his work in the first year since the seizure of power. The appeal from his loyal subordinate, however, may have put him in a receptive mood when in the second half of January 1934 he was surprisingly requested by Ley to agree to designate Rosenberg as his Delegate for Indoctrination. This move had been previously discussed between Ley and Rosenberg, but the documentation is inadequate to explain the former's motives. Ley knew, of course, that Rosenberg and Goebbels were inveterate enemies and he may have felt that an alliance with the former would strengthen him against the powerful Minister of Propaganda.

There is also evidence that Ley, who with Rosenberg was responsible for training the Indoctrination Leaders (Schulungsleiter) of the NSDAP, was genuinely concerned about what Rosenberg later described as 'the many rifts that have emerged in dealing with ideological questions'.[22] Ley would not have been the first to be alarmed by the vacuum at the heart of the ideology, which was particularly disconcerting to anyone required to devise training courses. The Nazi seizure of power had led to a sudden influx of new members, who were expected to show a grasp of Nazi political beliefs, in addition to their interest in lucrative employment. It was natural that Ley, in his perplexity, should turn to the man whom the Fuehrer himself described as 'our party dogmatist'. If this was indeed Ley's aim, he was to be disillusioned; Rosenberg was mainly interested in using his enhanced status to join the in-fighting on more equal terms. In February 1934 there were further negotiations between Ley and Rosenberg, which ended in June with Ley's financing the theatre organisation of the KFDK, which was renamed the National-Socialist Cultural Community (NS Kulturgemeinde). Relieved of his immediate financial problems, Rosenberg was able to set up a small unit (Dienststelle) for the execution of his new functions.

He had now acquired a right to intervene in a wide range of political, educational and cultural matters. It was not a right that his colleagues were much inclined to respect, nor Hitler and Hess to uphold; but his Dienststelle, combined with his access to publicity through the *VB*, gave him something more than nuisance value. The new Dienststelle was at first divided into sections concerned with indoctrination, art, literature and prehistory; at the end of 1934 sections for ecclesiastical and for scientific questions were added. It was not until 1938 that a section was set up to deal with Jewry and Freemasonry; even this step seems to have been taken for the fortuitous reason that Rosenberg had the opportunity to take over an anti-semitic publication in Frankfurt, named 'World Service' (*Weltdienst*).

It is a striking fact that Rosenberg who, with Streicher, is of all the Nazi leaders most closely associated with anti-semitism, should have made so little effort, when he had the chance, to pursue his speciality in any systematic way. It is as if the author of a manual on surgery, on finally entering the operating theatre, found that he could not stand the sight of blood. Reinhard Bollmus offers several plausible explanations. First, 'the problem of Judaism interested the Reich Leader only from an historical point of view'.[23] Secondly, 'the Reich Leader had scarcely any conception of medical anthropology'.[24] Thirdly, other organisations were already active in this field, though Dr Bollmus concedes that such a consideration never deterred a Nazi leader from setting up an additional one, if he had a mind to do so. In the present case, Rosenberg might have argued that the Ministry of the Interior was already working on the Nuremberg Laws, which were promulgated in 1935, and within the NSDAP Walther Gross was running the Office of Enlightenment on Population and Race Policy, which in April 1935 became the Race Policy Office (Rassenpolitisches Amt).

Gross was a satisfactory colleague in Rosenberg's eyes, possessed of that rare power of discernment that enabled him to assess the contributions to thought of the Reich Leader at their true worth. In an article written in 1942 Gross observed that 'Race policy is not natural science, but the political application of the discoveries of natural science'. As such, it required an historical perspective, which assigned to blood a decisive importance in the culture and destiny of a people. This perspective was concerned with an idea, or myth, propagated by such men as 'Gobineau, Woltmann, H. S. Chamberlain and Alfred Rosenberg, to name only the most important and best known'.[25] With such a colleague as Gross to bark for him, it may well be argued that Rosenberg had no need to keep a dog.

Setting aside the organisational aspect, however, one may note certain indications that, when it came to anti-semitic measures, Rosenberg lacked the enthusiasm with which Himmler and Goebbels carried precept into practice. He was well aware, as a result of his visit to London in 1933 (see Chapter 8), that his great objective of improving relations with Britain could not be realised so long as attacks on Jews were given full rein in the Reich. Even if one discounts his disapproval of the 1938 pogrom (Reichskristallnacht), expressed in the memoir that he wrote in Nuremberg gaol, there is the evidence of his diary, which was not written for publication. 'Why these attacks against the Jews? Special issue of *Der Stuermer*! Goebbels' speech in the Sports Palace!'[26] Again, one may dismiss as a sexual aberration his apparent willingness to have intimate relations with Jewish women, though this distinguishes him from Streicher, who believed that Aryan virility was irreparably impaired by intercourse with a Jewess. But some weight must surely be given to his intervention with the Baden Minister of Education in May 1933 to secure the release of the well-known educationalist, Kurt Hahn, who had been arrested at Salem.[27] That Hahn was known in Britain, and Rosenberg believed his detention might damage Anglo-German relations, does not exclude more generous motives; in a dictatorship the cause of humanity, if it is to be pursued effectively, must appear to be grounded in arguments compatible with the nature of the regime.*

Rosenberg's new appointment brought him back into the political arena at a critical moment. It was a period of acute tension between the 'old fighters', of whom he was one, and the forces of the state, which held that the Nazi revolution had served its

---

* A case is known to the author in which Rosenberg on the basis of earlier personal contacts intervened successfully in 1943 with Sauckel on behalf of a young man scheduled for an extermination camp, where his father had already died. The young man, who is alive today, was then in Thuringia, the former Land of which Sauckel was Gauleiter.

purpose and now needed to be stabilised. To the latter, Rosenberg's nomination was a warning; to the 'old fighters' it was a sop. The most powerful of them was Ernst Roehm, backed by his *SA*, who resented Hitler's reliance on the Reichswehr and its Generals, and his disinclination to embark on any meaningful socio-economic reconstruction. Roehm, who had no use for ideology, as such, was apprehensive about his power base within the state. Rosenberg had similar apprehensions, but he also saw the issue in theoretical terms: were the army, the bureaucracy and the ecclesiastical hierarchies to be allowed to use the achievements of the NSDAP in order to entrench themselves more securely, or were they to become the servants of the party? He had never respected the state; in a passage in the *Mythus,* attacking Hegel and bureaucratic traditions in Germany, he concluded, 'The state today is no longer a self-sufficient object of veneration, before which we must all bow down in the dust; the state is not an end in itself, but only a means to the preservation of the people. . . . The form of the state changes and its laws decay; the Volk remains.'[28]

Rosenberg feared that, now that the state had fallen into Hitler's hand, the Fuehrer had become content with the power it provided. A short time before his nomination Rosenberg had cautiously voiced his fear in an editorial in the *VB*. 'The revolution of 30 January 1933 does not continue the absolutist state under a new name; it places the state in a new relation to the people. . . . What has taken place in 1933 . . . is not the establishment of the state's totality but of the totality of the National-Socialist movement. . . . The state is a tool of the National-Socialist philosophy of life.'[29]

On 27 June 1934 Rosenberg complained to Hitler about reactionary forces in the state, as represented by Vice-Chancellor Papen and Foreign Minister Neurath. The Fuehrer was sympathetic; he had himself been greatly irritated by Papen's recent speech at Marburg, condemning all who spoke of a second revolution, and he had put under arrest one of the Roman Catholic advisers, Dr Edgar Jung, who was believed to have drafted the speech. But, Hitler said, he was not as yet prepared to tackle reactionary forces; because of the prospects of the Saar plebiscite nothing unnecessary should be attempted against the Churches, 'but otherwise – an unshakable ideological attitude.' Rosenberg commented in his diary that the Fuehrer, so far as he could, had for many years 'extended his protection over my consistent point of view. He more than once stressed with a laugh that he had from the old days been a heathen; now the time had come that the poisoning of life through Christianity was nearing its end.'[30]

Three days after this conversation Hitler struck out both to the left and the right in the 'night of the long knives'. Roehm and Gregor Strasser, men of the second revolution, were killed; but so were men regarded by the Nazis as standing on the right, such as Schleicher and certain protégés of Papen, including Jung. Rosenberg had long been critical of Roehm's morals and there was no friendship between them; but Strasser's death troubled him and he sought refuge in the evasive supposition that Hitler could not have ordered it. Many years later he wistfully observed that, if Hitler had made Strasser Minister of Interior, 'many things would perhaps have gone differently'.[31]

At first sight it might seem that the massacre of 30 June 1934 was a victory for the state in its battle against the lawlessness of the SA. This would indeed have been the case if Hitler had used the power of the state and its laws to achieve his ends; instead he used the long knives of Himmler's SS and never allowed any legal proceedings of any kind to take place. He treated the law with contempt by declaring before the subservient Reichstag that at the moment of crisis he had himself been the sole and supreme judge. At the beginning of August the death of the aged President opened up new vistas. Hitler, instead of becoming President, declared himself Fuehrer of the Reich, an office unknown to constitutional law. Rosenberg wrote in his diary, 'All Germany is in deep mourning. A great man is gone. But the NSDAP has now got a clear passage to complete the Reich it wants.'[32] At the Nuremberg rally in September 1934, staged in part as a reconciliation with the rump of the SA, Hitler made a highly significant declaration: 'The state is not our master; we are the masters of the state.' It was a reaffirmation of the view Rosenberg had always held.

Whatever the Generals may at first have thought, the real beneficiary by the decapitation of the SA was Himmler and his SS. For the next decade they grew steadily in power, until by July 1944 Himmler became the mightiest man in the Reich after the Fuehrer. It may therefore be appropriate at this juncture to discuss his relationship to Rosenberg, which displayed contradic-

6. *Reichsleiter Rosenberg, 1933*

7. *Rosenberg in London, May 1933. Right: Norman Davis, roving US Delegate to the Geneva Disarmament Conference*

tory features. Rosenberg at the end of his life looked back upon an exchange of views with Himmler at one of the peasant rallies (Bauerntagen) at Goslar: 'Our thoughts ran along similar lines; he always stressed that his attitude was close to mine.'[33] This was true; in addition to their romantic attitude to peasants, they shared a keen interest in prehistory and interpreted German history as the long struggle of Aryan heroes against sinister Judaeo-Christian forces. Both men, unlike Hitler, had a smattering of Indian philosophy; they also cherished ideals connected with Orders of Knighthood, which we shall discuss in the next chapter. Whether Himmler, who was seven years younger than Rosenberg, derived these ideas from him, or from Darré,* or whether all three drew upon common sources, cannot now be satisfactorily determined. Of greater interest is the fact that, in spite of this congruence of ideas, Rosenberg remained close to Darré, but became increasingly estranged from Himmler and finally came to rank him with Martin Bormann, Erich Koch and Goebbels as 'the decisive symbols of the sickness of the NSDAP'.[34]

One reason for this development is that, while Darré lost Himmler's support and faded out as a power in the Reich, Himmler went from strength to strength and, as he did so, attempted to put into practice ideas which, for Rosenberg, could retain their attraction only within the covers of a book. Secondly, while both Rosenberg and Himmler were anti-Christian, the former believed that Christianity should be allowed, with some encouragement, to die a natural death; he did not claim to have a gospel to put in its place. Himmler, on the other hand, finding the SS malleable in his hands, began more and more to promote among them a cult of ancestors, combined with the revival of pagan festivals. Rosenberg, who could always recognise absurdity in others, regarded Himmler as no better fitted to be the Grand Master of Nazi occultism than Ludendorff and Dinter had been. When Himmler began to propagate Hans Hoerbiger's cosmology of eternal ice, Rosenberg sent a circular to all NSDAP offices, assuring them that adherence to these theories was no part of being a National-Socialist.[35]

In 1934, however, the antagonism between the two ideologists was still in its infancy; Rosenberg welcomed an ally against the Churches and noted in his diary: 'The SS, together with the

* See Chapter 8, p. 165.

I

Peasant Leadership (Darré) is openly educating its men in the Germanic way, that is, anti-Christian.'³⁶ The rise of Himmler and the relegation of Papen to the sidelines was a severe blow to Roman Catholics, who were already perturbed by non-observance of the Concordat and by Rosenberg's appointment. The Vatican had reacted in February by placing the *Mythus* on the Index and in the same month Cardinal Schulte, Archbishop of Cologne, complained about the book to Hitler, who took much the same line as before. 'I have no use for the book; Rosenberg knows it. I have told him so myself. I do not want to know about heathen things, like the cult of Wotan and so on.' But when Schulte persisted, Hitler at last stated clearly, 'Rosenberg is our party dogmatist', and proceeded to accuse the episcopate of having boosted sales of the *Mythus* by their attacks upon it. Schulte did not reveal that more attacks were planned in his own diocese, where a 'Defence Staff' had been set up, comprising Father Neuss and six other young priests determined to expose errors in the *Mythus* and neutralise its effect. By the autumn of 1934 they had produced a series of anonymous pamphlets, of which the most substantial was entitled *Studies of the Myth*. To evade the attentions of the Gestapo, these were printed simultaneously in five different cities. When they were ready for distribution and needed only the episcopal imprimatur, Schulte lost his nerve; but at the last moment the Bishop of Muenster, Count v. Galen, stepped into the breach. Although the bulk of the issue was confiscated, a good many copies slipped through the hands of the secret police.³⁷ In 1935 Rosenberg felt obliged to publish a vindication of the *Mythus*.*

No methods of attacking the Churches were too crude for Himmler, who early in 1934 had taken over the Gestapo from the less ideologically minded Goering and was running it in harness with the Party Security Service or Sicherheitsdienst (SD). There is evidence that in the Rhineland as early as March 1934 lists were being compiled of suspect priests by means of abuse of the confessional; Roman Catholic Nazis were instructed to confess to having listened to readings from the *Mythus* and then to report back whether the priest had spoken against the ideology of the NSDAP.³⁸ In later years Rosenberg wrote, 'The Church is not without blame for what took place in Germany, only the Himmler-Heydrich

* *An die Dunkelmaenner unserer Zeit* (Munich, 1935).

police, as has now become clear, later reacted in an unworthy and deceitful manner.'[39] This is no more than the usual attempt to offload responsibility onto the SS–SD; we now know that at least as early as 1935 Rosenberg began receiving reports from the SD about Church affairs;[40] if he did not know how such information was acquired, it was because he preferred not to enquire.

As soon as the successful outcome of the plebiscite in Catholic Saarland was known in January 1935, attacks on the Churches intensified; the tactics included accusing priests of acts of immorality and smuggling foreign exchange. Bishop v. Galen emerged as the most outspoken of the Catholic episcopate; learning that Rosenberg planned to come to Muenster to address an open-air meeting of NSDAP leaders, he wrote to the civil authorities of Westphalia, strongly recommending cancellation, on the ground that the indignation of the pious people of Muenster would be sure to lead to disorder. His recommendation was not accepted, of course, and on 7 July 1935 Rosenberg spoke at a mass meeting, at which Frick and the new leader of the SA, Viktor Lutze, were also present. Rosenberg accused Galen of trying to deny freedom of speech and suppress points of view differing from his own; he claimed that, in spite of the outcry in the foreign press, generated by charges of religious persecution, the Church was being treated with marked tolerance.[41]

Such moderation as the Nazis showed at this time in their dealings with the Churches was in great measure attributable to the strong disapproval voiced in other countries. At the same time the official anti-religious campaign aroused considerable disquiet in Germany, not only outside the NSDAP, but even within it. In April 1935 Rosenberg found it necessary to issue confidential guidance to NSDAP officials for use in reply to current criticisms. The first of these took the form of maintaining that Nazism was no more than a political movement; if, however, it claimed to be more, its ideology must be either for, or against, religion. Rosenberg in his circular prudently evaded the issue; Nazi ideology was not a religious dogma, but an attitude, characterised by the fight for specific values. The second main criticism harked back to the 1920 programme, which had endorsed 'positive Christianity'. Rosenberg's answer to this was that every new movement reinterpreted Christianity in its own way and all must be free to do so, including those 'who believe that to strive for the honour and freedom of Germany signifies fulfilment on this earth of a religious duty'.[42] Finally, there was the criticism that Nazi teaching on race and on the need for sterilisation of the unfit was anti-Christian. Here Rosenberg again evaded the point and merely commented, with a side reference to Copernicus, that the Churches had always opposed new ideas.

Was there an element of sincerity in Rosenberg's repeated claim that he stood for religious toleration? There can be no doubt that he worked for the disintegration of the Churches and held their creeds to be incompatible with Nazism. On the other hand, he frequently affirmed, even in the closed circle of party comrades, that the process of disintegration would be a long, slow one; on one occasion, for example, he spoke to Hitler of a hundred years.[43] In the meantime, he was astute enough to see that the life of the Churches would only be prolonged through the death of martyrs. He must also have been aware that, even within the NSDAP, opinion was divided; for example, Hans Schemm, who was Kultusminister in Bavaria until his death in 1936, used the political slogan, 'our policy is Germany, our religion is Christ'. Hans Kerrl, originally a protégé of Goering, who became Minister for Church Affairs in July 1935, was a convinced Protestant, even if, like some of the German Christians, he was also capable of blasphemous comparisons between Christ the Redeemer of men and Hitler, the redeemer of Germans. His effort to create a regime acceptable to a majority within the Protestant Churches, although doomed to failure by withdrawal of Hitler's support in 1937, was undoubtedly well meant, according to his lights. Hitler, after his death, said of him to Rosenberg, his sworn enemy, 'Kerrl's motives were certainly noble, but it was a hopeless attempt to try to unite National-Socialism with Christianity.'[44]

Surrounded, as he was, by a confused babel of conflicting voices, Rosenberg's public stand for toleration of all varieties of religious opinion was tactically the only sound one to adopt. The case for holding that it may have been something more rests largely on his attitude to the trial of Niemoeller. The dissident Church leader was arrested in July 1937, after attempts to unify the Protestant Churches had been temporarily abandoned and repressive measures were being applied more intensively. His case did not

come before a court until February 1938, when in spite of the fact
that it was tried by a special court (Sondergericht) a decision was
reached which was far from satisfying the prosecution. Niemoeller
was sentenced to seven months' detention, which implied immediate release; thereupon the SS carried him off to a concentration
camp, where he remained till the end of the war. Rosenberg sent
one of his staff, Dr Ziegler, as an observer to the trial.[45] On the
first day Ziegler was approached by the prosecution in the vain
hope that he would provide some valid evidence against the accused.
All that the prosecution had been able to collect was statements by
Niemoeller attacking his opponents on theological grounds, which
was not enough to satisfy the court that he had been acting against
the interests of the state. In addition, there were a few statements
critical of Kerrl and Goebbels.

Immediately after the verdict Rosenberg sent to Hess Ziegler's
report, containing remarkably forthright comments on the proceedings, which were described as 'an offensive to relieve pressure on
Minister Kerrl. In my view, such trials ought not, for the sake of
what the German character holds dear, to take place in Germany.
Here is at work a piece of cold, interfering state machinery,
which has lost sight of people and fellow citizens – Niemoeller is
a fellow citizen and, before the court, not one jot less so than
Kerrl.'[46] Rosenberg's covering letter to Hess supported this report
and concluded that such cases could damage the prospect 'of
bringing the idea of National-Socialism to its realisation'. He also
claimed to have taken up the case with Hitler.[47] Even if we
attribute Rosenberg's reaction in great measure to his antagonism
to Kerrl and Goebbels, one can hardly dismiss it as entirely hypo-
critical.[48]

Although Hitler came to no firm decision between those who
favoured close links between Church and state and those opposing
them, 1937 began with an indication that Kerrl was losing ground.
On 13 January, Rosenberg's birthday, he lunched with Hitler in
the uncongenial company of Kerrl and Goebbels, both of whom
attacked the anti-religious Gauleiter of Oldenburg, Karl Roever,
one of Rosenberg's few close friends. Hitler, however, turned the
attack against the Churches, which, he alleged, exploited people's
faith for their own political ends. When Kerrl tried to put in a
good word for the Protestant Churches, Hitler silenced him by

demanding to know, 'Did we come to power with, or without, the Churches?'[49] Near the end of 1937 Kerrl attempted to introduce regulations giving the central authorities in the Evangelical Church disciplinary powers over provincial Churches and breakaway groups. Rosenberg pointed out to Hess that, as under Kerrl's proposal the state would stand behind the Church authorities, this would identify the NSDAP, against its own principles, with the group of German Christians to which Kerrl belonged. 'In 1933 this identification was extremely difficult for the party to bear and now the same situation could arise in aggravated form from these regulations. . . . In the last analysis the aim of these regulations is nothing less than what the Fuehrer has already rejected once, namely the creation of a state Church.'[50] In May 1938 Hess informed Kerrl that his proposal was unacceptable.[51]

If Rosenberg was making progress in his fight against religion, he was losing ground in his struggle to control cultural life. Although he was sometimes successful in his attempts to make Goebbels and Ley follow a hard ideological line against backsliding painters and musicians, both resented his interference. In the summer of 1936 the conflict with the more choleric Ley reached the point at which funds were withheld from Rosenberg's Cultural Community. In August he appealed to Hitler and two months later, having received no reply, took the despairing step of bringing accusations against Ley before the High Court of the NSDAP. A few days later Hitler received Rosenberg on the Obersalzberg;[52] but instead of coming to a decision on the conflict between his two subordinates, he dangled before Rosenberg's eyes the vision of becoming his Commissioner against World Bolshevism, which Rosenberg had bitterly attacked at the Nuremberg rally in September. Nearly five years were to elapse before this vision acquired substance with his nomination as Minister for the Eastern Occupied Territories. Meanwhile Hitler himself must have realised that the project was incompatible with the current anti-Comintern activities of Ribbentrop, who in August 1936 had become a highly peripatetic Ambassador in London.

In January 1937 Hitler received Rosenberg again, this time in the company of Ley and Schirach, whose main business concerned the Adolf-Hitler Schools, which will be discussed in the next chapter. The question of the overlapping jurisdiction between Ley and the Delegate for Indoctrination was not solved; Ley stood firm and in the following month Rosenberg had to dissolve his Cultural Community. In return, the NSDAP Treasurer took over the financing of his Dienststelle.[53] Although its future was now assured, Rosenberg had suffered a loss of prestige and it may have been this consideration that led Hitler to award to him later in the year the National Prize for Art and Learning, which he had just created in token of his rejection of the international Nobel Prizes. Rosenberg's prize was worth 100,000 Reichsmarks and another prize of similar value was divided between two distinguished surgeons. For Rosenberg, some of the gilt was stripped off by the fact that he received the prize at the hands of Goebbels. Hitler, who was present, presumably intended in this way to minimise the feuding within the NSDAP. He then himself delivered a long speech, in which, instead of eulogising the recipients, he treated them to a tedious dissertation on degenerate art and characteristics of German genius.[54] You never knew in the Third Reich what you were in for.

We have a picture of Rosenberg at this period of his life from the pen of Sir William Teeling, who was on a visit to Germany to study the compatibility of the Nazi creed with Roman Catholicism. 'His office was not a particularly imposing one, being an ordinary converted private house, not far from the Tiergarten. He kept me waiting only a very short time. . . . I found a rather podgy but tall man, handsome to look at but also looking very ill. I understood he had only just recovered from a long and painful illness and he showed every sign of being in a rather unhealthy state. Many people have told me that they did not find him particularly intelligent. . . . As far as I was concerned I felt I was looking at a handsome man with a clear-cut face, quite frank and neither particularly intelligent nor unintelligent. His conversation was very matter of fact, without any particular brilliance. . . . He spoke with a slight Baltic accent and was, I gather, rather shy, which at first gives the impression of his being curt and cold; but later he becomes much franker and pleasanter. . . .' Later in the same narrative Sir William refers to 'the almost total lack of cordiality with which Hitler greets him [Rosenberg] on . . . public occasions.'[55]

Rosenberg, in spite of constant exposure to political pressures,

never evolved into a skilled political operator. He staked everything on his loyalty to the Fuehrer, whose favour was, at best,
uncertain and, at worst, mere recognition of the claims of the
strongest contender. At the beginning of 1938 it seemed as if some
of the original friendliness might be coming back into the personal
relations between the two men. On Rosenberg's forty-fifth birthday
Hitler visited his home in Berlin and presented him with a bust of
their old friend, Dietrich Eckart, and a photograph with the inscription: 'To my old and most loyal fellow fighter, Alfred Rosenberg,
with best wishes for his forty-fifth birthday in cordial friendship.'[56]
Irene Rosenberg, now aged seven, made her bow in history by
giving a bunch of red roses to the Fuehrer, who loved to be photo-
graphed with young girls.

At this period Rosenberg was also able to improve his standing
with Goering, who praised his speech at the 1938 Nuremberg
rally and ordered for himself a copy bound in leather.[57] Rosenberg
had stressed the need to act with tact towards the Churches,
because of their influence upon foreign opinion. In a reference to
the religious struggle in the Second Reich, he added, 'We do not
want to make the same mistake as Bismarck.'[58] Goering was growing increasingly doubtful whether Kerrl's defence of German
Protestantism was justifiable. In August 1939 he put to Rosenberg
the question: 'Do you believe, then, that Christianity is coming
to an end and that later a new form, conditioned by us, will come
into existence?' When Rosenberg replied in the affirmative, the
befuddled Reich Marshal said he would ask Hitler privately what
he thought.[59] If he did so, there can be little doubt what answer
he got.

Rosenberg had for some years been receiving requests that he
prepare a shortened and more easily digestible text of the *Mythus*.
In 1934, for example, he had rejected a suggestion that extracts
be made from the book for use in the schools.[60] Proposals of this
kind were rooted in the impression that, in attacking the Churches
and all they stood for, he was undermining the foundation on which
society and, indeed, the state itself were based. Even those who
criticised the Churches and believed that they had corrupted
primitive Christian doctrine wanted to know what Rosenberg
would put in their place. This doubt was implicit in questions put
to him in May 1938 by a Jugoslav journalist, who first asked

whether the NSDAP had a particular attitude towards the Gospels. Rosenberg replied that the quest for 'the pure teaching' of Christianity had been going on for a thousand years; nations had even come to blows on this account. 'National-Socialism does not feel itself called upon to restore this so-called pure teaching. ...' His interrogator then expressed the view that many young people wanted advice on metaphysical problems and were getting no answer to their questions. Rosenberg replied, 'Youth cannot be exempt from the struggle to find answers. Everyone must have the courage to go through a period of uncertainty lasting even as long as a decade. Young people do not have to be given immediate, ready-made answers to their questions. ... It is open to them to read all that has been written in different quarters and from that to shape their own viewpoint. The important thing is that they should always confront their fate with an attitude showing strength of character.'[61]

Rosenberg's own response to the question was, in fact, little more than an attitude; nor was it an honest one. In April 1936 he had congratulated himself in his diary on the fact that a speech made by Hitler on the previous day at the opening of the Nazi Ordensburgen* had accorded exactly with his own ideological pronouncement on the previous day. 'Right at the beginning he affirmed that at one time the Churches had supplied leadership for the people. Today they had become incapable of doing so. That had shown itself in the struggle against Marxism; therefore National-Socialism was inheriting this task.'[62] But what Rosenberg was saying two years later was that young people were to be left to their own devices; supplemented, no doubt, by intensive listening to the state-controlled radio.

Even Martin Bormann seems to have doubted whether this was enough. In February 1940 he wrote to Rosenberg on the subject of religious instruction in schools, pointing out that the NSDAP had not tried to influence this teaching because there could be no compromise between National-Socialism and Christianity. The Churches would only be overcome 'through a new ideology, the coming of which you have announced in your works'.[63] In the long run, this would be taught in the schools, but the time for this had not yet come. Meanwhile, Bormann felt it necessary to point out,

* Castles of the Order; For an account of these institutions see Chapter 7.

religious instruction embraced not only Christian dogma, such as those relating to the creation of the world and the immortality of the soul, which were repugnant to Nazism, but also the ten commandments, which fulfilled an important function in the moral and social order. If these were eliminated and not replaced by something else, would not the NSDAP be blamed for the demoralisation of youth? It was a shrewd question; indeed, although Nazism has disappeared, it is still a valid one today.

Bormann's immediate remedy was that Rosenberg should produce a short guidance on the Nazi concept of life, which could be used for educational work in the NSDAP and Hitler Youth, in anticipation of the day when the school system as a whole was ripe for it. Rosenberg had, in fact, overcome his scruples some months before and had put his hand to a condensation of his thought, which he entitled *Ideological Theses*.[64] We need not quote from these at length, partly because they do not merit it and partly because we examined Rosenberg's views in connexion with the *Mythus*. The *Theses*, however, do embody a new emphasis on his challenge to Kerrl's contention that ideology and religion are different things. Rosenberg maintains, on the contrary, that 'ideology embraces religion, science and art'. A Germanic attitude, manifesting itself in all three, will determine the form of expression and impose a unity. The Germanic element is the essential factor. 'Every great spiritual force of the past is ennobled only by the fact that Germans have believed in it.' The significant feature of Gothic cathedrals is not that they were built by Catholics, but that they were built by Germans. 'Belief in the spiritual value of honour and freedom as the highest values for living and dying signifies the greatest religious revolution in world history since Christianity.' But not everyone is ready for the freedom of thinking about such matters for themselves; those who are not should remain with their Churches. The future lies, however, not with those who make pilgrimages to the graves of saints, but with those who march proudly by the resting places of those who died fighting for Germany and for the Nazi movement. For them, 'the National-Socialist, Germanic idea of comradeship has replaced the Christian concept of love'.[65]

It will be seen that Rosenberg does not succeed in explaining in positive terms what it is that he intends should take the place of the Christian ethos; he merely advocates that one should be born a German and should become a Nazi. In default of anything more explicit, he simply reverts to his negative attacks upon Christianity. Indeed the most striking feature of the *Theses* is that in them Christianity has replaced Judaism as the principal enemy. Apart from one reference to the Jew as 'a creature without religion', the only mention of Jews is in connexion with 'Syrian-Jewish Church dogma', 'Jewish-Asiatic Church creeds' and the like. It seems as if the counter-attacks of the Churches, both Catholic and Protestant, against the *Mythus* had diverted him from anti-semitism, if only temporarily, and concentrated his enmity in one direction. He can hardly have been encouraged by the figures revealed by the census of 1939: 95 per cent declared themselves adherents of the Churches; 1.5 per cent atheists; only 3.5 per cent were 'believers in God', the form of registration favoured by the Nazis.[66] Only in the ranks of the SS was the proportion of 'believers' substantially higher.

Within the leadership, as within the SS, Rosenberg's views were gaining ground. In particular, Hitler was moving into his final ideological phase, which remained with him till his death. At the end of the year he banned a book by Kerrl entitled *Weltanschauung and Religion: National-Socialism and Christianity,* which had already been announced in a publisher's list.[67] In mid-January 1940, on a day when Rosenberg was lunching with him, Hitler finally admitted that his attempt to unite the Protestant Churches had been 'a great mistake'; he had wanted them to be a counter-weight to the Roman Church, but had misjudged the possibilities, because 'he still had certain preconceptions acquired in the borderland, where Protestantism had constituted a national Church'.[68] It was rare for the Fuehrer to concede that he had erred, especially in the presence of someone who had consistently upheld the other viewpoint. When Kerrl died in 1941, he was not replaced, though Hitler jestingly offered the post to Rosenberg;[69] it was probably the one Minister's portfolio that he felt obliged to decline.

The outbreak of war seemed to him to offer new ideological challenges; in October 1939 he wrote to Schwarz, the NSDAP treasurer, that his work as Delegate for Indoctrination had become even more essential, 'in order to make the purpose of our struggle as plain as possible, to re-establish it again and again on ideological, scientific and historical foundations, to intensify our fighting spirit and will to conquer, and – last but not least – to ward off systematically the attempts of our ideological opponents to take advantage of the "spiritual crisis" at our expense'.[70] This letter skated discreetly over two inconvenient facts; first, the war was not popular in the country as a whole; secondly, a war against the West in alliance with the USSR flew in the face of everything that Rosenberg and his wing of the NSDAP had stood for. We shall examine in more detail in Chapter 8 his reaction to Hitler's opportunist reversal of traditional Nazi foreign policy.

All this was bad enough; but Rosenberg saw a further danger that the Churches would exploit the situation; as he wrote later in the war, the heightened interest, especially among young people, in questions of life and death had given a new opening to 'Church propaganda'.[71] At the same time, renewed popular concern about religious matters to some extent inhibited the Gestapo from taking openly repressive measures. In an interview between Hitler and Rosenberg at the end of 1941 both men ground their teeth over the courageous attitude of Bishop v. Galen, which was actually being exploited by British propaganda;[72] but popular support for him was so strong that neither state nor party dared to arrest him. The need to maintain solidarity on the home front was paramount. Rosenberg was particularly apprehensive about the activities of chaplains in the armed forces. Goering backed him by excluding them from the Luftwaffe; but the Army jealously guarded its independence. As Rosenberg wrote later in his memoir, 'I could not expect anything else from these circles dominated by the Churches.'[73] He recorded bitterly that Roman Catholics had sent to every Army Command copies of booklets attacking the *Mythus*. He was, therefore, proud of the fact that, shortly before the war, General (later Marshal) v. Kluge invited him to address the officers at his HQ in Muenster and had concluded the session with these words: 'Permit me, Herr Reichsleiter, to say a frank word. You were depicted to us as a specially fanatical person and I admit having had some misgivings. But what you have said is so interesting and reasoned that I am very grateful to you.'[74]

The 'spiritual crisis' seemed to Rosenberg to give him a new chance to break through the barrier that had hitherto confined his activities to party cadres. He prepared the ground by canvassing with Goering and Hess the proposal that he should have a new mandate to defend the ideology with authority to issue directives not only to party organs, but to those of the state also. He pointed out to Hess that the people were looking to the party for a lead, but many of the leaders (and he left no doubt that Goebbels, Ley and Bouhler came high in this category) 'had trampled on the hard-won achievements of the party; some were no longer National-Socialists.... The Fuehrer's authority still guaranteed unity. Afterwards the struggle among the satraps would begin.' He did not get much change out of Hess who, in his view, failed to exercise proper authority over the other Reichsleiters, although himself 'a decent person, unconditionally devoted to the Fuehrer'.[75]

It was true that Hess' influence had markedly declined; but Rosenberg's proposal would have been a further infringement of his field of action. Nor was Hess the only one who felt his authority threatened by this proposal; Goebbels, Ribbentrop, Kerrl, Rust and Bouhler, a leading party bureaucrat, were soon up in arms. Early in November 1939 Rosenberg explained to Hitler the powers he wanted and seemed to win his assent;[76] but as soon as the quarrel began over the decree drafted in Rosenberg's Chancery, Hitler withdrew, as he preferred to do, from the field of controversy. In February 1940, as the matter dragged on, he told Lammers to call a meeting, which was attended by the interested Ministers or their representatives. Some two hours were taken up mainly by the familiar argument between Rosenberg and Kerrl about the relationship between religion and ideology. The decisive opposition, however, came from Goebbels and Weizsaecker, who was representing Ribbentrop; the Foreign Office view was that to enhance Rosenberg's status would offend – at the extremities of the spectrum – both the Vatican and the Kremlin.[77] When at the beginning of March Hitler administered the coup de grace, he tactfully mentioned neither, but told Rosenberg that Mussolini had three times asked him not to take any measures against the Roman Church. 'Later, after our victory, it would not matter; he could do what he liked with the Church. . . . Your appointment now, just before the great offensive begins, would have the impact of a bomb.'[78] Whilst Hitler was no doubt exaggerating the external repercussions in order to resolve a domestic difficulty, it should be recalled that Italy had not yet entered the war; Hitler's self-confidence was still well below the pinnacle it was to reach within the next three months.

All that Rosenberg managed to salvage from the wreckage of his new project was Goering's backing for increased ideological activity not only within the Luftwaffe, but also within the Wehrmacht. Although he was unable to secure the removal of Army chaplains, who were protected by the Concordat, he received full cooperation from General Reinecke, a time-serving, pro-Nazi officer, who had been brought out of retirement to head the Wehrmacht General Office (Allgemeines Wehrmachtsamt). Later, when Rosenberg's authority had been increased by his appointment as Minister, he concluded an agreement with Field Marshal Keitel for the supply of books for libraries in barracks and provision of itinerant speakers on ideological themes. In December 1943 a special staff of NSDAP Leadership Officers (NS-Fuehrungsoffiziere) was set up under Reinecke.[79] This was in accord with Rosenberg's ideas; but Bormann ousted him from control over it.

As far as the officer corps was concerned, these efforts seem to have met with scant success. A report reaching Rosenberg in 1943 about the attitude of the occupying Wehrmacht in Denmark bore witness to 'open rejection of National-Socialism on the part of senior officers' coupled with 'the greatest mistrust of every kind of propaganda'.[80] The fact was that the officers had been schooled in an older tradition, which had withstood the test of defeat in 1918 and had survived almost intact through the Weimar Republic. In some quarters this tradition, which the Nazis had outraged, was still smouldering in 1944; it burst suddenly into flame with the attempt on Hitler's life on the 20 July. The attempt failed, but it made a breach through which the SS was able to move into the one stronghold from which they had been so long excluded.

In the aftermath of these events certain members of Rosenberg's Chancery sent him a remarkable memorandum which, although it avoided directly criticising him, plainly implied that his ideological mission had been a failure. The attempt on Hitler's life was ascribed to 'insufficient initiative on the part of the NSDAP' and defects in 'the spiritual – ideological war leadership'. Errors had been made, which had discredited the party in the eyes of the people. For example, uniformed party members had continued to visit homes to collect for NSDAP charities, but had taken over from the priests and pastors the task of informing families of the death of their loved ones on the battlefields. Hence the widespread whispering campaign that 'The party takes your money and brings you death'.* The memorandum ended with an attack on Bormann, to whom Rosenberg had recently written complaining that the German people were being spiritually stunted.[81] The disarray among the leadership was being aggravated, of course, by the prospect of defeat.

If we admit that the NSDAP failed to penetrate the armour of senior members of the Prussian officer caste, the virtues of which have been underestimated – not least by British war-time propaganda – what of the juniors? There is, of course, no conclusive evidence on this point; but it is worth quoting the observation on the young Wehrmacht of a Prussian of the old school. 'These are the new generation, with the doctrinaire obstinacy and unteachability of the young. They are dangerous because they are fanatical; they are full of new principles of violence and determined revolutionism, and a source of incalculable ferment. In them spiritual nihilism has produced a positive attitude. Their contempt for the normal standards of civil life extends to the traditional standards of the nobility, the soldier's profession, and of legitimism. They have no more respect for Christianity than for any other "mythology". They have their own conception of heroism, the heroism of the modern mechanized arm. They heartily despise their commanding officers as respectable old gentlemen.'[82] We cannot with certainty say that Nazi indoctrination produced these men. We can say that the product exactly corresponded to Nazi requirements.

* 'Die Partei holt das Geld und bringt den Tod.'

# 7 Education and Elitism

The Third Reich lasted only twelve years, a lesser period than the 'Adenauer era' in the Federal Republic. Within this period of twelve years the conscience of the civilised world was grievously affronted and the map was changed in a drastic and, it seems, enduring manner. There has, therefore, been justification for treating the Nazi era as if it were a completed phenomenon, and studying its rise and fall, its overweening pretensions and their dire effects, as if these represented the full extension of Nazism. Yet it would be a mistake to suppose that the Nazis themselves saw their state as the fulfilment of their purpose in 1933, or in 1939, or at any other date. It was not merely a question of expanding frontiers or even of increasing the efficiency of totalitarian control; the Nazis had set themselves, like other ideological revolutionaries, the task of changing human nature. Their ideal state would not be finally achieved, until their ideas were so rooted in the minds of the Herrenvolk that their rule would last at least as long as the Roman Empire. The 'Thousand Year Reich' was no mere rhetoric; it was the enunciation of a clear objective. Meanwhile the Third Reich was perpetually in the process of development; as with the Communists, the aim would always be just out of reach, because only in this way could the dynamic of the movement be maintained. Nazism demanded constant struggle; this was the law of life; a people who ceased to struggle and fight had signed its death warrant. This was Hitler's answer to Speer, who had pointed out that his scorched earth policy in the last phase of the war was depriving the German people of future means of subsistence: 'If the war is lost, the people too are lost. It is not necessary to pay attention to the basis required by the German people for even the most primitive further existence. . . . For they have shown them-

8. *The Fuehrer congratulates Rosenberg on his forty-fifth birthday. Between them Rosenberg's daughter Irene, aged seven*

9. *Rosenberg at a lecture to Hitler Youth instructors on racial types*

10. *Hess* (left) *and Rosenberg at the opening of the APA. Himmler behind in SS uniform*

selves to be the weaker and the future belongs exclusively to the stronger Eastern peoples.'[1]

It is easy to write off Hitler's Alexandrine ambitions of conquest as fantasy; but there is a good deal of evidence to the contrary, especially in his conversations with Rauschning and in his early 'table talk'. He had been impressed by the success of the British in holding India for so long with such small forces and attributed this in part to the quality of the administrators produced by the English Public Schools. Etonians must blush if they read of the role that their predecessors were thought by the Nazis to have played in British Imperial history. It was the deliberate intention of the Nazis to breed a race of men who would rule with an iron hand the new worlds that the Wehrmacht would conquer for them. Except within the ss, the plans to produce this elite were not very fully or systematically developed. Hitler's impatience to achieve his immediate strategic and ideological goals led to a hypertrophy of the parts of his programme concerned with militarism and genocide. The long-term educational plans were relatively neglec-ted – not because they were less important, but because they were less urgent. As a result they remained to some extent in embryo. It is to these plans and Rosenberg's connexion with them that we now turn.

Nothing distinguished the Nazis more clearly from the tradi-tional conservative forces in Germany than the emphasis laid by the former on the need to fulfil the racial destiny of the Volk in terms of suitable human material. The conservatives, as their name implies, looked for nothing more than a return to the 'good old days' of throne and altar. If accounts of Hindenburg's last testament can be credited, he died under the illusion that the NSDAP might be willing to allow itself to be used for this purpose. He was not alone in thus misunderstanding the entire growth of the Nazi movement and the soil from which it had sprung. Although the NSDAP, for tactical reasons, had been willing to ally itself with the DNVP, it had no sympathy with the Second Reich and its objectives. As Rosenberg proclaimed, 'The old nationalism is dead.'[2] It had died with the German dynasties. In the *Mythus* he analysed the failure of Wilhelmine statecraft, which had been unable to create a type imbued with the spirit of the regime and capable of trans-mitting it to a future generation. Here Bismarck himself had failed

K

and, even if Wilhelm II had not removed him, 'the history of Germany would not in any essential respect have been different'. Only Moltke escaped this criticism, because he had been able to embody the quintessence of Prussianism in the General Staff, which had survived the disintegration of 1918 almost unscathed. Moltke represented 'the most powerful type-creating force since Frederick the Great'.[3] This was the road that the Nazis must follow: 'This is the task of our century: out of a new myth of life to create a new type of man.'[4]

The new type was, of course, to be a ruling type, a Herrenmensch. The Nazis in their propaganda encouraged the notion that all Germans were in future to be Herrenmenschen; but the Nazi elite knew very well that this would be neither practicable nor desirable. The NSDAP had not come to power in order to promote equality; it was itself best able to express the will of the inarticulate, non-political mass of its own people, just as the Communist party claims to do in a 'Socialist' society. The business of the Nazi elite was to rule and thus enable the Volk to fulfil its historic destiny, without being diverted from it by idle thoughts of a life of leisure, or more butter instead of guns. For this purpose, what was needed was a submissive populace, responsive to the new slogans of Nazism and re-educated so as to reject former, democratic slogans, especially those connected with liberty, equality and fraternity. At the Nuremberg rally of 1934 Rosenberg announced that, now that the NSDAP had overthrown the old, corrupt party system in Germany, its task was to purge 'Jewish-Marxist individualism and all so-called universal teachings'.[5] Not only political parties and religious groups, but all pluralist elements in society were to be suppressed, so that the atomised and undifferentiated herd would be wholly amenable to Nazi leadership. As Hannah Arendt has written, 'Total power can be achieved and safeguarded only in a world of conditioned reflexes.'[6]

Before considering how the Nazis went about their self-imposed task, we must briefly review safeguards against the totalitarian approach and the extent to which these were already built into the educational system that the Nazis inherited. In the first place, it was a federal system; there was no Reich Minister of Education; each of the constituent states had its own Minister, usually known as Kultusminister. At the same time it must be remembered that

Prussia practised a centralised administrative system and Prussia was two-thirds of the Reich. In the second place, there was a precious tradition of research for its own sake in German Universities – the tradition connected with the name of Humboldt. There had evolved two kinds of professors: those who considered that affairs of state were none of their business; and those who considered it to be their duty to uphold the state in every respect. The latter tendency, personified by such men as Treitschke, was further promoted by the fact that the professoriate was part of the civil service; not for nothing was it dubbed in Prussia 'the intellectual bodyguard of the Hohenzollerns'. In Prussian schools the influence of the state was even stronger, because since the time of Frederick the Great the practice had grown up of pensioning off NCOs by appointing them to teach in primary schools. Even in secondary schools the rank of reserve officer was more coveted than any academic distinction. Every effort was made to inculcate into pupils an attitude of undiscriminating loyalty to the King-Emperor.

The best potential safeguard lay in the predominance of confessional schools. In particular the Roman Catholics had become wary of the state in the course of the struggle between Bismarck and the Roman Catholic Church, known as the Kulturkampf. Although the same could not be said of the Protestant Churches, they also wished to preserve their denominational schools. Both religious groups had been able to protect their interests against the Weimar Republic, which had been unable to enact comprehensive educational reform, as foreshadowed in the Constitution, because no majority could be found in the Reichstag excluding both the Protestant DNVP and the Centre Party.

The educational system was not only sharply divided along religious lines; it also split along class lines. Pupils who went to Grammar Schools, or Gymnasia, as they were called, did eight years of Greek and Latin before passing the school-leaving examination (Abitur), which took them to university. There studies were further prolonged partly through the German tradition of frequent movement from one university to another and partly because there was no degree available below that of doctorate or PhD. Evidently only the upper class and bourgeoisie could afford to finance so lengthy a period of education before embarking on a career.

Towards the end of the nineteenth century this concentration on classical study and research had begun to attract criticism and, as the result of a conference convened by the Kaiser, some modifications were introduced into the curriculum of schools. These only served, however, to make the teaching more nationalistic; more German history, geography and folklore was taught, as well as more physical training with a view to producing fitter reserve officers.

If Prussian Generals, industrialists and civil servants were inclined to think that the system did too little to prepare young people for the realities of the world about them, the students' complaint was against the reality itself. The stern discipline of parents and teachers offended them; they saw little attraction in the life of profit-making or unswerving service to the state for which they were being prepared. Their disenchantment was illustrated by the Wandervogel (bird of passage) movement, which flourished before the First World War. Groups of young people, travelling light – both in terms of baggage and intellectual equipment – wandered through the German woods under leaders distinguished more by charisma than status. They were escapists rather than rebels, living in a shadowy world between an imaginary and heroic Nordic past and a visionary future, which they had read between the lines of Nietzsche and Stefan George. Opposed, as they were on emotional grounds, to urbanisation and industrialisation, they were easily persuaded that these developments were due to Jewish influence, not to the general desire in Germany, as elsewhere, to make higher profits and raise living standards. By 1914, eighty-four per cent of all Wandervogel groups showed traits of anti-semitism. They were the forerunners of the students who in 1933 burnt Heine's books and drove Jewish and liberal-minded teachers out of German universities. In the euphoria of August 1914 their vague idealism was converted into war hysteria and most of them plunged gladly into battle as the solution to their problems and the fulfilment of their hopes. The symbol of their heroic, if useless, sacrifice, to which Nazis loved to allude, was the assault at Langemarck in November 1914, in which a reserve Division of untrained troops was decimated. Those who survived into the less heroic and even more disenchanted era of Weimar were demobilised into a civilian life that had no place for them. Many joined the xenophobe, nihilistic Free Corps under cynical, ruthless men, like the early SA leaders, Klintzsch, Goering and Pfeffer; they were perfect raw material for Nazi ideology.

The NSDAP programme of 1920 included the following article on educational reform: 'The curricula of all educational institutions must be adapted to the needs of practical life. The first aim of the school must be to develop the mind by enabling it to grasp the concept of the state through civics (Staatsbuergerkunde). We demand training for specially gifted children of poor parents at state expense, without regard to rank or profession.'[7] Rosenberg's commentary, written two years later, was scarcely more specific. He insisted that Jewish influence must be eliminated from education and that the alienation of the learned professions from the people must be remedied by developing 'the spiritual energies and character values' of the lower classes. Elsewhere he alluded unfavourably to 'one-sided interest in dimmest antiquity, the wisdom of the East and abstract doctrines'[8] – a striking phrase, when one reflects how closely it corresponded to the interests of the future Reichsfuehrer SS.

One looks in vain for an attack on the feature of the educational system that, as time went on, attracted the most severe assaults of the Nazis, namely the predominance of confessional schools. This is explicable in terms of the reluctance of the young NSDAP to foul its Bavarian nest by opposing the Roman Catholic Church on the territory that it was most determined to defend and had fenced off in the Concordat concluded by the Vatican with Bavaria. Later, when the NSDAP was represented in the Prussian and Baden Land parliaments, it opposed unsuccessfully the conclusion of similar Land Concordats, only to perform a *volte face* at Reich level on attaining power in 1933. By 1930, however, Rosenberg had made his own position plain: education must be reserved for the state and the influence of the Churches must be excluded. 'The religious denominations serve no purpose in themselves, but only in so far as they are applied in the service of national life and Germanic worth of character. . . . The basic assumption of all German education is recognition of the fact that our morality is not the product of Christianity, but Christianity owes its lasting value to the German character.'[9] Education was defined by Rudolf Benze, Nazi Director of the Central Institute of Education, as 'directing of growth';[10]

the Nazis did not intend to allow interference by any influence that had not first been shaped to their specification.

In 1933 eighty-three per cent of all primary schools were denominational and religious instruction was given in them according to creed. The Nazis objected to this on social and ideological grounds. They believed that religion was a divisive factor, especially in Roman Catholic schools, where children were taught, so it was alleged, that their first allegiance was to the Pope in Rome, rather than to their Fuehrer in Berlin. More fundamentally, the Nazis claimed the whole man; they could not allow him to seek spiritual guidance from his Church, while rendering unto Caesar the things that were Caesar's. The Fuehrer's jealousy for his people was akin to that of the Old Testament Jehovah. Once in power he was determined to take education out of the hands of the Churches, even if it meant head-on collision with them. By 1937 religious teaching in schools was largely entrusted to laymen and was being crowded out of the school timetable. In the following year Rosenberg could claim, 'The curriculum of all categories in our schools has already been so far reformed in an anti-Christian and anti-Jewish spirit that the generation which is growing up will be protected from the "black" swindle'.[11] The Reich Concordat had delayed but not averted this trend.

It was not only in the school system that rifts between class and class, and faith and faith had made themselves felt. In 1931, when Baldur v. Schirach became leader of the Hitler Youth (HJ) and Young Volk (ten–fourteen years), there were eleven major groups of youth organisations, split along political and denominational lines. The HJ, which took youths up to eighteen, had in origin been little more than a recruiting agency of the SA; but Schirach had other ideas. In 1928 he had become leader of the Nazi Student League (NSDSB), which required someone more persuasive than a drill-master. Schirach was a fanatical devotee of the Fuehrer, about whom he wrote ecstatic poems; ideologically he was close to Rosenberg and aspired to be a moulder of men's minds. A few months after his appointment the HJ was detached from the SA and its female counterpart (Bund deutscher Maedel) was also placed under his leadership. By October 1932 Schirach was able to bring together nearly 100,000 HJ members at a Reich Youth Day in Berlin. Further expansion naturally followed the Nazi accession to power; by June 1933 all the political youth groups had been incorporated in the HJ with Schirach as Reich Youth Leader. Towards the end of the year Reich Bishop Mueller handed over to him the surviving Protestant groups and there then remained, apart from the small, segregated Jewish group, only the Roman Catholic group, temporarily protected by the Concordat. In December 1936 this, too, was eliminated and the HJ was left as sole youth movement.

Rosenberg devoted his speech at the 1934 Nuremberg rally to 'The Uprising of the Youth of the World', claiming that the NSDAP, as the party of youth, was the wave of the future. A few months later Schirach, in a speech to his following in Berlin, defended Rosenberg against the criticisms of the Roman Catholic Church and won 'stormy applause' by declaring 'Rosenberg's way is also the way of the youth of Germany'.[12] He was regularly invited to address the annual conventions of HJ youth leaders. At the end of his life, confronted by the charges of the Nuremberg Tribunal, he wrote in his memoir, 'I have thought over my speeches: I have not poisoned the youth.'[13] The Tribunal thought otherwise.

The Nazi aim to produce a uniform type could not be attained solely by destroying the variegated pattern resulting from the existence of diverse kinds of schools and youth movements; it was also necessary to eliminate the federal character of the educational system and bring all teachers under central direction. In January 1934 the Land Kultus ministers lost their autonomy and became agents of the Reich Minister of the Interior; but this was a transition stage. In May 1934 the Nazi Kultusminister of Prussia, Bernhard Rust, himself a former teacher, became Reich Minister for Science and Public Education. When Rosenberg congratulated him on his new appointment, he replied – no doubt with more modesty than he felt – 'But it is you who have been our teacher, mine as well'.[14] Later Rosenberg had some regrets that he had not himself become Minister of Education; but in 1934 he was still trying to break into the chasse gardée of foreign affairs.

When the Nazis came to power, thirty per cent of the school teachers were already declared adherents of the NSDAP, a figure above the average by professions. A high proportion of these were primary school teachers, who resented the superior status of secondary school teachers, who had the benefit of four years at university, concluding with a state examination and two years probationary teaching. After January 1933 new adherents were incorporated in the Nazi League of Teachers (NSLB), which three years later claimed ninety-seven per cent of the whole teaching profession. The secondary school teachers' examination had included compulsory papers in Philosophy, Logic and Ethics; none of these were subjects with much appeal to Nazis, who substituted an obligatory politico-ideological test, for which Rosenberg's *Mythus* was a 'set' book. Both the period at university and the probationary teaching period were reduced by one year. In spite of this approximation between the qualifications of secondary and primary school teachers, the rate of recruitment fell sharply in both branches of the profession and, in order to keep the educational system going, unqualified assistants had to be employed in the primary sector. In 1939 Rust made all teachers subordinate to his Ministry, instead of owing allegiance to Land or local authorities.

The shortage of teachers cannot be ascribed to the elimination of Jews and Social Democrats among them, which took place at the outset of Nazi domination; it must be ascribed, rather, to psychological factors. Not only was Nazism anti-intellectual; its emphasis on the primacy of hereditary endowment necessarily tended to diminish the importance of what could be taught. In a speech in 1938, on the occasion of the opening of the Reich School of the Nazi League of Teachers at Bayreuth, Rosenberg felt himself constrained to deny that the NSDAP wished to disparage the teaching profession. On the contrary, he claimed, it was Marxism-Liberalism that had done so by relegating the teacher to a mere purveyor of facts. Teachers in the Third Reich had to concern themselves with character training. 'A teacher who will not educate the young person entrusted to him by training his inner nature, if necessary, indeed, by exercise of authority, can no longer be regarded as a teacher.'[15] He concluded that teaching was a fine task – for anyone who did not have the good fortune to be concerned with politics, weaponry and technical development. It is scarcely surprising that this speech failed to stimulate recruitment.

After purging the teaching profession, the Nazis' next step was to put the remainder through a short indoctrination course. This was done in Indoctrination Camps (Schulungslager) organised by the NSLB; by 1937 there were forty-one such camps in existence.

Similar camps were set up for other influential elements in the community, such as civil servants and businessmen. One of these camps was visited by Sir William Teeling, who was allowed to attend some of the lectures. The first of these was on the new Nazi science of 'race hygiene' and consisted of the usual attack upon miscegenation with advocacy of sterilisation of the unfit. There followed a version of the history of ancient India, Persia and Greece, which adhered closely to Rosenberg's outline in the *Mythus*. The writer added in his report, 'They made frequent use of Hitler's *Mein Kampf* and of the different speeches and writings of Rosenberg.'[16] The *Mythus* was one of the books ordered by Rust to be put in all school libraries.

At the Nuremberg trial Rosenberg denied that he had had 'any direct influence on school policies . . . or universities'.[17] He had, of course, strong motives for making such a denial before the Tribunal; but as far as the schools are concerned it is true that Rust was largely successful in preventing his interference in the running of the state system. It was through his ideas and theories that Rosenberg's influence was mainly exerted. It will be convenient to summarise these ideas before reverting to the universities.

First and foremost it was necessary, in Rosenberg's view, to instil into young Germans the idea of race purity and the need to preserve it. 'Today a whole race begins to realise that values are only created and sustained where the law of the blood still determines the thoughts and deeds of men, whether consciously or unconsciously.'[18] The prime duty of the state was to promote this understanding. 'Strength, spirituality and racial attitude must go together if the new type is to be created. To carry this through is the first and last task of the leader of the future Germany.'[19] If this was not done, the omission would revenge itself on the people. 'Either we raise ourselves, through revitalisation and refinement of breeding, to the level needed for purification, or the last Germanic-Western values upholding morality and statecraft will be submerged in the filthy human flux of cosmopolitan city-dwellers.'[20] These beliefs had to be inculcated by introducing eugenics and race hygiene into educational curricula, whilst banishing pornography and deflecting women from harmful thoughts of emancipation. The Nazis were opposed to co-education and higher education for women. Sexual licence, according to Rosenberg, went hand in hand with the wish of feminists to take on men's work. Abortion for women (except in the event of a misadventure with a non-Aryan) was as much anathema as homosexuality in men, since both limited the free flow of new life into the Reich. For the same reason, not only marriage to a racially inferior partner, but even cohabitation must be rigorously excluded. Information about a prospective partner's heredity could be obtained through the Ahnenerbe, the appropriate office of the SS. Part of the object of this teaching was to prepare the minds of the people to acquiesce in racial legislation, such as the anti-semitic Nuremberg laws and those for sterilising the unfit. It is evident that in 1939, when Hitler instructed the SS to embark on a discreet, but widespread, campaign for eliminating the incurably sick and insane, public opinion in Germany was by no means ready for it. The counter-attack, led by the Bishop of Muenster, slowed up the euthanasia programme and, even if it did not stop it, drove it further underground, thus showing how much effective resistance could be achieved by the Churches on an issue attracting the support of their flocks.

According to Rosenberg, not only was the Catholic Church opposed to racial hygiene, but it had also turned men against the ideal, shiningly expressed in Greek culture, of healthy, natural man with pride in his body. The cult of the male body was expressed in the films of Leni Riefenstahl, Hitler's favourite producer. The Nazis threw their entire weight behind the existing movement in favour of increased physical training in schools. This was in part attributable to the generally anti-intellectual prejudices of the NSDAP and in part to misapplied Social Darwinism; fitness to survive was equated to physical fitness. Walther Darré, who was close to Rosenberg, drew a frank parallel between breeding horses and humans. 'We shall gather together the best blood; as we have bred up again our former Hanover horses from the few remaining pure-blooded male and female animals, so we shall once more breed over the generations the pure type of Nordic German...'.[21] Himmler went further and confided to his masseur, Felix Kersten, that Nietzsche's 'superman' could be produced by breeding.

The arrogant assumption of such men as Himmler and Rosenberg that they knew for what purpose men existed on earth, and how this purpose could be promoted, is partly accounted for by the fact that they did formulate for themselves one very clear aim, namely that of raising healthy cannon-fodder. Engineers, factory hands, farmers and, above all, soldiers were the essential human material of the Third Reich. If only for this reason, corpus sanum came a long way ahead of mens sana; indeed the mind was required to fulfil little more than the function of a telephone exchange, capable of receiving orders and relaying them. Most Nazis had a horror of intellectual activity; lawyers, in conformity with the Fuehrer's prejudice, topped the list of undesirables. Preparation for the life of a soldier was not confined to the Hitler Youth (HJ) and Labour Service, but permeated education: geography was related to military map reading; mathematics to range-finding; chemistry to production of explosives. Nothing was studied for its own sake. Rosenberg did not believe that ideology should be directly taught in the schools; at a meeting in 1940 with Hess he expressed the view that it should interpenetrate all parts of the school curriculum.[22]

At the heart of the racial theory, as applied to education, was a paradox and a profound pessimism. The paradox was that, if heredity alone enabled a man to act as an Aryan should, education and indoctrination could, in logic, achieve very little. Rosenberg's pessimism was in sharp contrast to the nineteenth century belief that the state, by means of educating young citizens and improving their environment, could raise moral and cultural, as well as economic, standards. The experience of the twentieth century, with crime and violence accompanying rising standards of learning and living, has not borne out the hopes of the optimists; but this fact does not, in itself, make Rosenberg's contrary view more plausible. His whole pedagogic (if it can be said to merit the term) rested upon the abstraction of pure race and its determinative effect on human character and national virtue, for which no scientific evidence exists. This meant that, in the fields of biology, genetics, history and politics, in which the Nazis were chiefly interested, the inductive method, on which the expansion and deepening of knowledge had depended for some five hundred years, was largely abandoned. As in the Middle Ages, certain general, unproven ideas were enunciated as dogma and had to be accepted before anything further could be discussed. Strangely enough, Rosenberg, who never wearied of referring to the Inquisition and the persistence of the medieval Vatican in adhering to geocentrism, seemed incapable of seeing that this was precisely the attitude to which academics subservient to the regime had reverted. This was 'the science of struggle' vaunted by Professor Walter Frank, Director of the Reich Institute for the History of the New Germany. This was the message of Ernst Krieck, who became Rektor of Frankfurt University: 'In future we recognise no intelligence, no culture and no education which does not subserve the self-fulfilment of the German people and derive from that its significance.'[23] In the same spirit of the Inquisition, Rosenberg's protégé, Alfred Baeumler, who in May 1933 was appointed Professor of Political Pedagogy in Berlin, led the students in an orgy of book burning, which went on for most of one night and involved breaking into private libraries.

Rosenberg frequently maintained that intellectual freedom had never been so well served as by the Nazi state. In December 1937 he issued a statement on behalf of the NSDAP, relating to 'problems of research, in Kosmo-Physik, experimental chemistry and the geology of prehistory, which have lately come to the fore in a great number of publications ... the NSDAP can in no circumstances take towards these questions an attitude of ideological dogmatism.'[24] This sounded well; but ideology kept intruding even in the no-man's-land of pure science. Because of the prominent part played by Einstein and other Jewish scientists in research into atomic physics, the whole subject was condemned by the Nobel prize-winner, Philipp Lenard of Heidlberg.[25] Rosenberg, who was an admirer of Lenard, supported him. He thus became responsible in some small measure for the merciful dispensation by which Germany excluded herself from the possibility of becoming the first country to make the atomic bomb.

Second only in importance to acceptance of the dogma of race was that of the insignificance of the individual, which derived from it. The 1920 NSDAP programme had made a cautious beginning. 'The activity of the individual must not clash with the interests of the community, but must be carried out within the framework of the community and must be for the general good.'[26] The party had put this into practice in the demands made upon the membership, and the willing response, involving sacrifice of money, time and energy, encouraged the NSDAP to apply the principle in a more comprehensive fashion to the German people as a whole. In his 1934 Nuremberg speech, Rosenberg drew the moral. 'The secret of the success of National-Socialism and the secret of the tremendous strength of our movement is to be found – after our unshakeable faith in the Fuehrer – in the fact of the determination of all Germans ... not to think of themselves as private persons ... but in everything as executors of specific tasks and as the servants of a specific community.'[27]

Even this did not go far enough; what was needed was to condition minds in such a way that the injunctions of the regime became self-policing. For this purpose it was necessary for the individual to be robbed of the wish and capacity to form an independent judgment. It was at all times impressed upon him that, as a single unit, he counted for nothing; only as part of a herd did his existence acquire significance. As Rosenberg put it in the *Mythus*: 'A human being in himself (an sich) is nothing, he is capable of personality only in so far as he is integrated, mind and soul, into an organic succession of thousands of his race....'[28] The wearing of uniform was encouraged, so that the individual merged into the crowd; marching and singing, because thought was thus discouraged. Rosenberg described in one of his speeches 'the new German style ... it is the style of a marching column, no matter where, or to what end, this marching column may be directed'.[29] Theirs not to reason why had become an educational principle.

University students had to serve in the Labour Front and pupils in the special secondary schools run by the ss* had to spend some weeks in a factory or on a farm. This is the system known today in some Communist countries as 'polytechnic' education; its aim is connected not so much with the state of the economy as with ideology. It was exploited by the Nazis to impose communal living under uncomfortable conditions, which further served to weed out those who were not 'good mixers' and keep everyone in a mindless and gregarious state. Living in tents and hutments during refresher and indoctrination courses, which had at first been a necessity of improvisation, was continued for more subtle purposes. Professor Baeumler candidly admitted in 1942: 'The future teacher will emerge from an institution which has formed him by

* National Politische Erziehungsanstalten (NPEA), See p. 151.

means of its communal life.'³⁰ Camps removed the young from
the influence of their 'unreconstructed' parents and exposed them
to the conformist tyranny of their contemporaries. It was usually
possible for a young man to be brought into line by his fellows
without the threat of a concentration camp. Putting him for a
few weeks in a tent or hut, where he had no privacy and no time
to himself, emphasised his impermanence, his transitory membership of a nomadic tribe. If he also needed to be impressed by the
greatness of the tribal leadership, he could be taken to see the
monstrous pseudo-classical buildings which were being set up in
Berlin by Albert Speer, the Fuehrer's architect. As Rosenberg,
himself trained as an architect, expressed it, 'Monumental buildings are not houses, but the ideas in stone of a community.'³¹

University students had formed one of the earliest groups to
become dominated by Right-Radicalism; by 1931 the representative student bodies (Allgemeine Studentenausschuss) in all but a
few Roman Catholic universities were controlled by students belonging to extreme nationalist organisations, including the National-
Socialist League of Students. When the NSDAP came to power, it
decided to preserve the distinctive character of the latter organisation, whilst destroying allegiance to all other student organisations,
which accordingly became merged in the collectivity of those taking
orders (Gefolgschaft). Nazi propaganda about 'Youth led by Youth'
was never more than a slogan. In 1934 university students were
restricted to seventy-five per cent of the previous year's intake,
of whom only ten per cent were women. In fact, over the next
five years up to the outbreak of war, the student population fell
even more steeply. A modest scholarship scheme for sons of
manual workers, the Langemarck-Studium, was introduced.

In the speech delivered by Rosenberg in February 1934, on
taking up his post as Delegate for Indoctrination, he declared that
the NSDAP claimed the right to fill posts in institutions of higher
education 'with those who represent our spirit'.³² The purge
carried out among academic staff was, indeed, more drastic than
that in the schools. Rust had a veto over nomination of all university Rectors (Vice-Chancellors), whose staff were collectivised in
another Nazi 'front' organisation, the National-Socialist League of
University Teachers (Dozentenbund or NSDB). It was through this
body that Rosenberg chiefly exercised his influence in universities

and by 1941 he had secured at least nominal control over its activities.[33] It was never the intention of the NSDAP, however, to try to turn the universities into breeding grounds for their elite; as we shall shortly see, their plan was to conduct this operation altogether outside the existing educational system.

Even so, Rosenberg was disappointed by the failure of the NSDAP – usually ascribed to the weakness of Rust – to make greater inroads in the universities. In February 1942 he wrote in strong terms to Schwarz, the NSDAP Treasurer, justifying the continuation of the long-term ideological activities, which he was promoting concurrently with his more pressing duties as Minister for the Eastern Occupied Territories. Rosenberg explained that after 1933 the arts and sciences, tainted as they were with religion, liberalism and Marxism, had feared a strong, revolutionary assault on the inner core of the system of higher education. In practice, so much consideration had been shown that this had taken place only in the case of a few appointments. 'The intellectual activity of our universities in these years has scarcely altered.' Rust's Ministry had not carried out a systematic reform; the old Faculties were still operating and the staff teaching exactly as before. 'The historic task of the movement will therefore be not to change university activity as a whole, but rather to mobilise from within the movement itself the cadres for research, which can work on themes laid down by the movement and produce studies that will not be superficial, but will really be founded on strict scientific research and will provide the foundation on which the coming generation of researchers and teachers can build.'[34]

Even if one makes allowance here for that measure of special pleading used in all countries to wheedle money out of financial authorities, it emerges clearly that, in spite of the blood-curdling start, with book burning and expulsion of Jewish professors, nothing basic had changed in the universities. It cannot be said that, apart from individual acts of heroic desperation, such as the student movement in Munich associated with the Scholl family, the universities themselves put up serious opposition. Professor Rothfels has unearthed a couple of articles in *Historische Zeitschrift*, attacking Rosenberg's denigration of Charlemagne as 'slaughterer of the Saxons' and critically analysing his 'blood and soil myth'.[35] To write such articles in war time certainly required courage, but did not amount to effective counter-attack. The failure of the Nazis' ideological assault on the universities must be ascribed to other causes.

In the first place, Hitler's divide and rule tactics within party and state, which in some political fields contributed to his personal authority, produced in the educational and cultural area only confusion and uncertainty, within which elements of relative freedom were able to survive. Goebbels, Himmler, Ley, Rust, Rosenberg, Bouhler and others were too busy defending the indeterminate frontiers of their territory to concentrate on producing uniformity within it. After 1942 Bormann began to take a firmer grip on ideological enforcement, but even he, isolated at Hitler's HQ, could only act on such information as reached him there. Often it was no more than the complaint of one offended dignitary against another. When Rosenberg complained to him that Bouhler was censoring academic dissertations, it was more an attack on Bouhler than a defence of academic freedom; but some residual benefit to that deserving cause may have resulted.[36] The vendetta of the SS-Ahnenerbe against Rosenberg's protégé, Professor Hans Reinerth, had the effect of protecting more orthodox exponents of prehistory against the attempt of Reinerth to 'coordinate' his colleagues' academic activities.[37]

In the second place, the massive inertia of the university system served it better than any concerted attempt at defence, such as would at once have brought down upon it the vigilant repressive forces of the SD. In the final analysis, however, it was the incoherence, imprecision and irrationality of the ideology itself that defeated all efforts to drive out what remained of the humane and Christian values of earlier centuries. When Professor Walter Frank exclaimed at Tuebingen in 1936 that 'all German history ... must be seen only as the prehistory of National-Socialism',[38] this could only have the impact of rhetoric, not of a serious historical postulate. Nazi biologists, avid for promotion, might measure the long skulls of their prehistoric ancestors, but there would be others who knew that the size of the human head could be affected by rickets, as well as by race. The Nazis might treat as dogma their simplified and distorted version of theories put forward in the nineteenth century by such pioneers as Darwin, Malthus and Mendel; but to those whom a true spirit of enquiry had drawn into academic life these were hypotheses like any others, which in each generation had to be vindicated anew.

The Nazi interest in elitist institutions did not extend to the universities which stood condemned as the production-line of the despised intelligentsia; selection of future leaders had to be the function of the Party, which rejected the old traditions and was seeking to substitute its own myth. But when it came to deciding who constituted the Nazi elite, there was no unanimity. The competing elements were observed at an early stage of development by Konrad Heiden: 'The National-Socialist despises his fellow German, the SA-man the other National-Socialists, the SS-man the SA-man.'[39] Probably no one who was not an SA-man upheld its claims, which were in any case extinguished by the SS on 30 June 1934; but there was widespread agreement within the NSDAP that it was itself the elite of the German people. This was certainly Rosenberg's view, even before he fell out with Himmler. It was also the view of Ley, who became Organisation Leader of the NSDAP after Gregor Strasser's resignation; but neither he nor Hitler himself had foreseen the problem that would arise as soon as the NSDAP came to power. In the three following months new members flooded into the party at such a rate that by May 1933, when new membership was suspended, the number of 'Johnny-come-latelies' was almost double that of the tried and trusted, whose fitness to become the elite had been proved in the long years of struggle. It was in large measure this lack of a coherent theory of power within the NSDAP that left open the door for the SS.

The first initiative on behalf of the party was taken by Rust, who in April 1933 took over three former Prussian Cadet schools, designated National Political Educational Institutions (NPEA), to serve as boarding schools for boys from ten to eighteen who met certain tests of heredity, physical fitness and HJ membership. Fees were graded according to parents' capacity to pay and a number of free places was allotted to the Armed Forces. No special Teacher Training Colleges were set up, however, to train the necessary staff, some of whom were recruited from the SS, SA and the police; special courses were taught by serving army officers. Rust was unable to defend his initiative against the growing power of the SS and after 1936 control passed into the hands of SS

L

Obergruppenfuehrer August Heissmeyer. By 1943 there were thirty-nine NPEA for boys and two for girls.

The same lack of foresight had allowed the HJ to develop into a mass organisation, which by the end of 1936 numbered over six million members; it had lost all claim to be an elitist body. Schirach was therefore faced with the same problem as Ley, who in the summer of 1936 had asked Rust to hand over to him the NPEA, only to find that Heissmeyer had forestalled him. Ley and Schirach then concerted their plans for founding the Adolf-Hitler Schools, the first of which was inaugurated on 20 April 1937 – Hitler's birthday. There had been some talk with the SS about coordination of plans for the ideological training of the teaching staff of all the various institutions concerned, including the Ordensburgen, which we shall mention shortly; but nothing came of it.[40] Rosenberg, who had since 1935 been feuding with Ley about the training of Political Leaders for both the Ordensburgen and the Strength through Joy organisation,[41] alleged later that he had been 'deliberately excluded' from the plans for the Adolf-Hitler Schools.[42] The same was true of Rust; Ley and Schirach were determined that their elite schools should be entirely separate from the state system. Ten of these schools, financed from party funds, were eventually set up. Pupils were chosen by Gauleiters on the recommendation of the HJ; analysis of the intake has shown that in the first two years over eighty per cent came from middle-class families. This scarcely upheld Ley's claim that 'The most ordinary man of the people ... has the chance to rise to the most important posts within the party, in the state and in every organisation.'[43] Precept and practice rarely coincided in the Third Reich.

It was typical of the disorder of Nazi planning that the preparations for adult education of an elitist character in the Ordensburgen were undertaken by Ley before he had given any thought to the secondary stage. Indeed the first Burg at Kroessinsee in Pomerania was inaugurated almost exactly one year before the first Adolf-Hitler School came into existence. It was intended that one quarter of the best school-leavers should, after an interval, complete their training in one of the three Ordensburgen. Rosenberg criticised these plans as being on too massive a scale, which prevented 'the process of personal development'.[44] In 1936 it was envisaged that Rosenberg would select the teaching staff and eventually set up a High College (Hohe Schule) to train teachers both for the Ordensburgen and the Adolf-Hitler Schools;[45] but in the face of Ley's growing hostility it seems that these plans were later abandoned and by 1941 Rosenberg was describing his Hohe Schule, which in any case never came into being, as concerned with research.[46]

The concept of the Ordensburg was different from that of the traditional university; knowledge was not pursued for its own sake, nor was there training for any profession other than that of becoming a functionary in the NSDAP. This was, in fact, the ambition of sixty-seven per cent of those leaving the Adolf-Hitler Schools at Easter 1942; of the remainder nearly eleven per cent opted for a military career; only 4.6 per cent wished to become teachers.[47] The selective principle that would take them to an Ordensburg was not the 'Abitur' examination, which admitted to a university, but an estimate of their 'racial worth and ... fulfilment of their duty in the service of the community of the people'.[48] By the time they qualified for admission to an Ordensburg at twenty-five they would not only have passed through the HJ, the Labour Service and the usual pre-war period of conscription, but they were expected to have embarked on a profession. The Ordensburg was conceived of, therefore, more as a Staff College than as an institution of higher education. The nominal three and a half years assignment proved far in excess of requirements. It included some 'in-service' training as a junior party official and numerous tests of courage, such as parachute drops, and was designed to produce, in the words of a contemporary Nazi publicist, 'A sworn brotherhood of leaders ... who throughout the time to come will be able to control the destinies of the German people in the spirit of National-Socialism.'[49]

Whether such a system could have worked in more competent hands than those of Ley, Schirach and Rosenberg cannot now be known; there is reason to doubt it. In July 1939 an Indoctrination Leader in the Gau Aix–Cologne made a report to Rosenberg on Ordensburg Vogelsang in the Eifel. Ley had recently sacked the Commandant, named Manderbach, for having allowed one of his own children to be baptised; this had no doubt drawn Rosenberg's attention to the way in which the Junkers (as they were called) were being trained there. He had a legitimate interest because he

was partly responsible for the ideological teaching. His strong dislike of Ley may well have provided secondary motivation. The
physical standard set by Ley was (according to the report) higher
than that required by the army; about the intellectual standard he
was a great deal less particular. A disproportion between mental
and bodily effort was also noticeable in the day's work; as much as
four hours was often devoted to physical activity, while only one
lecture a day was usual, with a seminar or discussion group every
other day. In the circumstances, it was perhaps unnecessary on the
part of the author of the report to insist that, 'All attempts to
plagiarise the educational methods of Oxford and Eton must stop
at once.... Club armchairs, which, I hear, are to be provided in
considerable number for Vogelsang, certainly do not fit in with our
educational ideas.'[50]

The Nazis were up against the problem that must vex
educators in any totalitarian state: how is an adequate level of
intelligence to be achieved if, in addition to exacting the highest
physical standards, all independence of judgment and spirit of
enquiry is excluded? That Ley, for one, was unaware of the
existence of the problem is shown by a remark that he made when
greeting the first intake of Ordensjunkers: 'When I look at you my
men, I know that the principles on which we mustered you are
right. Externally you already look alike and in a short time you will
be alike inside as well.'[51] All Nazis were agreed that attempts to
teach their way of life were a poor substitute for the strains and
stresses of life itself and the instinctive reaction evoked by extreme
pressure on those who were racially of the right stock. Melita
Maschmann has written, 'we had no education. All we ever had
was experience – much too much of it. . . .'[52] In this sense war
was the logical culmination of the educational process. For those
who were too young, or had the misfortune to live in time of
peace, perusal of the lives of heroes was the next best thing. As
Rosenberg put it, 'A great man and his achievement seem to us a
thousand times more important and instructive than an apparently
clever theory, according with the law of reason. . . . For us, the
battle of Leuthen is as much a model for the training of character
as is *Faust* or Beethoven's *Heroica*.'[53]

Where Rosenberg, as always, remained theoretical, Himmler
applied his theory. The Death's Head units of the ss were method-

ically hardened by their service in guarding concentration camps to become indifferent to the suffering and death of the inmates, and to be instantly obedient to the commands of their superiors, however inhuman these might be. Likewise the Armed SS (Waffen-SS) was trained for war and expanded rapidly as soon as war broke out. The SS Junkerschulen at Brunswick and Bad Toelz were explicitly approved by Hitler in 1938 as schools for training officers. As such, they were more successful than the Ordensburgen in attracting men who wished to be officers, but lacked the bourgeois background and high educational qualifications expected by the German army. By the end of the war the Waffen-SS had acquired a very high reputation as a fighting force, though its claim to have been entirely separate from the Death's Head units cannot be sustained.

Himmler's concept of the SS as an elite was expressed in his notorious attempts to equate it with an Order of Knighthood. Some writers have suggested that Himmler, in creating the SS, also had the Jesuit Order in mind; ingenious analogies have accordingly been drawn between the two organisations. The comparison is not very instructive, however, since it ignores the fundamental divergence of aim, which in each case supplied the driving force and led in entirely different directions. Himmler himself never made this comparison, though there is admittedly evidence that in early life he had studied the history of the Jesuit Order.[54] But on more than one occasion he did draw a comparison between the SS and the medieval Order of Teutonic Knights,[55] which had fulfilled a civilising mission in the East and in its heyday had briefly ruled an area stretching from the Bay of Finland to the Vistula. As we have seen, this Order had long been an object of Rosenberg's veneration and he, too, invoked its memory, though not in connexion with the SS, which he would have regarded as utterly unworthy of the comparison.

The real prototype of the SS was neither the Jesuit nor the Teutonic Order, but a much more recent phenomenon in German history, namely the emergence after the war of two groups of desperadoes with inter-locking membership, the Free Corps and the 'Fehm' gangs (from an old German word, meaning lynch law). The Free Corps, rashly called into existence in the earliest phase of the Weimar Republic, had been animated by the urge to fight, by loyalty to their commander, who in many cases had led some of the same men in the Great War, and by hatred of Jews, Social-Democrats and the Republican regime. If these men be regarded as forerunners of the Waffen-SS, the Death's Head units, which did their evil work in obscurity and outside the law, mirrored the 'Fehm' gangs, which in the immediate post-war years moved furtively about the country, murdering political opponents and those who dared to disclose where the illegal arms of the Free Corps were cached. Whatever ideals Himmler might claim, his SS were fatally flawed from the moment of its birth as Hitler's bodyguard, which evolved to meet his need for a force, standing outside the law, through which he could dominate both party and people. By fulfilling this function the SS gained the independence to become a state within the state; but in doing so it assumed also the ignoble role of informer, torturer and executioner.

It was one of the paradoxical features of Rosenberg's career that the SS represented that section of the German people that was most receptive to what he said and wrote. They accepted his crude distortions of history; with him they turned their backs on all Christians, except a few chosen heretics against the medieval Church; with him and with Darré they believed that, by breeding, the ancient blood of the Aryan super-man could be renewed. They reprinted his articles and speeches in the SS *Guidelines* (SS-*Leithefte*). Yet Rosenberg regarded Himmler as his enemy and, instead of recognising his SS as an Order of Knighthood, came to refer to it contemptuously as 'the police'.[56]

Nothing illustrates this divergence more clearly than Rosenberg's theoretical application of the idea of an Order in the modern world, as contrasted with Himmler's crude, practical exploitation of the idea. Rosenberg tried to apply the idea to plug the void left by the failure of the Nazis to evolve a theory of the state. A ruling elite was a necessity for the NSDAP, because they had discarded the hereditary principle and rejected constitution-making as an idle pastime, contrary to the leadership principle (Fuehrerprinzip). To make the future safe for Nazism it was thus essential for the group that had acquired power in the years of struggle to renew itself by co-opting others who had been similarly indoctrinated. Rosenberg cherished thoughts about a Senate of the Order, which would be a repository of Nazi virtue. There is a passage in the first edition of the *Mythus* indicating that in 1930 he favoured some form of popular monarchy.[57] In later editions this was replaced by the following: 'The future will show what form the popular leadership, through the birth of a state based on an Order (Ordensstaat), will take, so embodying the yearnings of the present race of men for the fulfilment of the coming Reich.'[58] The retention of this passage in subsequent editions suggests an implicit criticism of Hitler for having made no move towards the fulfilment of the Reich by creating such an Order. Another passage in the *Mythus*, added after 1930, specifies that, 'It is the duty of the founder of the new state to form an association of men, on the lines of the Teutonic Order, consisting of personages who have taken a leading part in the re-constitution of the German nation.'[59] This addition plainly shows that, in Rosenberg's eyes, the existing SS could not be regarded as fulfilling this function.

On 30 April 1934 he visited the ancient castle of the Teutonic Order at Marienburg and delivered a speech on the theme of the state based on an Order. Rauschning was one of those present. 'I remember . . . a solemn announcement of the idea of the "Orders" as a fundamental idea of the state. Classical music, by candle-light, introduced and followed a respectable, literary lecture by Rosenberg on the history of the Teutonic Order in Prussia and the modern idea of orders; it was all read in the style of any of the despised provincial politicians of pre-National-Socialist times.'[60] The problem raised in this speech was one that was never solved – nothing less than the problem of the succession to the Fuehrer. Rosenberg pointed out that, while Hitler would not live for ever, 'it is our will that the National-Socialist movement should lay the foundation of the structure of the state over the centuries to come'. This meant selecting and assembling 'out of the totality of seventy million people a core of men to whom the special task of leading the state would be entrusted'. It was made clear that one function of 'the Council of the Order, or Senate of the movement' would be to choose the next leader, 'as in the East Prussian Germanic Order the Council of the Order chose the High Master'.[61] This proposal, like so many that Rosenberg put forward, fell on deaf ears; the Fuehrer had no intention of accepting any limitation on his own arbitrary power of decision. Exactly eleven years after the date on which Rosenberg spoke, Hitler committed suicide, having on the previous day written his last testament, in which, after expelling Goering and Himmler from the NSDAP, he bequeathed to Doenitz the state which he had himself destroyed.

It was typical of the frustrations and miscarriages of Rosenberg's career that Hohe Schule, which was to have crowned his ideological achievement, was never built. He had been slow off the mark and, when war came, Hitler wished these further educational plans to be deferred.[62] He imposed for the duration a firm ban on the building programme, thus saving posterity from the spectacle of an immense Speer-style erection on the shores of lake Chiemsee in eastern Bavaria, the main portal of which would have dwarfed such a building as the Frauenkirche, the symbol of Munich. Rosenberg persisted, however, and on 29 January 1940 induced the Fuehrer to sign a decree authorising him to undertake preparative work short of actual construction of the High College, as 'the central point for National-Socialist research, doctrine and education'.[63] Pending the conclusion of the war, Rosenberg was to concentrate on the establishment of extra-mural institutes (Aussenstelle) in university towns, which would be mainly concerned with research. Ten of these Aussenstelle were planned, complete with libraries, and six of these came into existence, if in some cases of a shadowy kind.[64]

It was one thing in the Third Reich to catch Hitler in a good mood and secure his signature; it was quite another thing to procure the necessary funds. Rosenberg still had to acquire premises for his Institutes and equip and staff them. In the spring of 1940 he noted in his diary that he foresaw 'hard struggles with the education-bureaucracy in the Ministry'.[65] Accordingly, he kept Goering and Hess informed, realising that he would either have to rely on party funds or on his own ingenuity. At some point during the summer of 1940, as German tanks swept across France, it occurred to him to take a leaf out of the book of Himmler's SD, who had for some years exasperated him by moving in behind the advancing Wehrmacht, first in Austria, then in Poland, and taking possession of property, chiefly Jewish and monastic, on the pretext that it might yield evidence of the supposed global conspiracy against Germany and of the activities of the conspirators. As this was exactly what Rosenberg wished to do, he concluded with the SD one of those intra-governmental treaties so typical of the

Third Reich, in accordance with which they would share the spoil. The SD, though they never respected the agreement, were supposed to confine themselves to 'political and police material'.[66] As Rosenberg, without an executive apparatus, would have been powerless against the SD, he got Hitler to approve in July 1940 a Striking-force Reichsleiter Rosenberg (ERR) – Einsatzstab Reichsleiter Rosenberg, which would travel to newly occupied countries, inspect libraries and archives and transport to the Reich all material the confiscation of which could be justified. In this way Rosenberg intended to equip his Institutes at minimal cost.

The NSDAP was used to operating without legal sanction; but the Wehrmacht liked to keep to the rules, even if these were only the rules of war. As these precluded indiscriminate pillage, Keitel had to be instructed by Hitler to issue apporporiate orders to Army Commanders in France, Belgium, Netherlands and Luxemburg; Scandinavia was later included and eventually the whole Eastern front. What was not explicitly stated in these orders was that all Jewish property was to be treated as ownerless; that this was well understood between Hitler and Rosenberg is clear from a conversation between them in September 1940, when the latter reported with glee having abstracted from the Palais Rothschild in Paris not only sixty-two cases of documents and books, but also a chest of porcelain, which had belonged to Frederick the Great.[67] Once works of art were included it was inevitable that Goering would be involved; indeed, as soon as the prior needs of his mansion at Karinhall had been recognised, he proved very cooperative in arranging transportation through the Luftwaffe.[68] What had begun as an attempt to supply free research material for Rosenberg's Institutes turned into one of the great looting operations of modern times. It soon spread far beyond Jewish property; for example, Rosenberg made a haul in the Louvre and selected for the Fuehrer Boucher's Madame Pompadour, which was sent to him together with a Vermeer from the Rothschild collection. Hitler's speciality, however, was corrupting others, while remaining himself uncorrupted. According to his friend and photographer, he refused both pictures, the right place for which was, he said, an art gallery.[69] Later he allowed Bormann to use the spoils of Europe to indulge his wish to turn Linz into a rival cultural centre to Vienna in the Danube valley. It was not established at Nuremberg that Rosenberg profited financially by his traffic; among the quick-fingered gentry of the NSDAP he stood out as one of the few who did not openly enrich himself. However three valuable pictures from the Netherlands including a Franz Hals were removed from his well-appointed house in Berlin, when he was bombed out in 1943.[70]

The most important of his Aussenstelle was the one inaugurated in March 1941 for Research into the Jewish Question and Freemasonry; it was set up in Frankfurt, which was regarded as badly infected, because in the days of Weimar it had housed the School of Cultural and Social Criticism, where Professors Adorno, Marcuse, Horkheimer and others had flourished. The Institute, which within a short period amassed a library of 40,000 books, also assumed responsibility for production of the anti-semitic periodical *Weltkampf*. At the beginning of 1941 Rosenberg had proposed to Amann that the Institute should also absorb Streicher's *Der Stuermer*, which had long been an offence to leading Nazis, as well as stinking in the nostrils of all decent people.[71] This proposal was not accepted, in spite of the fact that Streicher had been disgraced in the previous year. Hitler was known to be an avid reader of *Der Stuermer* and preferred its lively pages to Rosenberg's more staid treatment of the Jewish problem.

The Institute operating in closest cooperation with a university was the one at Halle, concerned with the rise of Christianity and the development of 'German piety', which gave Rosenberg scope for his veneration of Meister Eckhart. He was friendly both with the Gauleiter, Joachim Eggeling, and the Rector of the University, Professor Wiegelt, who specialised in prehistory. These two men founded the Halle Society of Knowledge, which awarded an annual prize named after Rosenberg.[72] Another of the Institutes was that at Hamburg, which concerned itself with colonialism, including the sinister influence of Christian Missions in Africa and Asia.[73] In October 1941 Rosenberg was still arguing with Schwarz about expansion of his Institutes; but early in 1943 Hitler at last issued a decree which enabled the advocates of total war to put a stop to these peripheral activities.

The ruthless pursuit of Nazi aims turned out to mean not, as Rosenberg had hoped, the permeation of German life with the new ideology; it meant concentration of the combined resources of party and state on total war. The ideology was pitted with obscurities, but the threat of defeat by an alliance of enemies, outraged by attempts to put part of that ideology into practice, was something all could understand. At the end of January 1943 Rosenberg resentfully confirmed to Bormann that he had closed down both the APA and the office for setting up the Hohe Schule.[74] As his cherished projects faded out and the occupied Russian territory, which he claimed to govern, rapidly diminished, his old rival Goebbels, came into his own as the apostle of total war. Goebbels, who had once described Rosenberg's *Mythus* as 'an ideological belch',[75] had always been primarily a man of action. He confided to his diary 'After the war we can talk again about ideological education. At present we are living our ideology and don't have to be taught it.'[76] It is Rosenberg's contribution to foreign policy and the great ideological war that must now occupy us.

# 8 Nazi Foreign Policy and 'The Struggle for England'

If Rosenberg's views on religion were more mystifying than mystical, there was a chill clarity about his views on foreign policy. The bold outline, which changed very little after 1922, can be summarised quite briefly. The Second Reich, as a result of mistakenly seeking colonies and world trade and in the process acquiring a large navy, had fallen foul of its natural allies, Britain and the USA. These two powers were natural allies in an ideological sense, since both were Anglo-Saxon in origin and, although a good deal corrupted by Judaism and humanism, were both in their different ways shouldering the White Man's burden by keeping coloured peoples in subjection. In return for being permitted to pursue their imperial policies without hindrance, the two Anglo-Saxon powers should give Germany a free hand in Central and Eastern Europe. To do so would in any case benefit Britain, whose hereditary enemy – because of the need to defend India – was Russia, whether ruled by a Tsar or by the Communist Party.

The main obstacle to German eastward expansion was France – the other colonial rival of Britain – which was maintaining the *cordon sanitaire* of Slav states created by the post-war treaties. France was also an object of German hostility on racial grounds, having progressively fallen from Aryan grace since 1789. Although France was a colonial power, she had abandoned the White Man's commanding role by arming Africans and other coloured peoples and using them against Europeans. (The bitter resentment against the French for using coloured troops in the occupation of the Rhineland has often been underestimated.) Accordingly, France must be hemmed in by German alliances not only with Britain but also with Italy; although the Italians were of dubious racial quality, they became ideologically respectable in Rosenberg's eyes after Mussolini's march on Rome (1922). If France were outflanked north and south, she would have to drop her anti-German policies in Central and Eastern Europe. Abandonment of the Germanic peoples of the South Tyrol, whom the Treaty of St. Germain had basely assigned to Italy, would be a small price to pay for Mussolini's friendship. Until 1939, when Rosenberg reluctantly concluded that all hope of alliance with Britain must be surrendered, he held to the foregoing views with great consistency. Nor did the outbreak of war disprove his general thesis; it proved only (apart from the fact that Ribbentrop was a disastrous Foreign Minister) that Jewish influence had finally taken over in London, as in New York and Washington.

The only major modification in Rosenberg's outlook concerned Russia and this we must look at more closely. When he first came to Munich, he was anti-Communist and anti-semitic, but not anti-Russian; he denied that the Bolshevik leaders were Slavs at all. He favoured the restoration of pre-revolutionary government in Moscow and in his first booklet accused 'the Jewish regime' there of persecuting 'everything that was truly Russian'.[1] In 1921 at a time when Hitler was praising the Treaty of Brest-Litovsk, which Ludendorff had imposed in 1918 on the USSR, Rosenberg condemned the Treaty for conceding 'self-determination' to Russia and giving recognition to Bolshevism, 'instead of helping a strong national Russian government to combat it'.[2] In a booklet published in the following year, he blamed the British for their failure, as a result of Jewish influence, to give adequate support to the White Russian counter-revolutionary Generals, Judenitsch, Denikin and Wrangel.[3] It was at this period that Rosenberg was in touch with Russian emigré groups in Munich. Later he became estranged from all except the Ukrainian nationalist faction, led by the former 'Hetman', Paul Skoropadski, and the leader of the Ukrainian Cossacks, Colonel Poltawetz-Ostanitza. In 1927 the policy of applying ethnic particularism, especially in the Ukraine and Caucasus, emerged fully fledged in his book on the future of German foreign policy.[4] This remained his policy till the end, though he feebly allowed it to be overruled by the apostles of Slav expulsion and elimination and even continued to serve as Minister of the Eastern Occupied Territories after Hitler had come down on the side of the latter.

Rosenberg's changed attitude in the early 1920s is explained partly by his growing obsession with Lebensraum as an ideological, as well as a geopolitical, concept. He believed that throughout the history of the vast area to which the designation Russia was for convenience applied the only constructive and cohesive force had been that supplied by successive injections of Germanic blood, taking at first the form of waves of Nordic invaders and later that of settlers and immigrants. The latter had been especially influential along the Baltic coastline and had been encouraged by Peter the Great, Catherine and other Tsars and Tsarinas of German extraction. The early Germanic wave had included the Goths, who founded a Caucasian state, and the Varangians, who had set up the kingdom of Kiev, described by Rosenberg as 'the foundation of all future attempts to create a state'.[5] But these achievements had been constantly threatened not only by Jews, but by Huns, Avars, Tartars, Mongolians and other 'people of the steppes'. It was these mixed and undesirable races that had finally got the upper hand in 1917 and set to work to drive out or exterminate the remnants of Germanic influence. While Rosenberg at first thought that, with the help of Germany, this trend might be reversed, he later came to the conclusion that it had gone too far. It was therefore necessary to weaken the Muscovite-Bolshevist state, which could best be done by appealing to separatist traditions, which were particularly strong in the Ukraine and Caucasus, where there had been Nordic blood and creative achievement.

Those who have failed to understand this sequence of thought have formed the conclusion that Rosenberg's anti-Russian policy was predicated on the hatred of a Baltic German for his Slav neighbours, and that his war-time efforts to moderate the brutality of his nominal subordinate, Erich Koch, in the Ukraine were attributable to the squeamishness of a man confronted with the logical results of his own thinking. This view that he was anti-Slav in the same sense that he was anti-semitic is not correct. Rosenberg accepted the hideous implications of anti-semitism, even though during the Nuremberg trial he claimed, like the others, that the mass murder of Jews had been the fault of Himmler and Heydrich, both of whom were conveniently dead. But Rosenberg's attitude towards the Slav peoples was different; they were capable of producing great art, as Dostoevsky and Tolstoy had shown. They were inferior to Nordic peoples, but able to cooperate with them; the kingdom of Kiev, which he so much admired, was an example of 'immediate coexistence between Slavs and Normans'.[6] He praised 'the magnificence of old Slavic stature' in contrast to 'the crooked-legged, pock-marked Mongolian type', the confrontation between them exemplifying the continuous struggle between European and Asiatic peoples.[7] It was suggested to him in 1942 that he might like to modify a reference in the *Mythus* to 'the yellow peril' (presumably for fear of giving offence to the Japanese); but he refused to do so.[8] It was never his wish to destroy the Slav peoples; they had their place as a buffer against Mongolians and the like. Unfortunately, they had strayed too far west and were blocking desirable areas needed by Germans for their expansion. In particular, they must be made to evacuate lands where Germanic peoples had once lived, because blood and soil were inseparable. Thus Poland, as a state, must go.

The demand for Lebensraum was linked not only to the mystical union between Blut and Boden, but also to the anti-urban prejudices of ideologically minded Nazis, especially those in the SS. These are usually ascribed to the influence on Himmler of Walther Darré, who in 1931 became head of the SS Race and Settlement Main Office and in 1933 Minister of Agriculture. His book *The Peasantry as Prime Source of the Nordic Race** had a certain influence on the NSDAP at a time when it was in any case turning to rural areas for support; it was favourably referred to by Rosenberg in the *Mythus*. Darré's was not an original contribution; as we have already noted, a romantic attachment to the soil and those who cultivated it was part of the Germanic ideology. As such, it was proclaimed by Rosenberg long before Darré came on the scene. For example, his 1922 commentary on the NSDAP programme contains references to over-industrialisation and the need to embark on settlement in the East; 'the strength of the state, it is said, rests in its peasantry.'[9] Resettlement of depopulated eastern provinces of Germany was one of the aims of the Artamanen League, in which Himmler was interested before Darré left the service of the Prussian Ministry of Agriculture and threw in his lot with the Nazis in 1929.

There were two main reasons, apart from a purely romantic concern for the land and those living on it and by it, why the Nazis interested themselves in small farmers and peasants; both

* *Das Bauerntum als Urquell der nordischen Rasse* (1929).

are expressed in Rosenberg's *Mythus*. In the first place, a sturdy and abundant peasantry was traditionally the best recruiting ground for infantry; according to Rosenberg, the national honour of the Volk grew out of the soil – 'with sword and plough for honour and freedom'.[10] Secondly, he regarded the relationship between land-owner and peasant as an organic and harmonious one, which had been disturbed by industrial and urban life. Cities, he maintained, were centres of 'race chaos'; only a very few should be permitted to have populations exceeding 500,000 and towns should be planned with populations in prospect of not more than 100,000.[11] In the early years of the NSDAP, however, these views were at variance with the objective of building up the party on a mass basis, thus providing a non-Marxist alternative for the urban proletariat. In 1928 the election results indicated that this objective was not being achieved, but that Nazism had a strong appeal in the rural areas of Schleswig-Holstein, Hanover and Brunswick. The emphasis of Nazi policy accordingly underwent a change; Darré's agricultural 'apparat' was set up in the following year and the NSDAP declared itself determined to check the drift from the land.

Although Rosenberg and Darré both attended a rally of youth groups at Weimar in the spring of 1930, they seem to have become acquainted only at the end of the summer, when Rosenberg wrote to Darré a somewhat patronising letter, inviting him to call at the offices of the *VB*, so that he could receive enlightenment on a matter concerning youth groups, on which Darré had been conducting a public correspondence.[12] In spite of this somewhat unpromising beginning, the two men established quite a good relationship; their ideological views were certainly very similar and Darré may thus have become a channel through which Rosenberg influenced Himmler, who was five years younger than Darré and seven years the junior of Rosenberg.

The shift of the domestic policy of the NSDAP, to which reference has just been made, had the result of bringing it into closer alignment with the foreign policy that Rosenberg had been advocating. His proposed alliance with England, implying renunciation of German claims to colonies and overseas coaling stations, no longer represented in any sense a sacrifice of German interests, since the pursuit of colonies to absorb surplus population and provide markets for German industry was not in itself desirable. On the contrary, colonial policy merely diverted German settlers from their rightful homeland in the east and promoted expansion of an already overheated industrial system. In 1939 Hermann Rausch-ning, who knew Rosenberg, summed up his foreign policy as follows: 'His conception of a Nordic Pan-Europe is generally accepted where definite political aims are still considered necessary [i.e. by the Nazi leadership]. Nordic Europe is the solution of the future, with a German Central Europe, a racial and national state, as the central power on the continent, safeguarding the South and South-East; the Scandinavian states with Finland as a secondary alliance for safeguarding the North-East, and Great Britain safe-guarding the West and overseas, at points where this is requisite in the interest of Nordic man.'[13]

Before examining Rosenberg's attempts to make his views prevail, especially after 1933, when Hitler, at last charged with responsibility for German foreign policy and aware of his country's weakness and isolation, necessarily adopted tactical expedients departing from pure ideological doctrine, we must first glance at the parallel development of the Fuehrer's attitude to foreign affairs. We have already rejected the assumption that, when he began his political career in Munich, he had an outlook on the world that subsequently suffered little or no modification. Confirmation of this rejection is supplied by a recent book by Professor Eberhard Jaeckel, who has shown that in 1919 Hitler was still obsessed by the need to revise the Treaty of Versailles and thus regarded France as the chief foe. He did not display any strong ideological hostility to Russia; in 1919 he spoke frequently about the Treaty of Brest-Litovsk, but, as he himself made clear, this was in order to refute the argument that the severity of its terms had provided justification for the imposition of the equally severe Versailles Treaty upon Germany.[14] In a speech in July 1920 he considered the possibility of an alliance with Russia, though he concluded that it could only come about when the Jews had been expelled.[15] Two years later at Rapallo Germany concluded an agreement with USSR, which was vigorously attacked by Rosenberg in an editorial in the *VB*. Hitler, it seems, had not yet been won over to this ideological concept of foreign policy, since as late as April 1924 he wrote an article, published in *Deutschlands Erneuerung*, in which

M

he posed the alternatives of an alliance with Russia against England, or with England against Russia, leaving the conclusion open.[16]

Between this date and 1925–26, when he was writing the second volume of *Mein Kampf*, which was published in December 1926, a marked change in his views took place. For Chapter XIV of the second volume for the first time treats relations with Russia as 'the most important problem in our foreign policy'. He no longer poses an alternative, but states clearly that the NSDAP must 'put an end to the perpetual Germanic march towards the South and West of Europe and turn our eyes towards the lands of the East. . . . This colossal Empire in the East is ripe for dissolution.' There are two reasons for this; one is the familiar one that Russia has fallen under 'the Jewish yoke'; the other that 'for centuries Russia owed the source of its livelihood as a State to the Germanic nucleus of its governing classes'.[17] In short, he has accepted Rosenberg's argument, as well as his conclusion. In Hitler's unpublished book, written in 1928, he was even more emphatic and actually paid tribute to Baltic Germans. The doctrine of Lebensraum emerged at last without qualification: 'For the future an alliance of Germany with Russia has no sense. . . .'[18] Eastward expansion was necessary, because 'the foundation of the Aryan struggle for life is the soil. . . .'[19] Finally, he advocated an alliance with England, whilst admitting that 'the struggle [i.e. with Jewry] is undecided in Britain'.[20]

It would, of course, go too far to ascribe this progressive modification of Hitler's views on foreign policy exclusively, or even primarily, to Rosenberg's influence. Other influences were also at work. For example, the geopolitical concepts of Karl Haushofer, mainly transmitted through Hess, were also thrusting in the direction of a demand for Lebensraum. Moreover, as we have seen, the adoption of a fully ideological foreign policy at this juncture chimed in with the new emphasis on the land in domestic propaganda. But it is worth noting that there is contemporary evidence of Rosenberg's influence on Hitler, recorded by those in a position to observe it, principally Luedecke and Hanfstaengl, both of whom claimed to have tried in vain to counter the anti-Russian trend, which they attributed to Rosenberg. The expulsion of Otto Strasser from the NSDAP in 1930 had fatally weakened its pro-Russian faction and Rosenberg's views were gaining ground. A British undercover agent, whom Rosenberg had introduced to Hitler in 1931, recalled a conversation in the following year with the Fuehrer, who might almost have been quoting Rosenberg when he said, 'Russia is a mere geographical conceit. It is inhabited by a heterogeneous conglomeration of peoples, differing in language and characteristics.'[21] It will be necessary to bear in mind such indications of Hitler's thinking, when we come to discuss his later decision to appoint Rosenberg his Minister of Eastern Occupied Territories.

In the period 1930–32 Nazi leaders, hungry for power in the Reich, were busy cutting up the quarry they had not yet caught. Those already in possession of an 'apparat' were considering how to impose it on the state system, or at least ensure its survival as an organ of the party within the state system. Although Rosenberg's cultural organisation (KFDK) had branches in the Nazi administrative districts (Gaue), it was not an effective political 'apparat'. Nor indeed was the *VB*, since it was administered by Amann. On the other hand, Rosenberg's editorship of the *VB*, taken together with his membership of the Foreign Affairs Committee of the Reichstag, strengthened his claim to be the NSDAP candidate either for future Minister of Foreign Affairs, or at least for a State Secretaryship in the Ministry. This therefore became his objective and he sought to build up his candidature by visits to the capitals of the countries which, he hoped, would be Germany's future allies, namely to London and Rome. He also set up a Foreign Policy Archive to provide the nucleus of a future 'apparat'.

The improved finances of the *VB* enabled Rosenberg to insist that the newspaper should begin to retain its own foreign correspondents. Luedecke had for some time, until his return to Germany in 1932, acted in an unpaid capacity in the USA. Dr H. W. Thost was sent to London and in 1931 took up residence in Wimbledon. Consistently with his master's ambitions, Thost undertook duties going far beyond those of an ordinary correspondent. He reported, of course, on the scene in Westminster and kept the *VB* well supplied with stories about the development of anti-semitism in the East End; but he also cooperated in the founding of an Anglo-German Club in Oxford, under the Chairmanship of a Baltic German Prince, whose father had been murdered by the Bolsheviks. He was tireless in seeking out Englishmen who would write articles sympathetic to Germany in the British press and, if they subsequently visited Germany, arranged for them to be suitably received.[22] Interest in the NSDAP was growing in Britain; among those received in 1931 in the Berlin office of the VB were Rennie Smith, the Parliamentary Private Secretary of the Foreign Secretary, Arthur Henderson, and Thomas Jones, the former right-hand man of Lloyd George.[23] Both were given copies of Rosenberg's *The Future Course of German Foreign Policy*, which can hardly have reassured them. Later the author realised to what an extent his writings had given hostages to fortune and in 1932 forbade republication of this booklet.[24] Thost also made it his business to check, so far as he could, on the activities of the German Embassy in London; none of the Nazis needed much convincing that German diplomatists were unpatriotic and unrepresentative of the young, aggressive Germany of the future.

The most fruitful English contact, however, was made not through Thost, but through Schickedanz, who established excellent relations with another Baltic Baron, Wilhelm de Ropp; his family had also been victims of the Bolsheviks, who had seized their estates in Lithuania. 'Bill', as his friends called him, had an English wife, and since 1910 had been resident in Britain; in 1915 he had become naturalised, joined the Wiltshire Regiment, and later flown with the Royal Flying Corps in the Great War.[25] Afterwards he settled in Berlin as a freelance journalist and in this capacity contributed articles to *The Times*, which were more pleasing to pro-German elements in Printing House Square than those of the regular correspondent, Norman Ebbutt. Through de Ropp an even more useful contact was made with another former RFC officer, F. W. Winterbotham, who was doubling the overt role of staff officer in the Air Ministry with the covert role of Air Intelligence officer in Secret Intelligence (SIS). As the Air Ministry was presided over from 1931–35 by the pro-German Marquess of Londonderry, this was a particularly valuable point of entry from Rosenberg's point of view.

It was through Winterbotham, as he has related, that Rosenberg's first visit to London was arranged in the autumn of 1931. 'I met them off the Harwich boat train. . . . My first impressions of Alfred Rosenberg . . . were of a keen, intelligent and cheerful type, rather heavily built, in his late thirties, like myself, height about five feet-ten,* rather coarse features, anxious to make a good

* Rosenberg was, in fact, 5ft 11in.

impression and, above all, to talk of his beloved movement.' The high points of the visit were a meeting with Lord Hailsham, lunch with Geoffrey Dawson of *The Times* and another at the Savoy with Oliver Locker Lampson, who at that date was 'running an organisation called the Blue-shirts'.[26] Bill de Ropp presumably acted as interpreter, since Rosenberg did not speak English, though he claimed to be able to read the language.

His visit to Rome, which took place in November 1932, was a more public occasion. He accompanied Goering to an international conference of politicians and political scientists, called the Volta Congress, which discussed the future of Europe. Whilst Goering was given the seat of honour at the banquet given by Mussolini for the Congress, it was Rosenberg's speech that attracted his favourable comment and won space in the Fascist press.[27] It had been carefully tailored for his audience and at last showed awareness that a man who has aspirations to become Foreign Minister must not carry campaigns of open hatred into the international arena. The Fascist Party was not anti-semitic and Rosenberg omitted any direct attack on Jews. He did, however, attack the Pan-European ideas of Count Coudenhove-Kalergi, whom he had already stigmatised in his 1927 book on foreign policy as 'a half-Japanese, married to a Jewess'.[28] The Count's proposals were condemned as being based on an abstract idea of Europe; the reality consisted of the four national states, Germany, Britain, France and Italy, whose interests need not conflict. Britain's main concern was with her Empire, France's with Africa south of the Sahara, and Italy's with the Adriatic and North Africa. Germany was the barrier to Bolshevism and it was therefore against the interests of Europe to allow Germany to be weak. In the long run, not only the Bolshevik threat, but also that of the black and yellow races demanded solidarity between the four great nation states of the European continent.[29]

Rosenberg must have returned to Germany more than ever confident that he would receive high office as soon as the Nazis took over. It was not to be. Hindenburg, in accepting Hitler as Chancellor on 30 January 1933, insisted that his nominees should continue to direct the Foreign Office and the Ministry of Defence. In the game of musical-chairs Rosenberg and Roehm found that the chairs they wished to occupy had not yet been vacated. Roehm still had his power apparatus – the SA; but Rosenberg felt that he had been passed over, especially when in mid-March his hated rival, Goebbels, had a new Ministry created for him and began to take control not only of the press, but of cultural life as well.

Luedecke has recorded that Rosenberg admitted to him it was 'quite impossible to appoint me Foreign Minister'.[30] His career as ideologist and journalist virtually precluded this; he had made hard and hateful judgments and all of these were on the record. There had been alarm in Warsaw and Moscow, when Hitler came to power; Rosenberg's Lebensraum projects were well known there. Rauschning has written: 'At my first official visit to Warsaw in July 1933, I was asked by the Polish authorities to use my influence to prevent the public discussion of such stupid ideas as those of Rosenberg on the Ukraine. They were, for that matter, by no means Rosenberg's alone.'[31] Although the top post was beyond his reach, Rosenberg claimed to have had from Hitler a definite promise that he would become State Secretary.[32] This is probably true; Hanfstaengl has written that, when Hitler returned to the Kaiserhof after being invested with the Chancellorship, Hanfstaengl overhead him say to Frick, 'The best thing to do with Party-comrade Rosenberg is to put him as State Secretary in the Foreign Office.'[33] Hanfstaengl immediately warned the Foreign Minister, Constantin v. Neurath, whose influence with Hindenburg at that time would have been sufficient to block the move. The Vice-Chancellor, Papen, who was a Roman Catholic and an advocate of the Concordat with the Vatican, was another hostile influence.

This personal set-back aggravated Rosenberg's distress at the course of events. New members were pouring into the NSDAP, further diluting its character; the leadership seemed occupied with personal advantage and the conclusion of an alliance with the traditional forces of Prussian conservatism. Goering was busy organising the Gestapo along lines which Heydrich was later to develop so effectively. In addition to intercepting telegrams and telephone conversations Goering was sedulously building up dossiers not only on political opponents, but also on colleagues. In the process he acquired a packet of Rosenberg's love letters; what was worse, the letters were addressed to a beautiful red-haired Jewess, named Lisette Kohlrausch, whom the Gestapo had arrested. Rosenberg got her released, but his fear of being exposed to ridicule, in a way that would have severely damaged his status as Party ideologist, seems to have begun in him that subservience to Goering that so fatally afflicted him later as Minister.[34]

Rosenberg's state of mind early in 1933 is well illustrated by an episode related by Sefton Delmer, who was on the spot in February 1933, when the Reichstag building went up in flames. 'There under the trees of the Tiergarten, and just opposite the Reichstag entrance I saw a familiar figure: Dr Alfred Rosenberg, Editor of the Nazi *VB* and Hitler's No. 1 adviser on foreign affairs. He had been driving home through the Tiergarten in his car, Rosenberg told me, when he noticed the fire. "I only hope," said Rosenberg gloomily, "that this is not the work of our chaps. It is just the sort of damn silly thing some of them might do!" '[35] It seems not to have occurred to him to reshape the front page of the *VB*; this was done later that evening by Hitler and Goebbels.

It was not until 31 March that Rosenberg was finally received by the new Chancellor in his official capacity and authorised to set up the Foreign Policy Office (APA) of the NSDAP; but when he went to see Schwarz, the party Treasurer, he found that no funds were yet available. With the help of Luedecke, he made plans to raise money by means of contributions from German industry. Then, leaving Luedecke and Schickedanz in charge, he took advantage of Hitler's authority to pay a second visit to London. As soon as his back was turned, his old enemy, Goering, struck at him indirectly by having Luedecke arrested. He was released after a week, after learning from a talkative Gestapo agent: 'It's really Rosenberg they're after.... He has been watched for some time.'[36] However, that may be, the APA's American expert had been eliminated and Rosenberg had been warned not to try to challenge the top leadership.

Luedecke was arrested again in mid-July and, in spite of half-hearted efforts made by Rosenberg on his behalf, only regained his freedom in February 1934 by escaping to Czechoslovakia. His decision to escape resulted from final realisation that Rosenberg was too weak and indecisive to be able to help him. In their last interview, early in February, when Luedecke was in Berlin on 'French leave', Rosenberg admitted that, when he had attempted to intervene, he had been told by Hitler to mind his own business.[37] In a last appeal to Hitler for vindication, written in Geneva in April

1934, Luedecke bitterly described Rosenberg as 'unfortunately too feeble and passive either to assert himself effectively or to decline appointments and offices without executive function'.[38] No reply was sent to this letter; Himmler passed it on without comment to Rosenberg, who in his memoir gives a garbled account of the episode.

Luedecke's description of the two functions that by the spring of 1934 had been assigned to Rosenberg, although conceived in bitterness, is very close to the mark. We have already discussed his appointment as Delegate for Indoctrination; the APA was no more solid a power base. When it was first set up, Rosenberg had been told that it was not meant to supersede the Foreign Office, but to function in areas where the latter was relatively ineffective. He had officially announced that its aim was to increase under standing of foreign policy within the NSDAP; to make the NSDAP better understood abroad; and to train up a new generation of diplomatists The last point, on which, in fact, the APA achieved little or nothing, was a public statement, in polite language, of the NSDAP's distrust of the Foreign Office, the class that had tradition ally staffed it, and the policy of 'fulfilment' (i.e. of the Treaty of Versailles), with which it was popularly associated. Hitler fully shared this prejudice; in a talk with Rosenberg in May 1934 he described the Foreign Office as 'a society of conspirators'; their conspiracy was directed against the new Germany.[39] On the other hand, the very retention of representatives of the old Germany seemed in other countries to mean a continuation of Stresemann's policies under new management and this made the Foreign Office a valuable stalking-horse in the dangerous game that Hitler was play ing. Above all, he needed time to rearm under cover of peaceful protestations. In the pursuit of this essentially opportunist policy, he found Rosenberg a liability. The first two international agree ments concluded by the Third Reich were the Concordat with the Vatican – in Rosenberg's eyes one of the centres of the great anti-German conspiracy – and the pact with Poland, a country that he wanted removed from the map of Europe.

Although nothing had been said about relations with England when the APA was set up, it is possible that Hitler at first thought that in this field Rosenberg might be able to accomplish something through the contacts that he claimed to have established. If so, the failure of his second visit to London in May 1933 must have disillusioned both of them. Rosenberg seems at first to have planned to by-pass the German Embassy, since he was convinced that the Counsellor, Count Bernstorff, was a foe of the Nazi regime; but Thost persuaded him that, if he was to be received, as he hoped, by the Foreign Office, he would have to use the orthodox channel.[40] Rosenberg was to blame his ill success impartially upon Bernstorff, Thost and his old enemy Goebbels, who had organised a boycott of Jewish stores at the beginning of April, so further exacerbating British opinion.

Rosenberg was very much on the defensive during his two interviews at the Foreign Office; in the course of the first, when Sir Robert (later Lord) Vansittart was questioning him about the numbers detained in concentration camps, he tried to move onto the offensive by means of an allusion to repressive British measures in India. He concluded by assuring the Permanent Under-Secretary that 'the revolution in the Reich was purely a social one, and the government of Adolf Hitler had no aims in foreign policy that were not peaceful'.[41] His subsequent interview with the Foreign Secretary, Sir John Simon, followed much the same lines. Rosenberg began by stressing the threat of Bolshevism, but Simon showed himself more interested in persecution of Jews and concentration camps in Germany. The German government, he maintained, had now completely isolated itself from public opinion in Britain.[42] As if to prove Simon's point, a crowd formed outside Claridges, where Rosenberg stayed, and a man chanting anti-Fascist slogans was arrested and later fined for disorderly conduct.[43] An even more distressing episode occurred when a wreath bearing a swastika, laid by Rosenberg at the cenotaph in Whitehall, was taken away by the chairman of the Aylsham Branch of the British Legion, who hurled it into the Thames.[44] There was considerable publicity and HMG expressed regrets to Ambassador Hoesch, who reported to his government that the visit of Rosenberg, who was regarded as the 'incarnation of the new Germany', had 'caused England's hostility . . . to break out with full force'. A new waxwork figure of Hitler in Madame Tussauds was disfigured. Hoesch, like Bernstorff, was no friend of the Nazis, but he added in his report that the unfortunate effect of Rosenberg's visit was 'in no wise due to the personality of Rosenberg'.[45] At the same time his personality scarcely helped to remove prejudices; Vansittart described him as 'a Balt who looked like cold cod'.[46] Fears within the German Embassy that Rosenberg might be nominated to succeed Hoesch subsided. It is in any case improbable that Rosenberg would have accepted the post, if offered; it is more likely that he was sincere in saying to Luedecke, 'In London I'd be well out of the way! – I've every intention of staying right here in Berlin.'[47]

The repercussions of the abortive visit were not confined to London; in Moscow Litvinov seized the opportunity to complain to the German Ambassador of Rosenberg's 'relations with Russian and in particular Ukrainian emigrants'.[48] The professional diplomatists had scored a success at the expense of their new masters in Berlin, and Rosenberg had plenty of enemies to rub in the salt. Even in his own field of press relations he was unable to remove the regular *Times* correspondent, Norman Ebbutt, whose anti-Nazi reports were even more painful to Hitler than they were to Geoffrey Dawson. Rosenberg and Thost had had the ingenious idea of conveying to the well-known teetotaller, Lady Astor, the message that Ebbutt must be removed because of his heavy drinking.[49] But there is no evidence that Rosenberg did call on Lady Astor, or even got to Cliveden; another four years elapsed before the Nazis, their patience finally exhausted, expelled Ebbutt. In only one respect was Rosenberg able to claim to have acted with tact and discretion; he deliberately avoided meeting Sir Oswald Mosley on the ground that Fascism was not in the British tradition. As he later recorded, 'I thought it wrong that Sir Oswald Mosley called his party the "British Fascists".'[50]

Although Thost had some suspicions about the *bona fides* of de Ropp, this channel survived the misfortunes of the London visit and in February 1934 Winterbotham came to Germany under Rosenberg's auspices. He was taken, unaccompanied by anyone from the British Embassy, to call on Hitler, who blandly assured him that Germany would have 'some 500 first-line aircraft in squadrons by the end of 1934', and then launched into his familiar demand that 'the British Empire ... the Americas and the Germanic Empire of the future' should between them rule the world.[51] These stirring words alerted Winterbotham to the need to inform the British Embassy of his activities and he reported the conversation to the Air Attaché, before leaving Berlin in Rosenberg's

black Mercedes for Weimar. There Rosenberg addressed a Nazi
rally and they afterwards adjourned to a beer cellar, where Winterbotham was intercepted by an urgent call from the British
Ambassador, Sir Eric Phipps, who wished to see him as soon as
possible. Before returning to London, however, Winterbotham
attended a lunch given by Rosenberg and graced by two future
Field-Marshals (Kesselring and v. Reichenau), who frankly
discussed German rearmament with him. Back home he proceeded
to arrange for another old friend, Ken Bartlett of the Bristol
Aircraft Co., to go to Berlin to show de Ropp's German friends
'the latest (not quite) Bristol engines still on the secret list'.[52]
It is strange that the SIS, which came under the Foreign Office,
had failed, it seems, to warn Winterbotham that in the previous
July Vansittart had instructed the Embassy in Berlin that the Air
Attaché must not discuss with the German government the sale
of British aircraft.[53] At that date the conversion of civil aircraft
into bombers presented no technical or other problems.

The episode, related after many years with such candour by
Winterbotham, sheds a flood of light on the conflicting attitudes
adopted in Whitehall towards Germany at this period. He seems
surprised that he was afterwards reprimanded by the Foreign Secretary. 'Why should authentic information about German air rearmament in violation of the Treaty of Versailles be apparently the last
thing the Government wanted?'[54] Yet the intelligence value of his
report can hardly have outweighed the reassurance given to the
Germans by the fact that a British Air Force officer should discuss
their rearmament plans with them in so friendly a way. When one
considers that it was the avowed aim of Nazi policy to secure
British sympathy and support against the shackles of Versailles and
to drive a wedge between Britain and her French ally, it looks as
if this was less a case of SIS exploiting the APA than the other way
round.

Neither Rosenberg's contacts in aviation circles, nor his attempts
to build up a connexion with Lord Rothermere in England and
William Randolph Hearst in USA served to convince Hitler that
the APA was a going concern. Because Rosenberg's star was not
in the ascendant, his APA failed to attract ambitious and able men;
he was left with men like Horst Obermueller, who until sacked in

1935 was head of the English section. At the end of June 1934, Rosenberg, in the course of a discussion with Hitler about the replacement of Hoesch in London, put forward Obermueller as a candidate.[55] It was an inept suggestion, since Obermueller had commanded a U-boat in the war and had been accused of war crimes; his assignment to the Court of St James could hardly have failed to create a furore in London. However the Air Ministry had no scruples about doing business with him; early in 1935 he accompanied two German air experts to London, visited the Bristol Aircraft works and was received at the Ministry by Lord Londonderry who, according to Rosenberg's report to Hitler, explained to Obermueller how the Ministry functioned.[56] There must have been many in England at that time who would have been glad to have an explanation.

The man who was waiting in the wings was Joachim v. Ribbentrop, whose Bureau in Berlin was moving into the APA's preserves and who was himself to become Ambassador in London in August 1936. Ribbentrop was a late comer among the top people of the NSDAP; but, unlike Rosenberg, he had prudently aligned himself with Himmler. His earlier career as a champagne salesman had made him an expert 'name-dropper'; Hitler was the more impressed because, like Hess and Ribbentrop himself, he was convinced that Britain was governed by a small, aristocratic clique. It was true that in the 1930s germanophiles were disproportionately represented in the House of Lords; it did not follow that they were governing the country. In March 1935 Rosenberg wrote in his diary that Ribbentrop was trying to secure a State Secretaryship in the Foreign Ministry;[57] it was the post that had been denied to him earlier. Three months later Ribbentrop was given the rank of Ambassador and was instrumental in getting Britain to sign a naval agreement, when Europe was still resounding with echoes of Hitler's defiance of Versailles in the form of an announcement of his intention to rearm and introduce conscription. It was a triumph for elements in Britain that had listened only to the siren song of German propaganda. Ribbentrop's assignment to the Embassy in London put an end to his half-hearted attempt to reach agreement with Rosenberg on a demarcation of territory between them. The APA, playing an ever diminishing role, found itself virtually confined to the Balkans and Scandinavia, though Goering excluded it from any effective link with Sweden.

Although in 1936 relations with Italy were at last beginning to prosper, as a result of Anglo-French antagonism to Mussolini's invasion of Abyssinia, it must have seemed to Rosenberg that the policy being pursued was still not sufficiently ideological. At the annual Nuremberg rally in September 1936, under the influence of the outbreak of civil war in Spain, he made an intensely anti-Russian speech, in which it is possible to detect a faint note of criticism of German foreign policy. 'Short-term foreign policy, whose decisions vary from day to day, is the most fatal way of guiding the destinies of modern nations. . . . The decisive world conflicts of our time require that men who are always inclined to compromise shall be replaced by men who are vividly conscious of the whole past history of a people as of a heritage, which at the same time implies a duty. . . .'[58] Two months later Ribbentrop signed the Anti-Comintern Pact with Japan, to which Italy adhered a year later; the great anti-Bolshevist front was at last being formed – or so it seemed.

There followed Hitler's *annus mirabilis* – 1938. In March he moved into Austria, returning, like the prince of a fairy-tale, to the homeland of his dishonoured youth. In the elections that followed in April in the enlarged Reich Rosenberg spoke in several Austrian cities, taking de Ropp with him to show him how welcome the Nazis were. In Graz the Gauleiter presented him with a bound volume of the letters of Austrian Nazis, who had suffered imprisonment, with the inscription, 'To the man to whom we owe the inner strength to withstand.'[59] At the end of September 1938 at the Munich Conference Hitler secured the Sudetenland without striking a blow. But 1938 was no *annus mirabilis* for Rosenberg, since in February Ribbentrop was made Foreign Minister. Rosenberg drafted a letter of bitter complaint to Hitler, petitioning for a seat in the Cabinet (which had, in fact, ceased to meet).[60] A copy of this letter was produced at the Nuremberg trial, though Rosenberg in his memoir denied that he actually sent it.[61] In any case, Hitler remained unmoved. At the 1938 NSDAP rally Rosenberg opened an exhibition under the rubric: 'Struggle in the East'. He little knew that it was to be the last of the great Nuremberg rallies, nor that by September 1939 the USSR would be an ally of the Reich.

In March 1939 Hitler occupied Prague. He could no longer claim that he was revising the Treaty of Versailles or applying the Wilsonian doctrine of self-determination to German minorities; this was naked aggression. By the end of March the British and French had given their guarantee to Poland, which had already rejected Hitler's hints that Germany and Poland might profitably do a deal at the expense of Russian Ukraine. If the Anglo-French meant their guarantee to be taken seriously, they now had to come to an understanding with the USSR. While in London the implications of this were being faced at last, signs multiplied in Moscow that Stalin might be prepared to offer Hitler another alternative – a Russian-German deal at the expense of Poland. If Hitler could forestall the Anglo-French negotiators, he would be able to overrun Poland before the winter; he set a provisional date – 1 September 1939.

In mid-May two representatives of an Estonian peasants' organisation came to see Rosenberg, bringing with them a symbolic fragment of their black bread. They enquired whether the Reich would be willing to assume a protectorate over their small country, while permitting them to keep their own language and cultural life; if the Russians moved in, they feared that they would suffer the same fate as had overtaken the Russian kulaks. Rosenberg replied 'We have no interest in seeing Russia once more in Reval and Riga. We respect the individuality of every nation. We do not want to intervene; you must yourselves muster the strength to carry through a change of attitude.'[62] It is unlikely that he knew how rapidly events were moving in the direction feared by his Estonian visitors. Ribbentrop was in his pro-Soviet phase; in so far as Hitler needed an expert adviser on Poland, he consulted Albert Forster, the Gauleiter of Danzig.

Later in May Rosenberg had a long, friendly conversation with Goering, an event rare enough for him to record part of it verbatim in his diary.[63] As always when two Nazi leaders met, they joined in criticising a third – in this case Ribbentrop. Goering, like Rosenberg, was perturbed at the speed at which events were moving, though neither trusted the other enough to indulge in overt criticism of the Fuehrer's timetable. Rosenberg pointed out that soldiers' lives could be saved by making full use of the many disaffected ethnic groups that abounded in the borderlands of Poland

and Russia; but time was needed in order to evaluate the possibilities and work out coordinated appeals to the different groups. Already Ribbentrop had offended the Carpatho-Ukrainians by allowing Hungary to occupy Ruthenia. Both men spoke bitterly of the way in which the Foreign Minister had made himself disliked in London.

A few weeks later the APA sent a long memorandum to Hans Lammers, the head of Hitler's State Chancery, with detailed maps showing eighty-seven ethnic groups extending as far east as Siberia. Rosenberg had always insisted that Russia was not a national state, but a state composed of many nationalities; Poland should be split in the same way into component ethnic groups, of which West Ukraine and West White Ruthenia were the most important. He assumed in his memorandum that the USSR was in no condition to embark upon war and, if Stalin came to an agreement with the Anglo-French negotiators, it would be for the purpose of setting them and the Germans at each other's throats. 'Moscow would only come on stage at the end to play the part of body-snatcher.'[64] In the plans that were being made to invade Poland and reinsure by means of an alliance with Russia he was completely ignored.

Rosenberg was in the Harz on 18 July 1939, after fulfilling a speaking engagement, when he received a message that Hitler wished to speak to him about a draft speech on England's present situation, which Rosenberg was due to deliver on the following day. Hitler, speaking on the telephone from the Obersalzberg, told him to hold up the speech, 'since it might be regarded in London as a broad hint, and the Russians might then perhaps jump over into the British camp quicker than expected'. Presumably the speech would have implied that the way to reconciliation between London and Berlin was not yet closed and that Hitler was not sincere in his rapprochement with Stalin. Rosenberg chose to put a hopeful construction on Hitler's words: 'So the Fuehrer is still not entirely of Ribbentrop's way of thinking, but, while taking all necessary severe measures and preparations to confront the British with the gravest consequences, nevertheless has the old attitude: everything possible to be done....'[65]

He still hoped to convince Hitler that conciliatory forces in Britain might win the day. One week after their telephone conversation he sent him an urgent note of a talk that he and State

Secretary Weizsaecker had had with Lord Kemsley,* who was visiting Germany with his wife and was due to be received later by Hitler. According to Rosenberg, who found the conversation encouraging, 'Lord Kemsley repeated constantly: England and Germany must never go to war, for that could only benefit Russia and would lead to the destruction of European culture.' Lord Kemsley, from whom Rosenberg derived the impression that he had been commissioned by Neville Chamberlain to plead his case, maintained that the Prime Minister was negotiating in Moscow most unwillingly and was ready to break off the talks, which had been begun in order to take the wind out of the sails of those opposing him in Parliament. Chamberlain was 'England's Fuehrer' and would remain so.[66] Hitler must also have found this report encouraging, though not necessarily for the same reasons as Rosenberg; a foe so divided against itself could hardly be expected to impress the Russians as a firm ally, nor to keep its promise to Poland. Lord Kemsley's later talk with Hitler must have followed different lines, if we are to judge by the former's report to the Cabinet, which did not perturb either Lord Halifax or Sir Alexander Cadogan.[66a]

Just as the lights were going out all over Europe, Rosenberg had a final, futile talk with de Ropp, who told him that, in the event of war, he had been appointed adviser on Germany to the Air Ministry. There must, said Rosenberg, be 'a joint statement in London directed against the whole policy of the Churchill and Eden group'. On the assumption that Poland would soon be disposed of, they then discussed how to prevent 'a European struggle from breaking out'.[67] Shortly before midnight on the same evening (21 August) Rosenberg received the news that the terms of the pact soon to be signed in Moscow between Molotov and Ribbentrop had been approved. It was a shattering blow to everything for which he stood. In his diary he struggled to find reasons to justify the Fuehrer's decision 'to switch course 180 degrees'; but his distress constantly broke through. 'The journey of our Minister to Moscow is a moral loss of face in view of our twenty-year fight, of our party rallies, of Spain. ... Ribbentrop will feel none of this, as he has no political principles, apart from hate for

---

* Gomer Berry, first Baron (1936) and first Viscount (1945) was Chairman of Kemsley newspapers and editor-in-chief of *The Sunday Times* (1937–59).

England. . . . History perhaps will one day clarify whether the situation that arose had necessarily to come about, that is, whether there were no decisive forces in England that could have been mobilised to cooperate with us.'[68] Three days later he came back to the same theme: 'And again the question arises: did this situation have to come about? Did the Polish question have to be settled now and in this way? Today no one can provide an answer.' In a flash of insight he added: 'I have the feeling as if this Moscow Pact at some future date will take its revenge on National-Socialism.'[69] It would indeed; but first a great deal of blood would flow, that of the guilty and of the innocent.

The invasion of Poland began at dawn on 1 September. Later that day Rosenberg had another talk with Goering, while both were waiting for Hitler to address the Reichstag. 'I have the feeling', said Rosenberg, 'that England has been wilfully underestimated; in recent years she had not been spoken to in the way one talks to a great power.' Goering replied that that very night he had 'fought like a lion to get the decision put off for another twenty-four hours. . . .' They went on to speak of the vain intervention of Goering's Swedish friend, Dahlerus, and Rosenberg added that 'the political adviser to the British Air Ministry' (i.e. de Ropp) would be getting in touch with him from Switzerland in case, after the fall of Poland, anything could be done to restore peace.[70] Rosenberg then retired from the scene for a few weeks with an inflammation of the joint of his left foot. The great 'struggle for England' had been lost.

One frail thread still held. On 23 September Rosenberg received a postcard from Squadron-Leader de Ropp in Switzerland, suggesting that an emissary of Rosenberg should meet him in Montreux. Six days later Hitler received Rosenberg to discuss the project, but spent most of the time describing his plans for conquered Poland and for creating a Jewish reservation, into which the Jews from the Reich, as well as from Poland should be driven. He agreed that Rosenberg should send someone to Montreux to bring de Ropp to Berlin, adding – almost flippantly – that he would himself receive him. He was about to make the British a peace offer in any case. Rosenberg cautiously enquired whether the Fuehrer eventually meant to take the offensive against the West and received the reply: 'If the English did not want peace, he would

N

use every means of attacking them and would destroy them.'[71]

Gradually Rosenberg began again to accustom his mind, as he had so often done, to acceptance of the Fuehrer's infallibility. If England was determined to work for the destruction of Germany, he confided to his diary, 'there can, in line of duty, be only one answer. Ways stood open to the English, even without Ribbentrop; they did not have the wish.'[72] He stiffened up the instructions for the emissary whom he sent to meet de Ropp in Montreux with authority to invite him back to Berlin. When the pessimistic Squadron-Leader opined that the result of the war 'would only be the decline of the West, of the Aryan race, and the era of the bolshevisation of Europe, including England', his German interlocutor replied sharply that 'Stalin had now ousted the Jews from all posts'; he emphasised how much the Soviet alliance had contributed to the strength of the Reich. During this curious conversation a telegram arrived from 'Fred in London',* saying that he considered a talk with leading Germans premature 'at present'. It was an unexceptionable conclusion, which might have been even more forcibly expressed. Regrettably, however, it was accompanied by a message for Rosenberg to the effect that the Air Ministry 'by no means wished to be a party to the present policy of England of waging the war to the finish', but was not yet strong enough to assert itself, pending the creation, through defeat at the hands of the Luftwaffe, of a basis of negotiation.[73] This attempt on the part of sis, to keep open a channel of communication with Germany, after the outbreak of war and the overrunning of Poland, seems to have been carried to astonishing lengths, even if one does not accept at face value the German record of the interview.†

By the end of the year even Rosenberg had abandoned the hope he had once pinned on Britain as an ally and was pondering how best to attack her. The renewal of an old Norwegian contact offered the possibility. He had first met Vikdun Quisling, a former Minister of War, in connection with the Nordic Society, which he had fostered since May 1933 in order to close ranks with the Aryan peoples of Scandinavia. Now Rosenberg, anxious for a new field of

* Presumably Fred Winterbotham
† This account of de Ropp's interviews is the German version; no official British account has been made public. His version in *I Spied on Hitler* reads: 'Six times they sent an emissary to me to see whether a way could not be found to end the war. Always I told him: England will never make peace with Hitler.'

activity, was actually trying to extend the war to Scandinavia. In December 1939 Quisling appeared in Berlin, asking to see Weizsaecker, who refused to receive him.[74] Rosenberg, seeing a chance to act behind the back of the German Foreign Office, took charge of Quisling and interested Hitler in the possibilities of direct intervention in Norway. Admiral Raeder gave his support and, before Quisling returned to Oslo, he had extracted a promise of help in the event of intervention by Britain. In mid-February Rosenberg learned with great satisfaction of the cutting out of the 'Altmark' by the Royal Navy, which had thus violated Norwegian neutrality. It was now possible to convince Hitler that he ought to attack Norway and Denmark in order to forestall a move by Britain. The new invasion took place on 9 April 1940 and in his diary Rosenberg wrote, 'This is a great day in the history of Germany'.[75] He congratulated Hitler, who solemnly (and somewhat inaccurately) replied, 'Even as Bismarck's Reich originated out of the year 1866, so the Great German Reich will originate out of this day's work.'* Disillusionment with Quisling's lack of support in Norway ensued; but Rosenberg had the satisfaction of feeling that his despised APA had at last played an active part in foreign affairs.

The final episode in the ill-fated struggle for England was one in which Rosenberg's role, if indeed he had one, remains obscure. He had always kept on good terms with Hess, who with his friend Haushofer had long shared his belief that Germany's true destiny lay in joining with Britain in an attack upon the USSR. On 10 May 1941 – less than six weeks before Hitler's invasion of Russia – Hess invited Rosenberg to an unusually early lunch at noon. Ilse Hess was unwell and did not come downstairs; her husband had given instructions to the domestic staff that he and Rosenberg were not to be disturbed. The latter left soon after one o'clock. Hess then had a rest, changed into Luftwaffe uniform, said a normal good-bye to his wife and took off on his solo flight to Scotland.[76] After their lunch together, the two men were not to meet again until both found themselves in Nuremberg gaol. Hess' flight gave rise to a flood of rumours in the Reich, including one to the effect that Rosenberg and Darré had been shot.[77]

It must be said that the policy of the Anglophile wing of the NSDAP was ill-conceived; it assumed on ideological grounds a

* Presumably Prussia's invasion of Denmark in 1864 was meant.

congruity of interests that never, in fact, existed. It was true that in those quarters in England through which Rosenberg sought to operate there was an almost pathological fear and suspicion of the USSR; but in other circles the feeling was steadily growing that Hitler – at least in the immediate future – was even more dangerous and less trustworthy than Stalin. After March 1939 this latter current grew immeasurably in strength. In Berlin it was attributed to Jewish influence. It was impossible for Nazis who thought like Rosenberg to admit to themselves how much antagonism they had aroused not only by specific acts of aggression, but by the crude brutality of their whole performance in the international arena. They had finally themselves eradicated in Britain the spirit of appeasement that for so long had served them so well.

# 9 Rosenberg and the Ideological War

Since historians are by no means all agreed that ideological motives led Hitler to invade the USSR, we must begin by explaining in what sense the term 'ideological war' is here used. Primarily, it is used to signify that his decision was based on irrational and pre-conceived ideas about the drama of history and the respective roles played by the German and Slav peoples. The slaughter of Slavs, as of Jews, was ritual murder, which not only contributed nothing to military victory but, as we shall shortly see, severely handi-capped the Wehrmacht in its task. Not only was the war conducted in a manner consistent only with an ideological explanation of Hitler's ultimate aims, but planning for it was begun at a time when the invasion of the USSR was the least rational of the alterna-tives with which Hitler was faced. This was immediately clear to the Planning Staff of the OKW, when on 29 July 1940 Hitler's intentions were made known to them by General Jodl, implying that dreaded two-front war which German statesmen and soldiers had always sought to avoid. As Colonel (later General) Warlimont put it, 'Jodl's word had the impact of a stroke of lightning. The bewilderment became, if possible, even greater, as the first ques-tions revealed that it was not proposed first at all costs to conclude the struggle with England, but on the contrary to conquer Russia ... as the best means of forcing England ... to make peace.'[1]

Hitler, in order to provide for his Generals a plausible explana-tion of his intentions, was indeed making use of what might be called the 1812 syndrome, according to which the road to London passed through Moscow. Yet Hitler was using this argument at a date when he had not yet accepted Raeder's contention that he could not transport sufficient German divisions across the Channel and when Goering's related attempt to win air supremacy over the

South coast of England had not even started. Although the cross-Channel operation 'Sea-lion' remained on the books, the transfer of troops from West to East was begun. These moves took place at a time when Stalin was refusing to listen to British insinuations that Hitler was not to be trusted, and was over-fulfilling the Russo-German economic agreement, which supplied more of the Reich's basic needs than Hitler was ever able to secure by conquest. Instead of pursuing 'Sea-lion', consolidating his rule in subject Europe, or embarking with Stalin on a partition of the Near and Middle East into spheres of interest, thus cutting off the British from their Indian and other Asiatic possessions, Hitler on 18 December 1940 gave the order for operation 'Barbarossa' and set a date in May of the following year. 'Those whom the gods wish to destroy they first drive mad.'

In suggesting that Hitler's was an ideological war, we must make it plain that this did not mean that all members of the Nazi top leadership saw it in the same light. This could scarcely have been the case, if only because, as was pointed out in Chapter Four,* no two Nazis saw the ideology in the same light. Immediately after the invasion began, Hitler spoke of it as a crusade and encouraged European client states to send contingents.[2] Later, when Germany saw herself faced by a long war, Himmler carried the crusading idea so far that he permitted the armed SS to recruit in a country such as Estonia, where even Rosenberg, who was born there, did not claim that Aryan blood amounted to more than fifty per cent. But was it a crusade against Pan-Slavism or a crusade against Bolshevism? In Poland it had clearly been the former, since Hitler and Himmler ruthlessly exterminated those elements in the Polish State and Army that would have been of most value in later cooperation with the Nazis against the Bolsheviks. It is significant that it was at Stalin's prompting that Hitler decided to eliminate all trace of Polish autonomy, while Mussolini argued in the opposite sense. Rejecting the policy of backing a Quisling-type administration, considered suitable for countries like Norway, which could boast Aryan blood, Hitler left the Poles no alternative between hopeless submission and irreconcilable hostility.

The issue in the Russian war was less clear-cut; the uncertainty in Hitler's mind is illustrated by the fact that, although he had

* Chapter 4, p. 65.

started the military planning in good time, it was the end of March 1941 before he instructed Rosenberg to draw up a blue-print for the administration and future political configuration of the territory that he expected would fall so easily into his grasp. At the end of September 1941, before the need to fight a long war had become fully apparent, Rosenberg already found it necessary to point out to Hitler the awkwardness of fighting an anti-Slav crusade with Balkan allies. Avoiding, as usual, any direct criticism of the Fuehrer, he drew attention to a speech made by the brother of the Roumanian dictator, in which the younger Antonescu had described the war as one against Slavdom; at that point, Rosenberg added, the Bulgarian Military Attaché had become red in the face and left the room.[3]

The concept of an anti-Bolshevist crusade eliminated objections from small allies, but did nothing to reconcile the German people to a prolongation of the war. Undoubtedly they would have preferred, if offered a choice, that the Luftwaffe should concentrate on suppressing RAF Bomber Command, which was beginning to be a nuisance, instead of supporting the Wehrmacht on the Eastern front. No one understood better than Hitler that even a dictator needs popular cooperation, especially in time of war. Nazi propaganda to the German people at this stage therefore did not so much stress anti-Bolshevism as material, if long-term, advantages. As R. L. Koehl has put it, 'Linking their conquests and their oppressions with nationalist values (strengthening Germandom), while providing for the future satisfaction of the material interests of millions of Germans (plans for future settlement, cheaper food, new industrial opportunities, cheap labour) the Nazis had no trouble holding the German people to their part of a bargain which they only half understood.'[4] This line was not followed only in public statements. On the day before the invasion, Rosenberg addressed the staff of what was soon to become his Ministry of Eastern Occupied Territories (RMBO): 'Today we are not leading a crusade against Bolshevism, solely in order to save the "poor Russians" for all time from Bolshevism, but in order to pursue German world policy and assure the safety of the Reich.'[5]

However much the views of ideologists might diverge, they could at least agree among themselves, and with the non-ideological Wehrmacht, that the common aim was, as Rosenberg expressed it in his draft general instructions to his Reich Commissioners, 'to free the Reich for centuries to come from the pressure of Great Russia'.[6] But how was this ultimate aim to be secured after the immediate military victory? Here again divergences at once arose. Even Nazis who, unlike Rosenberg, lacked the imagination to grasp the immensity of the space over which the Third Reich was now extending its control, had mastered the fact that the reproduction rate of the Slavs exceeded that of the Germans. The 'hard-liners', including Hitler himself, Himmler, Bormann and Erich Koch, intended to check this trend by keeping subject Slavs below the subsistence level, raising the legal marriage age, repealing penalties for abortion, allowing prisoners of war to starve and generally adopting genocidal methods; but even they realised that some Slavs would have to survive, if only to contribute by their labour to the high living standard of the Aryan Herrenvolk. The surviving Slavs would accordingly be kept in subjection by a resettlement policy, which began with the idea of a chain of Germanic fortified settlements extending from the Baltic to the Carpathians and patrolled by soldier-peasants (Wehrbauer), whose colonising function would be not to bring civilisation to the East, but to prevent civilisation from ever arising again outside their settlements. This project, in its later, more ambitious form, envisaged using Volksdeutsch communities even further East, for example the Volga Germans, and supplementing them by importations from the West. Thus Volksdeutsch from the Tyrol were to be withdrawn from Italian rule and transplanted to the Crimea and it was hoped to reinforce them with groups from Scandinavia, Holland and even England, when peace in the West had been restored.

Although at first sight this policy might seem to be consistent with much that Rosenberg had spent his life in preaching, it was not the one that he advocated; indeed, as responsible Minister, he resisted it in the devious and ineffectual way that was his hallmark as a man of action. This surprised some of his fellow Nazis and has continued to surprise historians, some of whom have done less than justice to the alternative policy, which Rosenberg outlined with complete clarity, even if his attempts to apply it were less clear-cut and, in the event, wholly unsuccessful. Gerald Reitlinger, for example, writes of 'long appeals by officials of the Eastern Ministry to Rosenberg. . . . And then, painfully and reluctantly, Rosenberg would try to wriggle out of his position.'[7] But this criticism ignores two facts: first, it was Rosenberg who carefully selected and in his half-hearted way tried to protect these officials, who so much disapproved of the conduct of the war. Secondly, it was Rosenberg, and not they, who came face to face with the malignant violence of Hitler, Himmler, Goering and Koch and had to try to dissuade them, by means of such arguments as might have some hope of success, that their policies were destructive not only of Slavs – a matter of total indifference to Hitler – but also of the war aims of the Reich. Neither of these facts is disputed by Dr Otto Braeutigam, who joined the RMBO in May 1941 at Rosenberg's request, remained with it until January 1945 and probably did as much as was possible to mitigate the effects of the anti-Slav, anti-Rosenberg policies.

These latter policies were strictly ideological in the sense in which the word is used in this chapter; that is to say, they were based on preconceived ideas having no rational relationship to history or, indeed, to contemporary reality. There was, for example, no evidence that German settlers wished to follow in the tracks of their medieval ancestors and go eastward, let alone emulate the Teutonic Knights in the fortresses of the Herrenvolk. It had long been a problem for patriotic Germans to prevent the depopulation of Prussia's eastern territory. Although not only Erich Koch, but even the Wehrmacht, argued in favour of setting aside land in the Ukraine for settlement after the war by German ex-soldiers, by 1943 only 237 had put down their names.[8] This would not have been of such importance but for Himmler's determination to embark on resettlement plans, in pursuance of his function as Reich Commissioner for Strengthening Germandom (Reichskommissar fuer Festigung des deutschen Volkstums – RKFDV), without waiting for the war to be brought to a victorious conclusion. His policy of mass removal and mass murder was incompatible with victory. It was also incompatible with Rosenberg's policy, though this should not be taken to imply that, if Rosenberg had had his way, Hitler would have overthrown Stalin.

What, then, was Rosenberg's policy and on what assumptions was it based? The first assumption was that, in order to win the war, particularist elements that had as a matter of historical fact resisted the hegemony of Great Russia must be put to work against

the centripetal force of Muscovy. Secondly, and consistently with
the first assumption, 'Russia was never a nation-state, but has
always been a state of nationalities'.[9] In enunciating these truths
to his staff on 20 June 1941, he might well have quoted no less
an authority than Lenin, who wrote in 1913 to Maxim Gorky, 'We
Great Russians have always acted like boors towards subject
peoples. All we can do is suppress them.' Rosenberg's idea was
to release the more important ethnic groups, from what Lenin had
denounced as 'the prison of nationalities'. If this policy were accompanied by one of granting religious toleration and breaking up the
collective farms for the benefit of the peasants, Rosenberg believed
that the people could be won over to accept the permanent disappearance both of the USSR and its predecessor, the Tsarist Empire.
That his policy represented a serious threat to the integrity of the
USSR, is sufficiently demonstrated by the mass deportation of ethnic
groups undertaken after the war by the Soviet authorities in areas
that the Germans had occupied.

In the first memorandum, which he had prepared for Hitler
on 2 April 1941, he had listed seven major areas, in which differentiated treatment was to be applied to the inhabitants.[10] Three of
these together (Ukraine and Crimea; the Don area; the Caucasus)
were to constitute a Black Sea Confederation, a unit of relatively
favoured treatment, though under German protection, to act as a
barrier against Great Russian expansion. To the north and west
the barrier was to be extended to include White Russia (though
Rosenberg had doubts about the possibility of constituting a state
in this area and soon abandoned it without a struggle), and a
confederation of the three Baltic States; but already in this area
much less favourable treatment was to be applied. He envisaged
expulsions from Latvia and Lithuania to make way for settlements of 'better blood'. For his failure to espouse the cause of
recreating fully autonomous Baltic units he was much criticised by
a member of his staff, Peter Kleist, whom he had taken over from
Ribbentrop as a Baltic expert.* His attitude has been ascribed to
the antipathy felt by a Baltic German towards the indigenous
majority. No doubt this played a part in his thinking; but it must
also be remembered that his prime object was not to revive the
statehood of ethnic groups, as such, but to create a solid structure

* See *European Tragedy*, P. Kleist (London 1965).

that would resist future Great Russian expansionist tendencies. In their brief lives as independent nations the Baltic States had shown neither the capacity to act together nor to survive singly.

The two remaining areas were 'Russian Middle Asia or Turkestan', which Rosenberg left out of account on the assumption that German conquests would not extend that far, and Great Russia itself, which he thought of as stretching from Moscow to the Urals. This, the worst-treated area, was to be forced to look eastward by being permanently cut off from the Baltic and Black Sea. It was also to be cut off from the great food and oil producing parts of the Black Sea Confederation, whose first duty would be to supply German needs. He regarded with equanimity the likelihood that this would very adversely affect the population of the Muscovite area, especially as it would have to accommodate 'inferior' elements expelled from points further west. If his plans were less brutal than those of Himmler, Goering and others, it was only a difference of degree; but it was a difference that, if combined with skilful propaganda and humane treatment of Russian prisoners of war and inhabitants of occupied areas immediately after the invasion, could have had an incalculable effect on the course of the war.

The invaders were welcomed in the Ukraine, as they had been in 1918. Whole divisions of the Red Army surrendered in the summer and autumn of 1941 almost without fighting; but Erich Koch was let loose on the population of the Ukraine and the prisoners were herded into camps to die of malnutrition or forced labour. It has been estimated that an astonishing total of 3.7 million Russian prisoners of war died in German hands.[11] While many deaths in the first winter of the war were due to the same lack of foresight that deprived the Wehrmacht on the eastern front of winter clothing, many more were directly attributable to the idea persistently instilled into German minds that Russians were an inferior race (Untermenschen), whose lives were of no significance. Much of the mortality occurred at a period when the German domestic economy was virtually on a peacetime footing. The Red Army soon began to fight; units which had been cut off became partisans, instead of deserters. The civilian population in occupied areas, terrorised after March 1942 by Fritz Sauckel's labour gangs, rallied to Soviet rule as the lesser of two evils.

Opposition to Rosenberg's policy stemmed from Hitler himself. Rosenberg virtually admitted this, even during the Fuehrer's lifetime, though he played down the implications, both in terms of the resulting contradiction and confusion, and in terms of his own policy being foredoomed to failure. In a confidential record for his own files, after his first visit to Koch's domain in June 1942, he wrote: 'Koch had heard some of the Fuehrer's general remarks detrimental to Slavs and thought himself safe in translating these remarks into practical politics.'[12] What Rosenberg has here left out is that Koch was Bormann's protégé and the latter's power resided in great measure in his system of converting the Fuehrer's rambling and prejudiced statements into policy directives. As if Bormann's backing were not enough, Koch also had that of Goering. The cards were so stacked against Rosenberg that historians should be surprised not so much by his failure as by the protracted, if unheroic, character of his obstinate resistance to the big battalions.

Erich Koch, who had been Gauleiter of East Prussia since 1928, was a stocky, ebullient man, only five feet six inches in height, with the fashionable small moustache modelled on the Fuehrer's. He had been a railway worker in the Ruhr and Rosenberg, in moments of exasperation, referred to him as 'that proletarian'.[13] Koch had formerly belonged to the left wing of the NSDAP and was, indeed, the author of a book, entitled *Reconstruction in the East* (Aufbau des Ostens), in which he advocated economic collaboration with the USSR. Rosenberg had thought his position at that time too close to that of the so-called National Bolsheviks. A man with such a background found himself faced after 1941 with the alternative of either retiring into the wings, where he would remain an object of suspicion, or of becoming demonstratively anti-Slav. Koch was not of a retiring disposition and had no difficulty in making his choice. Nor was he left in any doubt where the wind was blowing, as far as Hitler's Slavophobe attitude was concerned; he had been present early in October 1940 at an interview between the Fuehrer and Hans Frank, who had tried in vain to induce Hitler to modify his policy towards conquered Poland. Frank argued that German economic exploitation of his Government-General and deportation of Polish labour to the Reich were making his territory no longer viable. Hitler replied that it was a matter of indifference whether the population survived; indeed, he did not intend that the former ruling class should survive; the rest were just a reservoir of labour for their German masters.[14] That Rosenberg thought six months later that Hitler could be persuaded to treat the population of southern Russia differently shows only how estranged he had become from the real centre of power in the Third Reich.

At the end of March 1941 Rosenberg, who was at an international conference on the Jewish question at Frankfurt, was sent for by Hitler and put to work. By 7 April he had produced not only the memorandum discussed in the preceding paragraphs, but another in which he recommended appointment of Reich Commissioners for five of the areas to be detached from the USSR, and central direction of these satraps by a Protector-General of the whole occupied territory with HQ in Berlin. The need for this latter appointment (converted later into that of a Minister) was explicitly justified in terms of the need to coordinate the work of the Commissioners, especially during the military phase, and ensure differentiated treatment of the populations subject to their rule.[15] It should be noted that the interposition of a Minister between Hitler and the civil administrators of occupied territories was an innovation; for example, it did not apply in Poland, Belgium, Norway or Holland. Neither of the two Commissioners who actually took up their duties under Rosenberg's nominal supervision (Koch for the Ukraine – RKU – and Lohse for the Baltic area, known as Ostland – RKO) accepted subordination. Both, as Gauleiters, claimed direct access to the Fuehrer, whatever status Rosenberg might try to impose upon them in their capacity as Reich Commissioners.

Hitler had ample time to digest Rosenberg's proposals before proceeding to the next step, which was to appoint him on 20 April to be his Delegate for Central Planning for Questions of the East European Area. His office was to be financed from the budget of the Reich Chancery, so he at last achieved his ambition of moving into the state hierarchy. Only three high functionaries were at this stage informed and instructed to appoint liaison officers: Keitel, Goering and Funk, the Economics Minister.[16] Although Hitler had already decided to give Himmler's sinister SS Action Groups wide authority immediately behind the battle-line, the latter was not at first informed of Rosenberg's nomination. When in May he learned of it he complained to Bormann, 'To work with, let alone under, Rosenberg is surely the most difficult thing in the NSDAP.'[17] At the end of June, when Rosenberg reported to Hitler on the outcome of his consultations with Reich authorities, he optimistically claimed that a meeting of minds had been achieved with everyone except Himmler and Heydrich, whose proposals 'do not seem to me compatible with the overall authority of the Reich regime in the East'.[18] Hitler, in his usual fashion, postponed a decision; but, as he did nothing to check Himmler, and Rosenberg had no means of doing so, this was, in practice, a victory for the SS Action Groups.

If the invasion of RMBO's sphere by the SS did not immediately become fully apparent, there can never have been much doubt in Rosenberg's mind that he would have to play second fiddle to Goering in the latter's capacity as Delegate for the Four-year Plan. To have attempted to oppose Goering at the outset would have precluded Rosenberg's coveted appointment as Minister; indeed it is significant that the decree by which he was appointed was issued on 17 July 1941, that is, on the day after the crucial Angersburg conference between Hitler, Goering, Rosenberg, Keitel and Lammers, to which we shall revert shortly. Even the creation of the new Ministry was not publicly announced, since Hitler wished to couple the announcement with that relating to the capture of Moscow or Leningrad;[19] it was eventually made on 18 November 1941, by which time German hopes of a swift end to the war were fading.

Having briefly examined the circumstances of the appointment, we can deal with the vexed question why it was made at all, in view of the fact that the Fuehrer was clearly out of sympathy with Rosenberg's plans. We can at once discard Gerald Reitlinger's explanation that, 'In reality Hitler chose Rosenberg because he was the one-time deputy leader of the Party and he owed him a job.'[20] Although Hitler liked to have familiar faces around him, he did not hang onto old supporters who had become a liability; if he did not have them liquidated, like Roehm and Gregor Strasser, he let them be suspended from their duties, like Streicher after 1940, or languish in obscurity, like Feder and Esser. Both Streicher and Esser had been personally closer to Hitler than Rosenberg ever was. Hitler no more owed the latter a job in 1941 than he had done in 1933 or 1938.

The fact of the matter was that Hitler had to have a plan of some sort for the administration of the territories that he expected to conquer so swiftly and Rosenberg was the only party stalwart capable of producing one. The only alternative to creating a new Ministry would have been to hand the job over to Ribbentrop; but by 1941 the latter was even further out of favour than Rosenberg. Moreover this course would have meant giving fresh authority to the detested officials of the Foreign Office, whereas Rosenberg could at least be relied upon to provide jobs for members of the NSDAP and SA. The fact that Rosenberg's plan was less oppressive than Hitler's intentions was no disadvantage; it would tend to make the war more acceptable to the Wehrmacht and, in due course, to the reluctant allies of the Reich. To operate behind the relatively respectable facade of Rosenberg's eastern experts, some of whom had considerable experience in Russia and Eastern Europe, was reminiscent of Hitler's foreign policy from 1933 to 1938, the real nature of which had been temporarily masked by the continued employment of sober Foreign Office officials. In any case, Hitler had made sure that the vital fields of security, resettlement and the economy of the occupied territory would not be in Rosenberg's hands.

The gross contradictions inherent in German policy were maximised by the fatal miscalculation about the duration of the war. Otto Braeutigam has related how in an interview in May 1941 with State Secretary Weizsaecker about his transfer to the new Ministry, he was asked his opinion, as an old Russia hand, on the probable length of the war. When Braeutigam suggested three months, he was told to keep this view to himself, since in the light of current estimates it smacked of defeatism.[21] Here again ideological preconceptions proved misleading. It was assumed that the USSR would speedily collapse because of its Jewish-Bolshevist leadership, which was, by definition, incapable of sustaining a state. Russia, as Hitler had put it in *Mein Kampf*, was 'ripe for dissolution'.[22] Prolongation of the war at once began to produce strains that made even relatively mild treatment of captive soldiers and conquered territory unacceptable to hard-liners. Economic exploitation, which the milder men of the RMBO hoped would be of short duration, became the order of the day. Rather than demand sacrifice at home, for example by conscripting German women for work, Hitler appointed Sauckel to conscript labour in the occupied territories. This, in turn drove men, who were threatened by the press-gangs, into the ranks of the partisans, whose depredations further inflamed the ferocity of ss-D reprisals.

From the winter of 1941–42 the Germans were caught in a descending spiral which could only end in disaster. First the Wehrmacht, then Goebbels and at last the ss itself rallied at least partially to Rosenberg's basic thesis that Russians must be defeated by Russians; but by October 1944, when Himmler finally decided in favour of General Vlasov's Russian Liberation Army, he acted three years too late. Even then he failed to grasp the ethnic distinctions underlying Rosenberg's original plan. He is quoted as having said, 'What does it mean if such and such a White Russian or Ukrainian has his own troop? He is just the same a Russian. In other circumstances the fellow would seem to me just like some German emigrant, who comes from Baden or Bavaria and declares he is no German, but a Badener or Bavarian, fighting for the freedom of Baden or Bavaria. That's all nonsense. Only the fool Rosenberg has taught us such things.'[23] The eighty-seven ethnic groups, carefully computed by Rosenberg in the summer of 1939 as existing from Eastern Europe to Siberia, remained to the end a complete mystery to the high-priest of ss racialism.[24]

The eastern campaigns exposed the crude superficiality of Nazi racial theory. In prisoner of war camps the SD at once began killing off Turkestanis, who had surrendered in order to fight Bolshevism, on the ground that they were 'Asiatics'.[25] Heinrich Mueller, Head of the Gestapo, learned to his surprise at a meeting with Braeutigam that circumcision was practised among Moslems, who could not therefore be identified on sight with Jews and liquidated without further investigation.[26] A tribe of mountain people was discovered in the Caucasus, which obeyed Mosaic Law, but did not correspond in appearance to Jewish racial characteristics, as understood by ss racial examiners. The latter's expertise was negligible; as R. L. Koehl has it, ' "Refresher" courses hastily organised in the winter of 1939–40 could scarcely train the uninitiated to recognise anything but obvious blondness, blue eyes and pink skin.'[27] By these criteria most Nazi leaders would themselves have stood condemned. At a time when Koch was denouncing Ukrainians as 'White Niggers', the ss allowed themselves to be convinced that Cossacks

Diesmal wollte der Jude ganz sicher gehen. Er machte sich selbst zum Offizier, zum Kommissar, zum ausschlaggebenden Führer der Untermenschen.

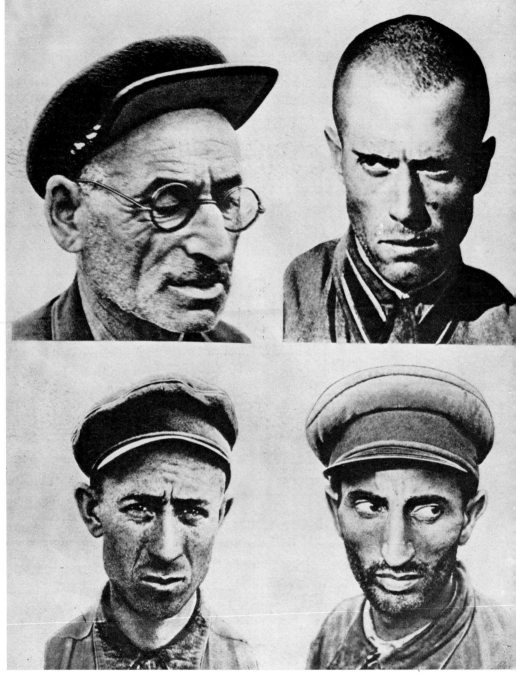

11. *Racial types from the SS pamphlet* The Subhuman, *of which four million copies were produced in 1942*

12-13. *Caricatures from the SS pamphlet* The Subhuman

14-15. *Contrasting racial types –* 'Two Subhumans' *and* 'Two Humans' *from the
same pamphlet*

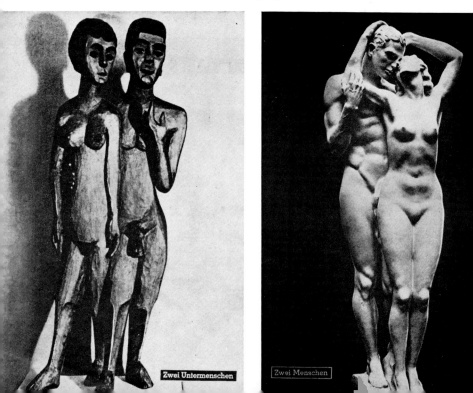

could not be wholly Slav, because their way of life had affinities with the SS ideal of the soldier-peasant.[28] On this shadowy assumption Hitler broke his own rule and allowed Cossack units to be equipped to fight the Red Army. A grotesque League Table was drawn up, beginning with races having a sufficient admixture of Aryan blood to be capable of Germanisation (Eindeutschung) and ending with Jews and Gypsies ripe for extermination.[29] The greater the wastage of 'good' German blood on the eastern front, the more determined Hitler became to eliminate racially 'bad' blood on the home front. Failure to pursue such a policy in the First World War had, in his view, had disastrous consequences. As he said in a speech in Hamburg in 1926: 'The war took the best elements of the nation while the very worst were kept almost intact.'[30]

As the war dragged on, the Nazis became increasingly alarmed both about existing shortages of Aryan manpower and about future demographic prospects. When the need to import metal workers from the Ukraine into the Reich became acute, the 'White Niggers' mysteriously became 'Germanisable' in the eyes of the SS Race and Settlement Head Office (RUSHA),[31] which also took a special interest in bastards fathered by Germans on non-Aryan women. Racial principles began to slip in favour of the contradictory theory that removal to the environment of the Reich would promote Germanisation. Skulls were frenziedly measured for new criteria and psychological ones were introduced. Himmler had declared that 'it was in the nature of German blood to resist'.[32] This led to the curious conclusion that Balts or Poles who did not wish to be Germanised were more likely to have Aryan blood than those who tamely submitted. By this time the ideology, which had never rested on any sure foundation, was in total disarray; but it continued to have the fatal effect of deciding almost every dispute – and disputes were a major product of the Nazi system – in favour of expediency, as against humanity. If Goering demanded more food from the Ukraine, the fact that people would starve there could be dismissed not merely as irrelevant but as an actual advantage. If Koch closed schools and technical colleges and shipped the inmates off to Sauckel, this course had the merit of depriving the Ukraine of an intelligentsia that might one day endanger German hegemony.

o

In the twilight area between those who ruthlessly applied the ideology and those who actively opposed it within the limits of their power stands the ambivalent figure of Alfred Rosenberg, the principal architect of the lethal doctrine. Faced at the climax of his career with an unrivalled opportunity to carry it into effect, he hesitated. There is no evidence that he intervened on behalf of the Jews, except in so far as his vendetta against Himmler, had it succeeded, would have indirectly improved their lot by leaving them in the hands of less rigorous men. Braeutigam has recorded an occasion on which Rosenberg condemned 'wild excesses' against Jews in Russia, who should merely be confined to ghettos as in Tsarist times.[33] But he never modified his basic anti-semitism. Faced with all other categories of humanity, however, whether Communists or Tatars, against whom he had so often inveighed, he began to compromise and make allowances. His tactics were devious, his motives obscure; he was never courageous and often evasive; but his interventions were usually on the side of sanity and even sometimes on the side of humanity. Above all, he gathered around him a group of men, some of whom, like Georg Leibbrandt, the head of his Political Department, had been born, like himself, in Russia and knew at first hand that not all Slavs were Untermenschen. Others, like Otto Braeutigam, had served in consular posts in the USSR and used their expertise in the interests of mercy by turning racial arguments against their proponents. He managed, for example, to reverse the judgment of the OKH that 'Armenians were even worse than Jews'.[34] The RMBO, basing itself on Rosenberg's principle that some ethnic groups were more deserving than others, saved lives of prisoners of war by getting separate camps set up for the more favoured groups and sending inspectors to tour them. Although the writ of the RMBO did not officially run in the Reich, it intervened there to secure better treatment for men imported for forced labour. The argument that these measures were undertaken less from a humane point of view than from that of prosecuting the war more effectively is only partly relevant; those who protested in the Third Reich in the name of humanity soon found their mouths stopped; arguments had to be couched in a form in which they had some chance of being heard.

Some of these men fell by the wayside. One of the first to go on Hitler's orders was Hans Koch, Rosenberg's liaison officer with

Army Group (South), who cooperated with the military in allowing a self-constituted provisional Ukrainian administration after the capture of Lwow at the end of June 1941. He had made the mistake of taking the war of liberation too literally and his Minister failed to back him. Peter Kleist was allowed to resign from RMBO early in 1943, after he had failed to induce Rosenberg either to promote further measures of Baltic autonomy or to force his General Commissioner in Lithuania to investigate the shooting of some farmers.[35] Later in the same year Himmler, who had long had a hostile eye on RMBO, at last got his hands on a key-post; a senior SS officer, Gottlob Berger, replaced Leibbrandt and the RMBO Press Officer, Major Cranz, who had incurred Hitler's displeasure by his comments on deficiencies in agricultural production in the Ukraine under the rule of Erich Koch, was also removed.[36] By January 1945 Braeutigam was under supervision by the SS and partly on this ground applied to return to the relative safety of the Foreign Ministry.[37] By this date, however, the RMBO had virtually ceased to exist, except on paper; even Rosenberg's conscientious Deputy, Alfred Meyer, the Gauleiter of Westphalia-North, had ceased to appear regularly, and their concern was confined to workers, prisoners and refugees from the East, who were living – and dying – in the Reich.

If the Ministry offered at least a temporary haven for a few men of integrity, the same cannot be said for its officers in the field; the cadre fell victim to the Minister's feuds and prejudices. His insistence in 1941 on Ribbentrop's withdrawing his liaison officers with the three main Army Groups led the Foreign Minister to refuse to release more personnel to RMBO.[38] Rosenberg negotiated with the Minister of the Interior for release of state officials, but according to Braeutigam was reluctant to employ any.[39] He shared to the full the antagonism felt by the Nazis for the Civil Service. He was thus thrown back on recruitment primarily from the SA which he had long favoured above the SS; but the SA under Roehm's successor, Viktor Lutze, had declined into a dumping ground for third-rate party hacks, to whom the Herrenvolk philosophy had a correspondingly strong appeal. Rosenberg wanted to equip them in field-grey to make them barely distinguishable from the Wehrmacht; but there was surplus stock of the gold-brown uniforms made for graduates of the Ordensburgen and, clad in this material, the functionaries of the RMBO earned from the fighting men the unenviable soubriquet of 'golden pheasants'.[40]

Rosenberg's willingness to modify in practice the pure ideological doctrine with which his name was associated was based partly upon his accurate appreciation of the ethnic complexity underlying the monolithic surface of the USSR and partly on his belief that, in order to destroy the Colossus, it was necessary to conquer a very large expanse of territory, within which his separatist ideas could be given full scope. In his first memorandum for Hitler in April 1941 he predicated an 'extraordinary quick occupation of a substantial part of Russia', and went on to pose the question: 'Should the occupation be determined by purely military and economic needs, or, for extending the occupation, should political grounds be co-determinining factors for shaping the future territories?'[41] In recommending that full weight be given to political factors, he was speaking a language highly acceptable to most professional soldiers, who were less inclined than were party leaders to under-estimate the immensity of their task. A barrier of deep mutual suspicion, however, divided the non-ideological Wehrmacht from the ideologist who might otherwise have been their natural ally.

A clear indication of potential affinity of interest arose at the planning stage in relation to the notorious 'Commissar order'. On 30 March 1941 Hitler had convened a gathering of over 200 senior officers in order to inform them about the coming 'struggle of two ideologies'.[42] He told them that it would be part of their duty, although contrary to their tradition, to despatch on the spot as proven criminals all Soviet political personages, officials and Commissars falling into their hands, whether in uniform or not. Most officers heard this injunction with consternation; considera-tions of humanity apart, the probability of reprisals against German prisoners of war could scarcely be ignored. Colonel Warlimont, who was under instructions to draw up a military order based on the Fuehrer's injunction, learned that Rosenberg had sent to Hitler a memorandum in which he had pointed out that he would need civilian Commissars and other officials for administration of occu-pied territories and that only the most senior ones should be victimised in the manner proposed. Warlimont embodied this modification in proposals submitted to Jodl on 12 May 1941, which eventually received Hitler's approval and must have considerably reduced the wholesale slaughter. It is significant that Warlimont has denied that there was any direct collaboration in this matter between himself and Rosenberg.[43]

In the crucial economic field, however, Rosenberg had no potential ally against the overriding authority of Goering and from the very start he made crippling concessions. He had pointed out in his basic memorandum that the differentiated treatment, which he advocated, would be prejudiced by uniform administration grounded solely on economic considerations, 'as is at present planned'.[44] A few days later, however, in drafting instructions for the future Reich Commissioner, Ukraine (RKU), he placed first among his tasks the procurement of raw materials for the Reich. Only in third place came 'Setting up a free Ukrainian state in the closest alliance with the Great German Reich'.[45] By the end of June he was denying any intention of creating an Economic Department in the RMBO, since economics was Goering's field of responsibility.[46] (He did, in fact, create an 'Economic-political Department' under Walter Malletke.) Addressing his staff he used an argument more likely to appeal to them than to Goering: 'It makes a difference whether after a few years I win over forty million men to voluntary cooperation, or whether a soldier has to stand behind every peasant.'[47]

Whether anything could still be salvaged from Goering's rapacity would depend on the personality of the men nominated to the post of RKU. The decisive conference took place at Angersburg on 16 July under Hitler; Goering, Keitel and Lammers were present, as well as Rosenberg. It began badly. Hitler made clear his disregard of the proposal to conciliate the Ukraine–Caucasus area by detaching Galicia for the benefit of Frank's rump Poland and announcing that the Crimea was to be entirely cleared for German settlers. Rosenberg then proposed that Gauleiter Lohse should be Reich Commissioner, Ostland (RKO) and Sauckel, RKU. Goering countered that one of these two posts must go to Erich Koch, whom Rosenberg wished to reserve for the Great Russian area, in which harsh measures could be tolerated with equanimity. Rosenberg, after protesting that Koch had already said he would not take orders from Rosenberg, made a tactical error by putting forward two further names: one was that of his old friend, Schickedanz, whom Goering opposed; the other was that of an SA

leader, Captain Petersdorff, whom Hitler and Goering – no mean
judges – regarded as mad. In the end Schickedanz got the
Caucasus; but it proved a hollow victory, because he was never
able to take up his post. Lohse became RKO, but the bestial Koch
was confirmed as RKU.[48]

Lengthy discussion at Angersburg about Himmler's responsibilities ended with the Delphic decision that his jurisdiction in the
occupied territories must be the same as in the Reich.[49] This
meant nothing; citizens of the Reich still lived in theory under
the rule of law, even if it was frequently disregarded in practice.
As soon as partisan activity began in the East, the SS virtually
suspended all law there. Rosenberg had not yet abandoned the
struggle, but it was already a lost cause. His only success was one
of negligible importance over his old rival Ribbentrop, who was
excluded from the eastern territories. The disastrous conference
ended at about eight in the evening; Hitler and Goering, who had
imposed their rulings, were prepared to be gracious. Goering shook
Rosenberg by the hand in anticipation of their 'good collaboration'.
After dinner Hitler said to him, 'It is good to have you holding the
gateway to the East.' But Rosenberg had few illusions. He confided
to his diary, 'I have been given a giant task, indeed the greatest the
Reich has to give. . . . But I have not received full powers to carry
it out. . . . Moreover Koch is in Kiev, the most important city, and
he is more inclined to Goering than to me.'[50]

Even this summing up proved optimistic. When at the beginning of September Koch took up his duties, he went on Hitler's
instructions to Rovno, which had been part of Poland until 1939. It
is true that Kiev, the traditional capital of the Ukraine, did not fall
to the Germans until the end of September, but Koch, in spite of
Rosenberg's protests, never had the smallest intention of staying
there; he continued to spend the bulk of his time in his other
'capital' – Koenigsberg in East Prussia. At the end of August he
briefly visited Rosenberg in Berlin and did not leave without picking
a quarrel with the latter's protégé, Major Cranz.[51] Friction was not
confined to personal issues. The RMBO was trying to encourage the
'liberated' peasantry to cooperate against Bolshevism by breaking
up the hated collective farms, but was encountering resistance
from the Ministry of Food and Agriculture, whose nominal head
was Darré. Rosenberg was on good terms with the latter, but his

days as Minister were numbered, as he had incurred the hostility of both Himmler and Goering; in May 1942 he was replaced by Goering's man, Herbert Backe, the State Secretary in his own Ministry, who was a 'hard-liner', although born in Russian Batum. By that date Rosenberg had at last got Hitler to approve a decree granting some measure of private ownership of land; but in the Ukraine Koch sabotaged it.

Hitler's rejection of plans to build up the Ukraine was further shown by his handing over Transdnistria to Roumania and giving orders to the SS to destroy the cathedral and monastic buildings which were the pride of Kiev.[52] When Rosenberg went to see him on 29 September, the Fuehrer said that according to his information – no doubt derived from Koch via his friend Bormann – the Ukraine did not wish to be separated from the rest of Russia. Rosenberg, after protesting that, even so, the willingness of Slavs to work for Germans should not be discouraged by Draconian measures, weakly agreed that for the time being no pronouncement should be made about the future of the territory; that self-administration should only be permitted at district (Kreis) level and that no institutions of higher education should be allowed. After failing to elicit any support from Hitler in his efforts to curb the activities of the SS, he got approval for prisoners of war to be released for work on the land, and for an edict of religious tolerance to be issued, as a further mark of liberation from Communism.[53] Hans Frank's account of a meeting with Rosenberg in Berlin in mid-November indicates that at that date the latter had virtually abandoned his plans for an autonomous Ukraine.[54]

At the next interview with Hitler on 14 December 1941 Rosenberg reverted to the prisoners of war who, as he pointed out, were dying at a rate of 2,500 a day, so that few were likely to survive.[55] He got no response from Hitler and conspicuously failed to press home his point; but over two months later, after prompting by Braeutigam, he nerved himself to write to Keitel, condemning conditions in the camps, which differed so markedly from those for Western prisoners of war and were contributing to the stiffer resistance shown by the Red Army.[56]

The spectacle of Rosenberg, the avowed foe of the Churches, appealing for tolerance to be shown to all creeds naturally excited the ridicule not only of Koch, but of his old enemy, Goebbels, who wrote in his diary, 'Rosenberg wrote me a letter stating that he intends to oppose the idea of a fight against the religious denominations. That's really too funny for words!'[57] But some ten weeks later he had come round to the project, presumably in the knowledge that Hitler was in agreement. 'We have finally had the good sense to issue a decree guaranteeing absolute religious tolerance in the eastern areas. The Fuehrer decided that this decree is not to be signed by Rosenberg, but by the Commissars for the different sections.'[58] Hitler's decision was based on Bormann's argument that Rosenberg's signature on such a document would give encouragement to the Churches in the Reich.[59] It may be assumed that the real reason was that, since exclusive responsibility in the Ukraine would now rest with Koch, he could sabotage the decree with impunity.

In November 1941 Rosenberg was a silent, if disapproving, participant in a meeting presided over by Goering, who again insisted in Koch's presence that the Ukraine must be exploited as a colony. Rosenberg might have maintained his discreet silence if it had not been for the extravagant language and behaviour of Koch, to whom he wrote in the following month, denouncing talk of 'White Niggers' and the infliction of corporal punishment.[60] As nothing came of a memorandum to Hitler on this subject, he took up the issue with the Fuehrer in person on 8 May 1942. He pointed out that a Soviet diplomatic note about atrocities, which had received wide publicity, had actually quoted from instructions for exploitation embodied in Goering's plans. Moreover certain people had so misunderstood ideas of racial superiority 'that they were going round the country with the whip'. In order to make clear to whom he was referring, he submitted to Hitler a draft decree, addressed to Koch, which was approved. He went on to stress that large auxiliary forces could have been raised from the Caucasus and Turkestan, 'if the SD had not at the start called all these peoples "Asiatics" and shot them down or left them to their fate.' In response to a query from Hitler, he actually stood up for the Armenians. After criticising interventions in his territory by Speer and Sauckel, he concluded that 'In many cases methods of compulsion had at once been used . . . so that in many towns there had been a flight to the woods. . . . These men would certainly add to the numbers of the partisans.'[61]

Immediately after this interview he wrote both to Koch and to Lohse, drawing attention to the danger that the local population, basing itself on some of the extravagant remarks made by German officials, might come to believe 'that the rule of National-Socialism would have even worse effects than Bolshevist policy. . . . The standpoint of a master does not consist in going about with a whip and speaking about the inferiority of the subject peoples.'[62] Koch was bound to take offence at these injunctions; but what rankled even more was that Rosenberg repeated them to subordinate officials in the Ukraine, so that there could be no doubt in their minds what the policy of the RMBO really was. He set off on 18 June, in an aircraft on loan from the Fuehrer, on his first tour of the Ukraine and at Rovno, the administrative capital, impressed on a staff meeting 'the necessity for the attitude of our leading functionaries in the East to be above criticism'.[63] He illustrated what he meant by receiving from a group of Ukrainian men and women the gift of salt and bread traditionally presented to their ruler. After he had spoken next day in a similar strain to officials in Kiev, there occurred his first open clash with the attendant Koch.

Koch defended himself from criticism in a long screed and appealed to Hitler, who made no immediate reply. But on 22 July 1942 Bormann, who was with Hitler at Vinnitza on the central front, brought the conversation round to 'the unbelievable number of children' seen during a short tour of the Ukrainian countryside. What was worse, in his eyes, the children looked well fed and healthy. Three times he pointedly referred to them as 'these Russians or so-called Ukrainians'. Hitler, whose thoughts at all times turned readily to genocide, at once asserted that everything should be done to promote abortions and get trade going in contraceptives; there was indeed danger that, under German rule, the local population would multiply. It would therefore be madness to introduce preventive medicine and other health measures on German lines. Moreover only the most rudimentary schooling should be provided; if Ukrainians failed to understand railway-signs and got run down, it would be all the same to Germans.[64]

So strangely was the Reich governed, that on the following day these random remarks were embodied by Bormann in a directive addressed to Rosenberg allegedly coming from the Fuehrer. Rosenberg, instead of returning to the charge, decided to placate Hitler by claiming there was really no difference of principle between them, though as far as the health of the population was concerned, he pointed out that 'measures were taken to prevent the spreading of epidemics, not in the interest of other people, but exclusively to secure the German occupation and keep up the efficiency of the labour in the service of German war industry'.[65] Challenged later at Nuremberg with having given way all along the line, in spite of attempts by Dr Markull and others of his staff to stiffen his backbone, Rosenberg admitted, 'I wrote an appeasing letter so that I could bring about a pause in the constant pressure under which I was kept, and I would like to anticipate and say that my activity, and the decrees which I issued after this letter, did not change in any way.'[66]

In the late summer of 1942 he again went to Russia and visited the HQ near Smolensk of Field-Marshal v. Kluge, one of the few senior officers with whom he was on friendly terms. He found that Kluge also disapproved of Koch's goings on, but felt he himself had no influence on Hitler. The Rear Area Commanders actually believed Rosenberg could help them to promote at the Fuehrer's HQ measures of political warfare, which would diminish the flow into the ranks of the partisans and enable a Russian 'foreign legion' to be constituted for combat duties. Rosenberg, who badly needed an ally, was persuaded in mid-December 1942 to preside at a meeting at the RMBO at which the soldiers spoke of the realities of the military situation; the battle of Stalingrad was beginning to cast its long shadow. Among the staff officers present on this occasion were two Colonels, v. Staufenberg and v. Altenstadt, who harboured designs on Hitler's life.[67] Rosenberg duly presented to Hitler a memorandum with the recommendations of the conference only to be told a few days later not to meddle in such matters. The possibilities of an alliance between OKH and RMBO were in any case limited by the fact that the former was less impressed by Rosenberg's particularist approach than by hopes of raising a Russian army against Bolshevism under the captured Russian General Vlasov, without regard to the regional legionaries, in whom the RMBO was interested. The OKH eventually found a strange ally in Himmler, but only in the last phase of the war, when he rallied reluctantly to the renegade Russian General.

As Rosenberg's constant complaints about the independent activity of the SS in occupied territory encountered only requests that he discuss matters with Himmler, he finally braced himself to do so. In September 1942 he had had an unsatisfactory talk with Berger, who had counter-attacked by criticising the staffing of the RMBO. He objected to Leibbrandt and defended one of his own protégés as being 'one of the few National-Socialists in the Ministry'.[68] Towards the end of January 1943 a meeting between Rosenberg and Himmler was arranged at Posen. The latter seems to have made an effort to make himself agreeable, saying to Rosenberg, 'We two have not wavered in our ideological outlook these twenty years and must work together.'[69] No meeting of minds was possible, however; Rosenberg wanted resettlement postponed until after the war; failing that, he wanted to prevent direct communication between Koch and Himmler in his RKFDV capacity.[70] It was decided to set up a committee to coordinate RMBO and RKFDV requirements, but in practice the Russian advance was taking care of the problem. Whilst Himmler and Rosenberg were arguing, Field-Marshal v. Kleist's Army Group was beginning its withdrawal from the Caucasus and by the summer the days of German civilian rule in the Ukraine were virtually over.

The private war between Koch and Rosenberg grew hotter as the area in dispute became smaller. Koch had cut off his subordinates from direct communication with the RMBO and closed all schools, except for the four-class primary schools. All former pupils over fifteen, as well as their teachers, were summarily rounded up and delivered into the rapacious grasp of Sauckel.[71] Rosenberg, who was wrestling with Hitler for a further measure of private ownership in agriculture, decided at last to make use of information gathered by his staff, accusing Koch of having removed hundreds of foresters and burned their homes at Tsuman, in order to clear the area for his hunting parties. At the beginning of April 1943 Rosenberg sent the dossier to Himmler, asking him to investigate; he also informed Lammers.[72] Asking Himmler to investigate irregular acts of violence was like inviting a fox to safeguard chickens against marauders. Receiving no reply, Rosenberg then asked Hitler for authority to send Koch on leave during investigation of the complaint.[73] This brought matters to a head and on 19 May 1943 he was summoned to Hitler's HQ, together with Koch, who had had time to prepare evidence refuting the charges against him.

Hitler refused to decide between the two men; he merely enjoined cooperation upon them and left it to Lammers and Bormann to persuade them to shake hands. This Rosenberg, to his credit, refused to do.[74] On 1 June 1943 Lammers wrote to both men, repeating Hitler's general injunctions. Koch was told not to obstruct his Minister's decrees. Rosenberg was told 'to confine himself in his measures to matters which unconditionally require to be centrally regulated from above'. Although Hitler had said nothing to clarify the relationship between two state servants, one of whom claimed to be the superior of the other, they were instructed to meet for consultation twice monthly, once in the Reich and once in the Ukraine.[75]

Almost immediately after receiving Lammers' letter Rosenberg undertook his second official tour of Koch's domain, having first announced his new measures, which Koch still opposed, for dividing up the collective farms and apportioning the land. It was never to be implemented in the Ukraine, but Rosenberg counted it as one of his scant triumphs. His tour, however, was not to be a triumphal one if Koch could help it. He met his Minister on arrival at Rovno and prevented his again receiving from an Ukrainian delegation the gift of salt and bread. Rosenberg's intention to lay a wreath on the grave of an Ukrainian national poet was equally frustrated.[76] He could not be deterred from meeting his own officials, however, and at a gathering of senior staff in Rovno on 5 June he told them that the new agricultural decree was to be put into effect – it was not just propaganda; even if 'hard methods' had to be used in recruiting workers for the Reich, there must be 'correct treatment' of them. Even Koch, in concluding the discussion, admitted that Sauckel had set a high target; every office in the Reich, he said, 'tries to extract limitless labour forces from the Ukraine'.[77]

Although dogged at every turn by Koch's malevolence, Rosenberg could not be prevented from learning the truth about the partisans, who were the most plentiful product of Koch's disastrous administration; a full account of their depredations was given to him by Ernst Leyser, the District Commissioner in Zhitomir.[78] The District Commissioner in Melitopol, Alfred Frauenfeld, was another critic of Koch's methods. As a fellow Gauleiter, he was to some extent immune from Koch's rages and accordingly earned his detestation. As Koch refused to spend a night under his roof,

Rosenberg was, for once, relieved of what he later described as Koch's 'boorishness'. During that night a shot was fired at the house; Frauenfeld, who prided himself that his own humane methods kept partisans out of Taurida, explained later to Rosenberg that a drunken German soldier had thought the windows were showing too much light.[79] If the incident reminded the Minister that the war was not far away, he was not to be dissuaded from a brief escape into the past by visiting the Crimea, which lay outside Koch's jurisdiction. Twenty-six years had passed since he was last at Simeis, watching the moon rise and searching out the remote crags, where the ancient Goths had made their last stand. That span of time had witnessed the rise to power of the new twentieth-century Goths, the men with whom he now found himself at loggerheads – Koch, Goering, Himmler, Sauckel and Bormann.

The Fuehrer understood this antagonism very well; while his Minister was dawdling in the Crimea, he had been telling Keitel about his recent talk with Rosenberg and Koch. The trouble was, he complained, that, as soon as danger threatened, certain people lost their heads and began to see phantom armies of allies where none existed. 'We've got quite enough of these people now. Many of them are in Rosenberg's shop. But unfortunately we have them in the army too. They're former Baltic Barons and Baltic Germans of that kind. But also former emigrés from the Ukraine. . . .'

The words might have come straight out of the mouth of Erich Koch. 'Rosenberg is one of the most acute thinkers in questions of ideology', Hitler went on. 'Just this preoccupation with ideological questions has naturally allowed him, I must say, very little contact with ordinary day to day matters. Ideological and everyday questions don't go well together in one head.'[80] And for the next ten minutes he repeated to the harrassed Keitel the gist of everything that Koch had said. But it has been left to history – since Keitel was a 'yes-man' of no discernment – to answer the question whether a better understanding of everyday affairs was shown by those who tried to make friends of subject peoples in Russia or by those who tried to destroy them.

Rosenberg was so incensed by his treatment while on tour that, on return to Berlin, he instructed Koch to go to Koenigsberg on leave. When Koch refused and appealed to Bormann, Hitler sent to his Minister a curt request 'not to meddle in the internal admin-

istration of the RKU, but to confine yourself to broad, general directives, which are first to be cleared with me'.[81] At this point senior
staff at the RMBO advised their Minister that he should resign, but
he could not bring himself to do so. Instead, he gradually allowed
his old enemies, Goebbels and Himmler, to encroach further on his
dwindling functions. It is arguable that, if he had at this juncture
formally abandoned the responsibilities that he could no longer
exercise, it would have been difficult for the Nuremberg Tribunal
to have condemned him to death. As it was, a prescient comment
was made by Leibbrandt at the interview in August 1943, at which
he learned of his replacement by Berger. 'If the war is lost,' said
Leibbrandt bitterly, 'as a result of the unholy eastern policy, then
you, Minister, will be hanged.' Braeutigam, in recording this
remark, has rightly added, 'One could indeed say things to Rosenberg that would have led to the gallows, if addressed to other
party leaders.'[82]

If Rosenberg hoped that, by returning to Berlin, he was moving
back to safety, he was much mistaken. On 24 August 1943 his
house was destroyed in an air-raid, and he moved to an hotel in the
Potsdamer Platz. About one month later his General Commissioner in Minsk, Wilhelm Kube, was blown up in his bed by a bomb
placed there by a local servant. If he had been unpopular with the
partisans, he had been scarcely better loved by the SS, against
whose atrocities he had protested. It was an ironic comment on
the assassin's work that Berger exerted his increased influence
within the RMBO to see that SS General v. Gottberg took over
the vacant post. Rosenberg confined himself to making Kube's
funeral oration, which was roundly condemned by Goebbels, who
fancied he did such things better. 'Rosenberg', he said, 'is not the
man to touch the hearts of his listeners.'[83] The feud with Koch
dragged on, but no longer had much meaning or importance; Kiev
fell to the Red Army on 6 November 1943. Ten days later
Rosenberg had another inconclusive interview with his Fuehrer;
it was the last time they met and spoke together. Nothing came
of it, except approval for Rosenberg to organise an international
anti-semitic congress in Cracow.

We have concentrated in this chapter on the Ukraine, because it
was here that the clash of ideas was more intense and the results
of mistaken policies more disastrous; but it should not be assumed

that Lohse was an easy subordinate. He was, however, a much less forceful man than Koch and he did not have Bormann's backing. He had said to Rosenberg at the time of his appointment, 'I shall be no more than your political echo.'[84] But power soon went to his head and, during Rosenberg's first visit to Riga in May 1942, he admitted in a drunken moment to his deputy, Meyer, that he hoped to create a dukedom for his son.[85] He accordingly resented the very modest measure of self-government that Rosenberg had introduced in March 1942 and also objected to the breaking up of the collective farms.[86] On this latter point he had even less excuse than Koch, since collectivisation in most of his area was of recent date and in many cases former owners of land could still be traced. Rosenberg cut short his visit, which took him as far as Reval, in obedience to Hitler's order to deliver the funeral oration for his dead friend, Gauleiter Roever. In this he proved fortunate, since the train, which he was scheduled to take next day, ran off the line, where it had been cut by partisons.[87]

In February 1944 Rosenberg paid his second visit to Ostland, travelling this time in his special train 'Gotenland', and presiding over meetings with his General Commissioners and their subordinates.[88] While in Riga he received instructions from Hitler not to go on to Reval, as he had intended; he therefore never saw his birth-place again. In his absence the RMBO premises were destroyed in an air-raid and from this time 'Gotenland', parked in a suburban siding, was his office. This change of habitat seems to have made him increasingly itinerant; he travelled widely, delivering speeches and making plans which the course of the war rendered ever more irrelevant. At the end of March 1944 he visited Hans Frank in Cracow, where he was planning to hold his anti-semitic congress. Among those to be invited were the Grand Mufti; Quisling, Alexis Carrel, Leon Degrelle, the French writer Céline and John Amery. Rosenberg may have had some misgivings about the latter's anti-semitism, since he noted that 'his speech must be prepared for him'.[89] Later he crossed his name off the list on the ground that Amery was 'one-quarter Jewish'. In mid-June 1944 Hitler put an end to this nonsense by banning the proposed congress for the duration of the war.[90] In the latter part of May Rosenberg went to Amsterdam and The Hague, where he met the 'Quisling' of the Netherlands, Mussert.[91]

The fact was that his days as Minister were over; he no longer had much eastern territory to administer and rumours were prevalent that RMBO was to be disbanded. In July 1944 the Russians broke through to the Baltic and Lohse, whose behaviour had been increasingly erratic, collapsed and in September was sent on indefinite leave by Hitler, who without consulting Rosenberg entrusted Koch with the residual tasks of exploiting what remained of Ostland for the benefit of the retreating Germans.[92] When Rosenberg wished to protest, he was sharply informed by Lammers that the Fuehrer could not receive him; he wanted Koch to have 'far-reaching freedom and independence'; if Rosenberg failed to respect this, Koch might be given formal, as well as practical, independence.[93] As if this were not enough, in the same month Ribbentrop, Himmler and Berger, who had not attempted to consult his nominal Minister, agreed that Vlasov should have command of volunteer forces from all parts of Russia. It was the perversion of what Rosenberg had stood for; although it came too late to have any effect on the outcome of the war, it was the final blow to his self-esteem.

On 12 October 1944 he at last braced himself to write a letter of resignation. Even at this late hour, when it might have been thought that he was looking beyond the lost war to the future, he could not bring himself to set down a rousing denunciation of mistaken policies; it was a timid, hesitant document. In a covering letter to Lammers, he deplored the handling of Eastern affairs, about which he was not consulted, and asked him to lay his statement of grievances before the Fuehrer. This statement reminded Hitler that early in 1943 Rosenberg had recommended to him a call to arms against Bolshevism addressed to all the peoples of the East; but this had been rejected. Now, at the demand of Himmler, Vlasov had been permitted to call himself Leader of the Russian Army of Liberation.[94] 'I am asking you, my Fuehrer, to tell me whether you still desire my activity in this field for, since it has not been possible for me to report to you orally and the problems of the East are brought to you and discussed from various sides, I must, in consideration of this development, assume that perhaps you consider my activity as no longer necessary.'[95] Hitler did not even trouble to reply, so that his Minister's resignation was never officially accepted.

16. *The Minister visits occupied Ostland, May 1942*

17. *In the dock at Nuremberg: Rosenberg is sixth from left in the front row, between Kaltenbrunner (left) and Frank*

18. *Death by the rope: Rosenberg on his coffin in Nuremberg prison*

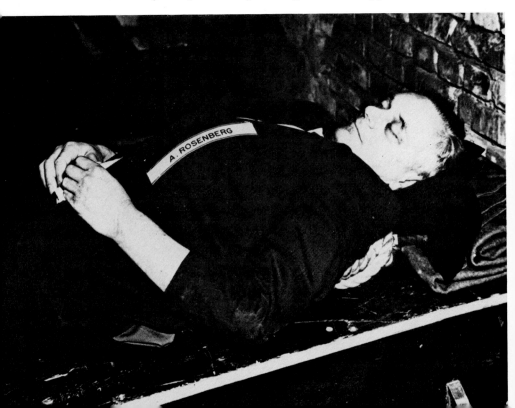

# 10 Appointment in Nuremberg

The last year of Nazi power dawned sombrely for the leadership still clinging to power in their diminished Reich. Himmler cherished the illusion that the Western powers would negotiate with him; Ley and others put their faith in the miraculous new weapons of revenge, about which the Fuehrer spoke. Rosenberg was more sceptical when he heard Hitler speak in this vein at a meeting of Reichsleiter and Gauleiter on 24 February 1945. A dinner followed the meeting, but the two men exchanged no word and Rosenberg never saw his Fuehrer again.[1] Since the previous November he had continued to try, without success, to fix an appointment; to avoid what he called Bormann's 'dicatatorship of the ante-chamber'[2] he attempted to reach Hitler through his female secretaries, who regularly took tea with him at his HQ, but the message he received was: 'I'll gladly ask Rosenberg to tea, but I think it will only lead to another business talk.'[3] This year there had been no message from the Fuehrer for Rosenberg's fifty-second birthday; he had celebrated it quietly over coffee and cakes with Meyer and Braeutigam. On the following day the latter asked his Minister to release him for return to Ribbentrop's rival concern. It was a painful request for Rosenberg, but he bore his former employee no ill will. Not long after, when Braeutigam was hurt in an air-raid, he received a bottle of red wine and Rosenberg's good wishes for his recovery.[4]

The temporary roof had been blown off Rosenberg's damaged house and the family retired to the basement rooms. He had never been much of a family man and his wife, Hedwig, had taken practically no part in his official life. Now that this life, which had meant so much to him, was coming to an end, he seems to have begun to notice her and his only daughter, Irene, whose fifteenth birthday was to have been marked on 22 March by a

P

small party. Instead she found herself confined to a dirty and cluttered basement, where she sat most of the day at her type-writer. Her father was proud of the verses and fairy-tales that she composed. Later in Nuremberg gaol he recalled how he had watched from the balcony, as she ran out of the house in the afternoon to see her girl friends, 'tall, young, with blonde hair to her shoulders . . . laughing as she turned round'.[5] Phlegmatically he dug his garden for the flowers and vegetables he would not see. In 1943 he had had bulbs sent from Holland; but those days were over and would not return. Soon even exercise was denied him, as he was laid low with his old trouble, an inflammation of the ankle-joint.

One of those who came to see him in April 1945 was the Hitler Youth leader Arthur Axmann, who told him about plans for carrying on resistance in the Bavarian mountains. Rosenberg said nothing, whereupon Axmann asked him whether the concept of Nazism had been at fault, or whether it was only the application. 'I said that a great idea had been misused by small men. Himmler was the evil symbol of that.' Axmann, mixing equally heavy doses of optimism and civility, said the young generation hoped Rosen-berg would stand by them.[6] Happily there has been no sign that his ideas, as such, make an appeal to the young in any country, even though racialism, which the Nazis did not invent, has gone from strength to strength. When one reads with astonish-ment that, according to neo-Stalinists in Czechoslovakia, 'the Prague spring of 1968' was a Zionist plot,[7] one wonders whether the people of Lidice died in vain and where Heydrich is now rein-carnated.

On 13 April, hearing rumours that the RMBO was to be evacuated to Bavaria, Rosenberg wrote to Hitler that this smacked of flight and he favoured staying in Berlin. He received a message that he could stay if he wished and he then released his remaining staff to follow their own inclinations. One of them had done so already; his old friend Schickedanz had shot himself, his wife and their small daughter. The same thought had occurred to Rosen-berg, who had provided himself with enough cyanide to save his family from falling alive into Russian hands. On 20 April came a telephone message from the Reich Chancery that all Ministers should leave next morning and report at Eutin in Schleswig-

Holstein. Rosenberg still had his car and driver; it was raining as they all climbed in. He took a last look round the garden . . . the newly planted birch trees . . . Irene's swing. He could not get a shoe on his left foot. They stayed only one night in Eutin, before going on to Flensburg, where accommodation was to be found for Hedwig and Irene, whilst he reported to Admiral Doenitz, the new head of state. 'We hear with deep emotion of the Fuehrer's death – he has been our fate.'[8] At this juncture the thought came to him that, 'I might possibly be an embarrassment to the Doenitz regime.'[9] According to Speer, Rosenberg wanted to dissolve the NSDAP believing that, as the senior Reichsleiter, he was the only one who could do so.[10] Even at this late hour he was still pursuing the struggle for precedence, which had been such a feature of the Third Reich.

Walking on the shore of the fjord near Flensburg, he finally decided to see his predicament through to the end, and threw into the water the vial of poison that he had been carrying.[11] Shortly afterwards he again twisted his ankle and had to be taken to the Naval Hospital.* There on 12 May he composed a letter to Field-Marshal Montgomery, placing himself at his disposal. The British Army were in no hurry to collect him; it was not until the morning of 18 May that the military police came to the hotel to which he had moved. In the meantime he had had a brief reunion with his wife and daughter, who had found their way to his hotel after being everywhere repulsed. The privileges of being married to a Reich Minister had vanished overnight; the German people were rapidly adapting themselves to their changed circumstances. He was not given much time to pack by the waiting detachment. He kissed Irene and Hedwig good-bye and hobbled out. They were not arrested, but at Christmas 1945 he still had no news of them. They disappeared into the obscurity in which, by choice, they have since remained.

A few days after his arrest Rosenberg was taken to Kiel and put on an aircraft in charge of an English Captain, who claimed to have read the *Mythus* and enquired whether Rosenberg stood by his conclusions. It was not in his nature in any circumstances

---

* Speer states that he was dead drunk, but does not claim that this statement is based on first-hand evidence. Rosenberg's version, used here, equally explains his being carried into the Hospital.

to admit error; he replied stiffly, 'Certainly there are some things that have been overtaken by events, but even now I regard the essential structure of thought as right.'[12] The spectacle of the ravaged country, as they flew south, seems to have done nothing to change his attitude of stubborn self-justification. Instead of reflecting where he might have gone wrong, he tried to find a point within himself from which to observe his predicament. 'Now we shall see how you, Alfred Rosenberg, close your life's adventure.'[13] The aircraft landed in Luxemburg and he was lodged at the Palace Hotel in Mondorf in American custody. There the major war criminals, who had been singled out for trial by special international tribunal, remained until transferred to Nuremberg in August 1945.

Rosenberg knew Nuremberg well. It was the city of the *Meistersingers*, Hitler's favourite opera, and of the Nazi cult of Durer; his *The Knight, Death and the Devil* had been presented to Hitler in Nuremberg in 1933. Rosenberg had often visited the famous Germanisches Museum. Every September he had supervised production of the *VB*'s special supplement in anticipation of the annual party rally, at which he had regularly spoken, besides presiding over a gathering of party officials concerned with the cultural programme. Which of the rallies was in his mind, as he arrived there in custody? Perhaps the one held ten years earlier and designated 'The Rally of Freedom'. But in the memoir that he wrote in prison he referred to two other rallies: that of 1933, at which he had spoken of 'a chivalrous solution' of the Jewish problem;[14] and that of 1937, at which he was awarded the Reich substitute for the Nobel Prize. He even spared a thought for Carl v. Ossietzky, formerly publisher of the radical *Weltbuehne*, whose acceptance of the Nobel Prize in 1936 had led Hitler to ban all Germans from receiving it in future and to establish the Reich award, which Rosenberg had received. Ossietzky had died in 1938 in the hands of the Gestapo. Seven years later Rosenberg, himself now in prison under conditions that Ossietzky would have regarded as indulgent, was still interested only in condemning him and claiming – quite falsely – that he had already been in gaol when the Nazis came to power.[15]

Rosenberg's memoir, like his defence at the trial, is marked by unshakeable faith in the validity of his own judgments. Wrong has, undeniably, been done; but it has been done by others; indeed their worst offence has been to destroy Rosenberg's vision of National-Socialism and so make a mockery of his life's work. Speer – no admirer of Rosenberg – admitted, 'Rosenberg made an impression of honesty and consistency. All the efforts of his lawyer both before and behind the scenes to persuade him to recant his so-called ideology came to nothing.'[16] Not for Rosenberg Speer's recognition of guilt or Hans Frank's hysterical repentance. He did not collapse under the strain, like Ribbentrop and Kaltenbrunner. Towards the end of August 1946 Lt. Col. W. H. Dunn made a medical and psychiatric report on him to the prison governor, Col. B. C. Andrus, who wished to be satisfied that no suicide attempts were imminent. Dunn was very pleased with Rosenberg's health and even with his mood: 'No evidence of depression or suicidal preoccupation. Mood was entirely appropriate.'[17] But was it, in fact, appropriate to be so sure, so calm? He had pleaded not guilty to all the charges against him; but certain facts remained and cried out for explanation. There were six million dead Jews and nearly four million Russian prisoners of war, to say nothing of those who had died in combat. It was not enough to say that the acts of terror and annihilation had been the acts of others, because of those other culprits the most violent had been acting in pursuance of a theory, and precisely the link between theory and action had been ideology – his ideology.

'He gave the impression,' wrote Dunn, 'of clinging to his own theories in a fanatical and unyielding fashion and to have been little influenced by the unfolding during the trial of the cruelties and crimes of the party. . . .'[18] When a film of atrocities was shown to the prisoners, 'Rosenberg was fidgety, could not sit still in his seat, and then turned away'.[19] He had always averted his gaze from that which he did not want to see, just as he had deflected his mind from contemplating what might be the impact of his doctrine upon the minds of men more literal and more ruthless than himself. It was significant that none of the men whom he most blamed for the distortion and subsequent disaster was present: Himmler and Goebbels were dead; Bormann and Koch were missing. Bormann is still missing. Koch was later picked up, living disguised in Schleswig-Holstein. The Russians, against whom his worst crimes had been committed, showed no interest in him;

to try him would only have been an embarrassment; they had in the meantime dealt with the Ukrainians in a manner of which Koch would not have been ashamed. He was handed over to the Poles.

There was one man at Nuremberg, however, whom Rosenberg might well have blamed for what had been ill done in the Third Reich: Hermann Goering, Reich Marshal. Not only had Goering constantly harried Rosenberg, but in the early part of the war he had been the force behind Koch, Sauckel and Backe. In his own very different way Goering had been just as much a force for evil as Himmler; indeed he had developed the Gestapo to a high degree of sadistic efficiency before Himmler took it over. Now that imposing presence was shrunken and the only gaolers who would come at his call were those who locked him into his cell. Yet, even in confinement, he continued to dominate not only Rosenberg, whom he had always dominated, but the other prisoners as well. He was still No. 2 in the non-existent Reich. When he was informed on 25 October 1945 that Ley had committed suicide, he said, in the tone of a Commanding Officer, responsible for his men, 'It's just as well that he's dead, because I had my doubts about how he would behave at his trial.'[20] He was still a formidable figure, so Rosenberg simply averted his eyes; very little direct criticism of Goering appears either in his testimony or in the memoir that he was currently writing.

There was one figure, however, which he still could not find it in his heart wholly to condemn and which it was impossible to ignore: the figure of his Fuehrer. Hitler's death had stilled some of the emotions he had always aroused in Rosenberg – the canine devotion, the fear of a harsh word, the longing to be taken on an expedition, or be given a good job. It was at last possible for him, as it had never been in a quarter of a century, to try to see Hitler for what he was. The analysis, it is true, began in the old, oblique fashion; Hitler had been the victim of less scrupulous men. 'And around the head of state was encamped an intelligence apparat, which deflected Hitler's will – already fatally twisted – towards a tragedy of world-historical dimensions, the result of which was the destruction of a thousand-year struggle for the Holy German Empire.'[21] But as his mind reverted again and again to the core of the problem, he was forced to see that Hitler had been responsible for the aberrations of his followers and thus for what had occurred. 'Under the unambiguous command of a far-sighted chief, whose leadership at once punished every disloyalty, the degeneration could have been prevented. . . . But it was he who permitted them to abuse their power and saw in criticism of this abuse only a judgment against himself. . . . Therefore all questions from every side always lead back to him.'[22]

Having made this admission, Rosenberg was able to make a reasoned analysis of the causes of Hitler's failure. One of the major ones he found in the Fuehrer cult, to which, though he did not say so, he had himself made a substantial contribution. After referring to Hitler's belief in a special providence watching over him, Rosenberg continued, 'This was noticeable when he came out of Landsberg in 1925 and then increased after he came to power, until at the end of the war this belief had begun to assume really distressing aspects.'[23] It was, one may well think, something of an understatement; but Rosenberg was shrewd enough to see that this cult of personality had come about in part because Nazism had never succeeded in stabilising its revolution; indeed, it had not wished to do so. Its volatile, dynamic nature had been one of its essential features; speed of movement had deceived NSDAP members into believing that the Fuehrer must be going somewhere.

Rosenberg, to do him justice, was not seeing this for the first time at Nuremberg. He was speaking the truth when he said at his trial, 'The practice of the German State leadership in the war differed completely from my ideas. To an ever-increasing extent Hitler drew persons to himself who were not my comrades, but my opponents.'[24] His lawyer, Dr Alfred Thoma, read into the evidence for the defence a passage from the speech that his client had made in Marienburg in 1934, in which he had advocated 'a monarchy on a republican foundation'. Rosenberg had gone on to say, 'From that standpoint the state will not become a deified end in itself, neither will its leader become a Caesar, a God, or a deputy of God.'[25] In prison he devoted space in his memoir to elaborating his now useless constitutional speculations, claiming to have bequeathed to the world an uncompleted work of some 400 pages, devoted to church and state, as well as to art and science. No copies of this work appear to have survived the post-war holocaust. As Dr D. M. Kelley, one of the psychiatrists, put it, he had 'always lived in a world of unreal philosophy. He is completely unable to organise his present very real situation and constantly seeks escape in aimless speech.'[26] He was given an *IQ* rating of 127; this was about average for the Nazi leaders, though well below that assigned (in descending order) to Schacht, Seyss-Inquart, Goering, Doenitz, Raeder and Papen.[27]

It is significant that of the six accused just mentioned two were acquitted and only Goering and Seyss-Inquart were sentenced to death; they were among the least ideologically motivated of the Nazi leaders. Many of their colleagues, including Rosenberg, had always lived in a world of fantasy; it had begun with the war that the army had never lost and continued with the peace that the Reich was never going to keep. Instead of the harsh, but solid, world of reality, they had preferred their ideological world, in which they were heroic figures, beleaguered by the sly, international conspirators – the Jews, the priests and the cosmopolitan financiers. Then, beyond their hopes, the illusion, as if obedient to the magic of an incantation, had begun to take on the firm outline of actuality. The mythical Fuehrer figure, who had been invested with powers that at first were imaginary, had miraculously gained strength and confounded his old enemies, whose defeat was taken as sufficient proof of the truth of their conspiracy. Finally, the Fuehrer, in a fury of self-fulfilling prophecy, had hurled himself upon so many new foes, far and wide, that they had massed their forces and destroyed him. Rosenberg had been the major architect of this myth and his memoir shows that, even at the last gasp, he had no intention of abandoning it.

The surviving Nazi leaders were accused of 'crimes against peace, war crimes and crimes against humanity and of a common plan or conspiracy to commit these crimes'.[28] It was a fourfold indictment, which most of them, including Rosenberg, regarded as unjust. In his eyes it was unjust because Hitler, the prime author of the terrible events under review, was not there to answer for them and, in any case, could only be brought to book by the Germans themselves. He had never attempted to look at the world through other than German eyes; seen in this way events had a tragic unity, which he summed up in his memoir in four short telling sentences. 'Never was the soul of Germany more at one with itself than in 1933. Never did the Great German dream seem nearer to realisation than in 1938. Yet never did the Reich collapse in more total ruin than in 1945. All that is summed up in one name, but a name answerable to the High Court of the German nation.'[29] Nazism had been something that only the German people had been able to comprehend – not a conspiracy, but a victim's reaction against a hostile conspiracy. The Allied aim to make Nazism appear to be the source of all evil was to Rosenberg mere revenge. As he said at his trial, 'Honest service for this ideology ... was not a conspiracy and my actions were never a crime.'[30]

It is, of course, true that from a strictly legal point of view there was no precedent for constituting a tribunal of victors to try the vanquished, and no accepted corpus of law by which the latter could be judged, apart from certain international conventions, not all of which were acknowledged by all members of the tribunal. The inevitable result was that the victors were judges, as well as prosecutors. This would have mattered less if all members of the tribunal had shared a common concept of what was meant by international law, justice and crimes against humanity. The medieval concept of the just war had some meaning when all the nations of Christendom at least claimed to observe similar moral standards; in the twentieth-century there had ceased to be anything in common between justice, as understood by Sir Hartley Shawcross and by Andrei Vyshinsky, who visited Nuremberg during the proceedings.

One of the Russian prosecutors, M. Y. Raginsky, waxed eloquent in his description of Rosenberg's authorisation of the removal to the Reich in the summer of 1944 of 40,000 homeless Russian orphans (Heu Aktion), but fell silent when Rosenberg alleged that a similar number of adults had been deported to the USSR in 1940 from each of the states of Latvia and Estonia.[31] It was all very well for the Russians to deny the existence of the secret annex to the Molotov–Ribbentrop pact of 1939, on which their seizure of these states was grounded, but copies of it had been found in captured German archives. If Ribbentrop's signature had been part and parcel of an international conspiracy against peace, what could be said about Molotov's? In 1945 the USSR was again occupying the Baltic States, which were recognised as independent countries by the USA. The SS and Gestapo were justly accused of maintaining concentration camps, but in 1946 it was well known not only that such camps existed in the USSR, but that the Soviet secret police had taken over the detention camps they found in the Russian occupied zone of Germany and had merely changed over the inmates. One of the American prosecutors, Thomas Dodd, heatedly accused Rosenberg of persecuting religion; the Soviet prosecutor did not cross-examine. There were many such awkward moments before the long trial was over.

It has since been argued that the Allies would have done better to leave it to the Germans to cleanse their own stable. The only valid comment on this argument is that it was never within the realms of historical possibility; those who have espoused it have overlooked certain important facts. First, in 1945 there was no German authority capable of legally setting up a court, let alone one that could try war crimes arising all over Europe. In any case the legal profession in Germany had been much corrupted by Nazism; the mass trials conducted after the 20 July 1944 conspiracy did not inspire confidence. Secondly, it must be remembered that in 1919 the victorious Allies had refrained from exercising the right they had at first claimed to try German war criminals, on the understanding that the Germans would deal appropriately with the matter. The dilatory and selfrighteous way in which the Germans had then gone about it had not encouraged the victors of 1945 to repeat the experiment. Thirdly, the student of history must use his imagination in an attempt to recapture the mood of liberated Europe in the aftermath of the Second World War. Crimes had been committed on an unprecedented scale; the war leaders could not ignore the demand for penalties to be exacted; this was one of the few post-war aims on which both East and West were agreed.

There had never been the slightest doubt that Rosenberg would figure on the list of criminals; his name had been among those mentioned in Molotov's note of 14 November 1942.[32] He was indicted on all four counts and found guilty on all of them.[33] Thoma did his best, but the defence was handicapped by the fact that it had access to documentation and to witnesses only through the indulgence of the prosecution. One week before the trial began Rosenberg tried to call as a witness 'Major Winterbotham of the

Air Ministry', in the hope that he would testify 'that I personally exerted myself for years (1931–39) in the interests of German-English understanding'.[34] There was no response. A good deal was made by the prosecution out of his share of responsibility for the invasion of Norway, although witnesses insisted that his APA had been of no real importance. In the final months of his life, after years of trying to emphasise his own importance, he found himself frequently obliged to deny it. Thus he disclaimed under cross-examination 'any direct influence on school policies ... or universities'.[35] This line of defence seems to have perturbed the Russians, who at one point read into the evidence Rosenberg's draft letter to Hitler of 6 February 1938, claiming that he ought to be in the Cabinet.[36] Accused by the Russians of having taken part in planning the invasion of the USSR, he could only defend himself by maintaining that, by the time he was brought in, the crucial decision had already been taken. Both prosecution and defence, for differing purposes, were able to quote from the speech that he had delivered to his staff on 20 June 1941 about the political objectives of the German offensive.[37] When he tried to off-load responsibility for inhumanity on to Koch, the prosecution was able to remind him that he had himself proposed Koch as future Reich Commissioner, Moscow. Rosenberg could only reply that Koch at an earlier period had been favourably impressed by developments in the USSR and had written a book on the subject.

The prosecution naturally made capital out of the memorandum by Dr Markull of the RMBO legal staff criticising the weak reply made by the Minister to Bormann's letter of 23 July 1942.[38] Rosenberg defended himself as best he could by insisting that, although he had appeared to acquiesce in severer policies in the Ukraine, 'the decrees which I issued after this letter did not change in any way'.[39] The record does, in fact, justify this contention in such important fields as health and education;[40] but Thoma was unable to produce documentation. Another weak spot in the defence was the Heu Aktion, which has already been mentioned.* Rosenberg could not deny that he had authorised the removal of the children to the Reich and was only able to maintain that he had cared for their welfare and visited their

* See p. 223.

camp near Dessau. Thoma insisted that his client had taken charge of them at the personal request of Field-Marshal v. Kluge, who feared they would otherwise fall into the hands of Sauckel's gangs.[41] There was a good deal of confusion about the numbers involved; the prosecution alleged from 40,000 to 50,000; Thoma admitted to 20,000, but expert opinion now holds that only 2,500 to 3,000 children had been collected before the German front broke in June 1944.[42]

The most serious charge against Rosenberg was, of course, that of collaboration in genocide. The Russians alleged that he 'was in favour of a systematic extermination of the Slav people';[43] but it cannot be said that they came even close to proving their case. More dangerous from the defendant's point of view, however, was the charge that he had conspired in the destruction of the Jewish people. Rosenberg could not deny that he had heard Hitler and others speak of extirpation (Ausrottung), but he claimed to have understood the word in a metaphorical sense; Churchill, he thought, must have used the word in this sense when he had spoken of rooting out Prussian militarism. He admitted that reports had reached him of 'terrible harshness' in camps for Jews; 'but that there was an order for individual annihilation of the entire Jewry, I could not assume. . . .'[44] This was not, of course, an honest answer. He had been invited by Heydrich to attend the Wannsee conference on 20 January 1942, at which the extermination policy was outlined. He did not go, but sent Meyer, who said nothing and, according to Braeutigam, took no note of the proceedings;[45] but that he made no oral report to Rosenberg is beyond belief.

In the summer of 1939 Rosenberg had made a ferocious speech, in which he demanded that 'the Rothschilds and Mandels ... the Albert Einsteins with the Hore-Belishas and the Kaganoviches' should be relegated to 'a wild island with a deadly climate, such as Madagascar or Guiana. Isolated from the outside world like lepers ... the obnoxious Jewish race will find itself isolated in a reservation from where there is no return, from where there is but one exit – death.'[46] For a brief period after the fall of France Nazi leaders did indeed toy with the idea of shipment to Madagascar as a solution to the Jewish problem; but by the autumn of 1940, when it was clear that Britain was staying in the war, this prospect had receded. On 6 March 1941, when Rosenberg was drafting the speech that he was to deliver at the opening of his new anti-semitic institute in Frankfurt, he consulted Bormann about including a reference to Madagascar.[47] Bormann evidently advised against it, since in the final draft of Rosenberg's speech, which was delivered on 28 March just before he was summoned by Hitler to assume new responsibilities in the East, a fresh page has been inserted at the following point: 'The Jewish question, which for 2,000 years has faced the peoples of Europe as their task and has not been dealt with, will now through the National-Socialist revolution find its solution for Germany and for the whole of Europe.' The solution would not be a Jewish state, since Jews were incapable of fulfilling the political function of creating a state. There must therefore be a Jewish reservation, where they would work under police supervision. 'The Jewish question will only be solved for Europe, when the last Jew has left the continent of Europe.'[48]

There is no word here of a 'chivalrous solution'. If Rosenberg did not from the first know what fate Hitler had in store for the Jews, it was because he did not wish to enquire. Later, as Reich Minister, he cannot have been under any illusions. In his final statement on 31 August 1946 he said, in relation to the genocide charge, 'I know my conscience to be completely free from any such guilt, from any complicity in the murder of peoples.'[49] In his memoir he was only prepared to concede that 'In the Jewish question I reproach myself only with not having protested in the same way' (i.e. as he had done on behalf of Eastern peoples).[50] As if to prove that he was incapable of revising his opinions or admitting his mistakes, even in the circumstances in which he now found himself, he devoted several pages to establishing to his own satisfaction that the difficulties experienced by the British government with illegal Jewish organisations in the mandated territory of Palestine were part of the same world conspiracy in which he had believed ever since, nearly thirty years before, he had first opened the pages of the *Protocols of the Wise Men of Zion*. One can but echo the verdict delivered on 1 October 1946 by General Nikitchenko: 'Upon occasion Rosenberg objected to the excesses and atrocities committed by his subordinates, notably in the case of Koch, but these excesses continued and he stayed in office until the end.'[51]

Rosenberg followed the proceedings closely in so far as these concerned him personally; on several occasions, whilst Russian prosecutors were examining him, he tried to intervene to check the translation, which seemed to him to be distorting what he had said. His answers were circumstantial – sometimes excessively so; even Thoma had to ask him to be more concise. When others were being examined, he tended to lose interest and spent part of his time in making pencil sketches of witnesses. In the court room he was seated between Frank and Kaltenbrunner, who at the beginning of the trial had shamed his fellow prisoners by his state of nervous collapse. The Nazi leadership had never been united in anything except in seeking Hitler's favours; the strain of defeat and exposure to universal censure heightened the friction among them to such an extent that they had to be separated in the luncheon intervals into relatively non-inflammable groups. Goering was isolated completely; Rosenberg was grouped with Kaltenbrunner, Frick and Jodl. Rosenberg had quarrelled at one time or another with nearly all those who were now in the dock with him. While his most severe criticisms were turned against fellow Nazis who were dead or absent, he also expressed his disapproval of those who, like Schirach and Fritzsche, had said in court that the Fuehrer had deceived them. Hitler might not be above criticism, but he was certainly above the criticism of such 'mediocre figures'.[52]

Rosenberg had decided to die in the faith in which he had lived. His lawyer tried unsuccessfully to introduce into his client's evidence a number of learned books designed to show that, as he wrote in his memoir, 'National-Socialism was a European answer to the question of our century. It was the noblest idea to which a German could devote his powers.... It was a true social ideology...'[53] The court was not interested; as Mr Dodd said, 'I think we are all, as a matter of principle, opposed to prosecuting any man for what he thinks.'[54] The Soviet prosecutor made no comment. The court was more interested in the devastation, the human misery, the holocaust of victims. Yet it was not, in fact, possible to separate cause and effect in the way that Dodd wished; his Soviet colleague would have been able from his understanding of ideology to explain, if he had wished, that men are liable to act on the basis of what they have been taught to think. As it was, it was left, by a curious irony, to an ss general, who had turned Crown's evidence, to press home the point that Rosenberg refused to perceive. Erich v. dem Bach-Zelewski remarked in the witness-box, 'I am of the opinion that when for years, for decades, the doctrine is preached that the Slav is an inferior race and the Jew not even human, then such an outcome is inevitable.'[55]

Rosenberg died without having grasped this truth. Many more intelligent men than he had equally failed to grasp it before him. One of these had been that prophet of racialism, Count de Gobineau, to whom a wiser compatriot, Alexis de Tocqueville had written, 'Do you not see that from your doctrine spring all the evils produced by permanent inequality: pride, violence, scorn for fellow men, tyranny and abjection in all their forms?'[56] This was the doctrine that Rosenberg had devoted his life to propagating and this was his main crime. Braeutigam has related a conversation held some years after the Nuremberg trials with Dr R. M. Kempner, a refugee from Nazi Germany, who had become one of the US assistant prosecutors. Kempner said 'Today we should no longer condemn Rosenberg to death.' Braeutigam's comment is that his former Minister nonetheless deserved to die: 'He held a high position as Minister and Reichsleiter, but did not use it to do everything in his power to avert the harm.'[57] It is a debatable judgment; Rosenberg's real offence was not that he acted like a weak man, but that he had written and spoken like a strong man. To what extent he had, in fact, corrupted the youth of Germany cannot now be measured; but that he had tried cannot be contested. For nothing corrupts a man more easily than to hear constantly the flattering statement that he belongs to a master race and has only to exert his mastery to prove himself a hero.

Rosenberg died in the conviction that National-Socialism was an attitude, as he had so often described it. It seemed to him to be an attitude of strength in contrast to the Christian faith, which taught a man to be conscious of his weakness and his liability to error. He had once been a Lutheran; but when the American Lutheran pastor went to see him, he said coldly to him, 'I don't have any need for your help.' Pastor Gerecke reported to Col. Andrus of Rosenberg, 'He thought it was nice if anyone could be so simple as to accept the story of the Cross as

I spoke of it.'⁵⁸ He maintained a Stoic outlook to the end. He was led to the gallows in the early hours of the morning of 15 October 1946 and said he had no statement to make. Those were his last words before he died by the rope. The bodies of the criminals were taken in secret to Dachau and incinerated in the ovens of the concentration camp.

The virus of Nazism in the world has not been disposed of so easily. In making this statement, we do not wish to imply that the phenomenon of Nazism, as expressed in the ideology propagated by such men as Rosenberg, could recur, either in Germany, or in some other country. Nazism, as such, was unmistakably cradled in a set of circumstances that could not repeat themselves in the same form. The very fact that the ideology was so successfully adapted to appeal at a particular point in time to so many dissatisfied and potentially violent elements in the Reich robs it of the possibility of more general application in time and place. The imaginary world conspiracy of Black, Red and Gold, which even at that particular time and place seemed unreal to many people, has at this remoter period become barely comprehensible. Indeed, this helps to explain why it has been comparatively neglected by historians.

Underlying Nazism, however, were two ideas which have universal application and are very much alive today. The first corresponds to man's basic need to think better of himself by thinking worse of some group of people different from himself. There will always be fertile ground for neo-Fascist and neo-Nazi activity so long as large numbers of men try to compensate at the expense of others for their feelings of insecurity and inferiority. Secondly, the belief seems fated to persist among large groups that their misfortunes must necessarily be due not to individual inadequacy or misdirection of effort, but to the malignant conspiracy of some other groups, which may at any given time be labelled 'the bosses', 'the Unions', 'the Commies', 'the colonial oppressors', 'the blacks' or, more simply, 'them'. So long as such states of mind recur – and their roots are very deep – a particular concatenation of political and economic pressures may lead to the eruption of violent and irrational movements and it will be premature to say: 'It couldn't happen here.' It is this apprehension that gives to the present study any value to which it can lay claim.

# Appendix:
# Rosenberg's Posthumously
# Published Memoir

The memoir written by Rosenberg in prison is an important document for anyone writing the history of National-Socialism and an essential one for anyone studying Rosenberg's life. It is therefore unfortunate that it has not yet found an impartial editor, who will treat it with the respect it deserves on historical grounds.

Enough has already been said in the Preface about the treatment of the memoir by Mr Lang and Mr Schenk. In 1955 an edition was brought out under the title 'Letzte Aufzeichnungen: Ideale und Idole der nationalsozialistischen Revolution' (abbreviation LA) by Herr Heinrich Haertle, who served under Rosenberg and has made no secret of his sympathy not only for Rosenberg, but also for the Third Reich. His text was severely criticised in Germany, although in an anonymous foreword he had admitted only to making 'isolated stylistic and formal corrections'.

In 1970, when LA was long out of print, Herr Haertle produced a new edition entitled 'Grossdeutschland: Traum und Tragoedie' (abbreviation GTT); it bore the subtitle 'Rosenbergs Kritik am Hitlerismus', which has only very limited application to the contents. He wrote in a new foreword, 'In order to exclude all suspicion of alteration in the contents, these have throughout been reproduced adhering faithfully to the sense, with corrections restricted to formal and stylistic changes and without even, in many cases, improving Rosenberg's brittle prose, complicated by his Balticisms.' This statement fails to explain, however, why certain passages, which now appear in GTT (e.g. three paragraphs about Kurt Luedecke) were not included in LA; even less why some phrases and even occasional sentences included in LA do not reappear in GTT.

Nonetheless, there can be no doubt about the authenticity of

Rosenberg's memoir as a whole. On the assumption that GTT is the more reliable text and is certainly more generally available, it is usually referred to in the footnotes. GTT, however, does not reproduce the first 75 pages of LA, covering the early period of Rosenberg's life before his arrival in Munich; for this period, therefore, reference has been made to LA in the footnotes.

# REFERENCES

Chapter 1 (pages 1–20)

1   Private information from relatives of a former employee in Rosenberg's Foreign Policy Office (*APA*)
2   *The Face of the Third Reich*, J. C. Fest (London, 1970) p.163
3   *Traum und Tragoedie*, ed. H. Haertle (Munich, 1970) p.120
4   BAK, NS10 – 62
5   *Hitler's Table Talk*, ed. H. Trevor-Roper (London, 1953) p.649
6   *Tendenzen und Gestalten der NSDAP*, A. Krebs (Stuttgart, 1959) p.166
7   BAK, NS8 – 7
8   USNA, EAP99 – 255
9   ibid.
10  *So Hat Es Sich Zugetragen*, O. Braeutigam (Wurzburg, 1968) p.150
11  BAK, NS8 – 144
12  BDC, Seell memo.
13  CDJC, CXXIXa – 722
14  USNA, EAP99 – 255
15  *So Hat Es sich Zugetragen*, op. cit., p.151
16  USNA, EAP99 – 255
17  ibid.
18  *Pest in Russland*, A. Rosenberg (Munich, 1922) p.41
19  *VB*, Munich, 28 July 1921
20  *Der Mythus des zwangstigsten Jahrhunderts*, A. Rosenberg (Munich, 1930), p.213
21  *Traum und Tragoedie*, op. cit., p.92
22  *Letzte Aufzeichnungen*, (Goettingen, 1955) p.10
23  ibid., p.14
24  USNA, EAP99 – 1020
25  USNA, EAP99 – 1020
26  USNA, EAP99 – 1004
27  USNA, EAP99 – 1020
28  Quoted in *Der National-Sozialismus: Ursprung und Wesen*, H. Grebing (Munich, 1959) p.14
29  USNA, EAP99 – 1020
30  Quoted in *Der Fuehrer*, K. Heiden (London, 1944), p.198
31  USNA, EAP99 – 1020
32  Quoted in the foreword to Friends of Europe pamphlet No.46 (Dec. 1936) Archives of Royal Institute of International Affairs, London
33  *Traum und Tragoedie*, op. cit., p.90
34  ibid., p.92
35  *The Face of the Third Reich*, op. cit., p.230
36  USNA, EAP99 – 1020
37  *Alfred Rosenberg: Der Mann und Sein Werk*, F.T. Hart (Munich, 1939) pp.37–38
38  USNA, EAP99 – 255

39  Diary: 19 January 1940; *Das politische Tagebuch A. Rosenberg*, ed. H-G. Seraphim (Munich, 1964)
40  Prozessregister No. 11E, Landgericht, Munich 1
41  *Letzte Aufzeichnungen*, op. cit., p.60
42  *Pest in Russland*, op. cit., p.16
43  *Die Spur des Juden im Wandel der Zeiten*, A. Rosenberg (Munich, 1920) p.116
44  *Der Fuehrer*, op. cit., p.9
45  USNA, EAP99 – 398
46  CDJC, CXLXIX – 21
47  *Letzte Aufzeichnungen*, op. cit., p.58
48  *Hitler Speaks*, H. Rauschning (London, 1939) p.132
49  *Die Spur des Juden*, op. cit., p.117
50  BAK, NS8 – 99
51  *Letzte Aufzeichnungen*, op. cit., p.63
52  BAK, NS8 – 99
53  BAK, NS8 – 8


Chapter 2 (pages 21–36)

1  *Letzte Aufz.*, op. cit., p.65
2  USNA, EAP99 – 1020
3  *Letzte Aufz.*, op. cit., p.79
4  ibid., p.14
5  *Dietrich Eckart: Ein Vermaechtnis*, A. Rosenberg (Munich, 1927) p.45
6  ibid., p.198
7  *Die Spur des Juden*, op. cit., p.88
8  ibid., p.133
9  ibid., p.36
10  USNA, EAP99 – 1020
11  ibid.
12  ibid.
13  *Mein Kampf*, A. Hitler (London, 1939) p.102
14  *Hitler – The Missing Years*, E. Hanfstaengl (London, 1957) p.123
15  *D. Eckart: Ein Vermaechtnis*, p.24
16  *Letzte Aufz.*, op. cit., p.72
17  ibid., p.78
18  *Entscheidungsjahr – 1932*, ed. W.E. Mosse (Tuebingen, 1966) p.81
19  BAK, N88 – 177 (*Meine erste Begegnung mit dem Fuehrer*) 1934
20  *Traum und Tragoedie*, op. cit., p.53
21  CDJC, LXII – 9
22  *Mein Kampf*, op. cit., p.559
23  *Mein Kampf*, op. cit., p.116

24  *Hitler's Mein Kampf: An Analysis*, W. Maser (London, 1970) p.59
25  *I Knew Hitler*, K. Luedecke (London, 1938) p.457
26  BAK, NS8 – 177
27  *Letzte Aufz.*, op. cit., p.83
28  *Fruehgeschichte der NSDAP:* W. Maser (Frankfurt, 1916) p.106
29  *Bevor Hitler Kam*, R.v. Sebottendorff (Munich, 1933) p.170
30  Quoted in *A History of National-Socialism*, K. Heiden (London, 1934) p.35
31  *VB*, 8 May 1921
32  ibid.
33  USNA, EAP99 – 358
34  *Lagebesprechungen im Fuehrerhauptquartier* (Munich, 1962) entry of 8 June 1943
35  *I Knew Hitler*, op. cit., p.82
36  *The Missing Years*, op. cit., p.41
37  *Hitler's Table Talk*, op. cit., p.218
38  *Nuremberg Party Rallies*, H.T. Burden (London, 1967) p.21
39  *I Knew Hitler*, op. cit., p.86
40  *Traum und Tragoedie*, op. cit., p.64
41  *The Gangsters Around Hitler*, O. Strasser (London 1942) p.21

Chapter 3 (page 37–60)

1   *VB*, 15 September 1923
2   *VB*, 21 April 1923
3   *Blut und Ehre*, A. Rosenberg (Munich, 1935) p.89
4   *Der Fuehrer*, op. cit., p.151
5   *The Missing Years*, op. cit., p.89
6   *Blut und Ehre*, op. cit., p.89
7   *The Missing Years*, op. cit., p.104
8   *I Knew Hitler*, op. cit., p.158
9   *VB*, 9 November 1923
10  *D. Eckart: Ein Vermaechtnis*, op. cit., p.60
11  *The Missing Years*, op. cit., p.104
12  Quoted in *Wenn die Goetter den Tempel verlassen*, K. Heyer (Freiburg, 1947) p.105
13  *Blut und Ehre*, op. cit., p.89
14  *Fruehgeschichte*, op. cit., p.406
15  *The Missing Years*, op. cit., p.108
16  *Traum und Tragoedie*, op. cit., p.69
17  BAK, NS8 – 99
18  *The Missing Years*, op. cit., p.122
19  *Wesen, Grundsaetze und Ziele der NSDAP*, A. Rosenberg (Munich, 1923) (Reprinted in *Reden und Schriften*, Munich, 1943) p.117

20  Quoted in *The Politics of Cultural Despair*, F. Stern (University of California, 1961) p.237
21  *Mein Kampf*, op. cit., p.183
22  *History of National-Socialism*, op. cit., p.84
23  *The Gangsters Around Hitler*, op. cit., p.22
24  *Hitler Speaks*, op. cit., p.80
25  *Nazi Fuehrer Sehen dich an*, W. Muenzenberg (Paris, 1934)
26  *I Knew Hitler*, op. cit., p.175
27  ibid., p.211
28  See A. Hitler to L. Haase, 16 June 1924, in *Nationalsozialismus und Revolution: Dokumente*, ed. W. Jochmann (Frankfurt, 1963) pp.77–78
29  *I Knew Hitler*, op. cit., p.218
30  *Nationalsozialismus und Revolution*, op. cit., p.78
31  *Traum und Tragoedie*, op. cit., p.73
32  *Nationalsozialismus und Revolution*, op. cit., pp.99–101
33  *The Missing Years*, op. cit., p.131
34  *Traum und Tragoedie*, op. cit., p.199
35  Quoted in *Hitler*, A. Bullock (London, 1962) p.129
36  *I Knew Hitler*, op. cit., p.257
37  *Traum und Tragoedie*, op. cit., p.150
38  *I Knew Hitler*, op. cit.
39  BAK, NS8 – 143
40  *Nationalsozialismus und Revolution*, op. cit., p.207
41  Three, according to Hart, op. cit., p.44; four according to *Traum und Tragoedie*, op. cit., p.100
42  CDJC, CXLIII – 379
43  *D. Eckart: Ein Vermaechtnis*, op. cit., p.64
44  *Traum und Tragoedie*, op. cit., p.278
45  *Prozessregister* No.11, E. Landgericht Munich I
46  *Traum und Tragoedie*, op. cit., p.69
47  *The Missing Years*, op. cit., pp.94–95
48  *The Early Goebbels Diaries*, ed. H. Heiber (London, 1962), 14 October 1925
49  ibid., 14 November 1925. See also *VB* of 14 November 1925
50  ibid., 15 February 1926
51  ibid., 6 July 1926
52  *Der Fuehrer*, op. cit., p.239
53  USNA, EAP99 – 358
54  Quoted from *Mit Hitler in die Macht*, O. Dietrich (Munich, 1934) p.195
55  *Weltkampf*, November 1925: quoted in *A. Rosenberg: Selected Writings*, ed. R. Pois (London, 1970) p.173
56  *Mythus*, quoted in *A. Rosenberg: Selected Writings*, op. cit., p.151
57  USNA, EAP99 – 254
58  *Wesen, Grundsaetze und Ziele der NSDAP* in *Reden und Schriften*, op. cit., p.152
59  ibid., p.145
60  ibid., p.148
61  *VB* of 1 February 1927

62   BAK, NS8 – 144
63   *H.S. Chamberlain*, A. Rosenberg (Munich, 1927) p.58
64   *Mein Kampf*, op. cit., p.183
65   *Account Rendered*, M. Maschmann (London, 1964) p.10


Chapter 4 (pages 61–81)

 1   *Ideology and Power in Soviet Politics*, Z.K. Brezezinski (London, 1962) p.5
 2   *Mein Kampf*, op. cit., p.151
 3   *First Letter on the Proposal for Peace with the Regicide Directory of France*, E. Burke (Selected Works, ed. E.J. Payne, (Oxford, 1892) p.24
 4   *The Last Days of Hitler*, H. Trevor Roper (London, 1947) p.196
 5   *Ich Glaubte an Hitler*, B.V. Schirach (Hamburg, 1967) p.87
 6   TMWC, 1749 – PS
 7   *The Politics of Cultural Despair*, op. cit., p.294
 8   Quoted in *The Politics of Cultural Despair*, op. cit., p.40
 9   Quotation reproduced in *Der Fuehrer*, op. cit., p.191
10   *Himmler als Ideologe*, J. Ackermann (Goettingen, 1970) p.60
11   *The Politics of Cultural Despair*, op. cit., p.56
12   Quoted in *The Origins of Totalitarianism*, H. Arendt (London, 1958) p.429
13   *Die Judenfrage als Rassen-, Sitten- und Kulturfrage* (1881)
14   Quoted in *Der Fuehrer*, op. cit., p.10
15   *Die Spur des Juden*, op. cit., p.152. The 1920 edition uses Feder's expression 'Zinsknechtschaft'
16   Quoted in *Immorality in the Talmud*, Friends of Europe pamphlet No.54 (1937), Archives of Royal Institute of International Affairs
17   *Die Spur des Juden*, op. cit., p.22
18   *The Three Faces of Fascism*, E. Nolte (London, 1965) p.332
19   *Mein Kampf*, op. cit., p.260
20   *VB*, 8 May 1921
21   *Himmler als Ideologe*, op. cit., p.26
22   *VB*, 25 August 1921
23   *H.S. Chamberlain*, op. cit., p.55
24   *Entscheidungsjahre – 1932*, op. cit., p.6
25   *Die Spur des Juden*, quoted in *A. Rosenberg: Selected Writings*, op. cit., p.175
26   *Origins of Totalitarianism*, op. cit., p.354
27   *Die Protokolle der Weisen von Zion*, (Munich, 1923) p.258
28   *Mensch und Gott*, H.S. Chamberlain (Munich, 1921)
29   *Himmler als Ideologe*, op. cit., p.30
30   *Traum und Tragoedie*, op. cit., p.249

Chapter 5 (pages 82–104)

1  Introduction by John Arendzen to Friends of Europe Pamphlet No. 44. Archives of Royal Institute of International Affairs, London
2  *Traum und Tragoedie*, op. cit., p.239
3  CDJC, CXLV – 537a
4  USNA, EAP99 – 403
5  *Mythus*, op. cit., p.74
6  ibid., p.414
7  USNA, EAP99 – 1020
8  CDJC, CXLII – 217
9  *Traum und Tragoedie*, op. cit., p.260
10  Quoted in *Traum und Tragoedie*, op. cit., p.89
11  *Mythus*, Introduction to 1930 edition
12  *Gestaltung der Idee*, A. Rosenberg (Munich, 1936) p.176
13  *H.S. Chamberlain*, op. cit., p.84
14  *Apocalypse*, D.H. Lawrence (London, 1932) pp.223–4
15  *Master Eckhart and the Rhineland Mystics*, J. Ancelet-Hustache (New York, 1957) p.176
16  *Mythus*, op. cit., p.221
17  *Grundlagen*, op. cit., p.751
18  *H.S. Chamberlain*, op. cit., p.26
19  ibid., p.73
20  *Der Mann und Sein Werk*, op. cit., p.19
21  *H.S. Chamberlain*, op. cit., p.73
22  ibid., p.83
23  *Mythus*, op. cit., p.23
24  *Der Nazismus: Ursprung und Wesen*, op. cit., p.64
25  Diary, 12 October 1940
26  *Traum und Tragoedie*, op. cit., p.95
27  USNA, EAP99 – 1020
28  *Grundlagen*, op. cit., Ch. 5, p.9
29  *The Evolution of Man and Society*, C.D. Darlington (London, 1969) p.298
30  *Mythus*, op. cit., p.700
31  ibid., p.71
32  ibid.
33  ibid., p.153
34  ibid., p.634
35  *Es Geschah in Deutschland*, S. v. Krosigk (Tuebingen, 1951) p.261
36  *Mythus*, op. cit., p.114. See also USNA, EAP99 – 254
37  *Deutsches Geistesleben und National-Sozialismus* (Tuebingen, 1965) p.99
38  *Account Rendered*, op. cit., p.208
39  *Blut und Ehre*, op. cit., p.204
40  *Mythus*, op. cit., p.701
41  ibid., p.450
42  Quoted in *Caesars in Goosestep*, W.D. Bayles (London, 1941) p.148
43  Quoted in *Wenn die Goetter den Tempel verlassen*, op. cit., p.109

44   BAK, NS8 – 185
45   *VB*, 1 March 1930
46   *Blut und Ehre*, op. cit., p.376
47   Quoted in *The Speeches of A. Hitler*, ed. N. Baynes, Vol. I (Oxford 1942) pp.106–7
48   *Cross and Swastika*, A. Frey (London, 1938) Preface by K. Barth
49   Quoted in *Kirche in der Krise*, V. v. Norden (Dusseldorf, 1963) p.94
50   *Traum und Tragoedie*, op. cit., p.58
51   *Mythus*, op. cit., p.599
52   *VB*, 10 September 1927
53   *VB*, 10 December 1926
54   *Traum und Tragoedie*, op. cit., p.95
55   ibid.
56   CDJC, CXLII – 333
57   *Hitler's Table-talk*, op. cit., p.422
58   *Zwischen Weissen und Braunen Haus*, E. Hanfstaengl (Munich, 1970) p.281
59   *The Speeches of A. Hitler*, op. cit., p.989
60   *Inside the Third Reich*, A. Speer (London, 1970) op. cit., p.110
61   Friends of Europe pamphlet No.26, Archives of Royal Institute of International Affairs, London
62   *Der Kampf gegen den Mythus*, W. Neuss (Cologne, 1947)
63   *Traum und Tragoedie*, op. cit., p.81
64   CDJC, CXLIII – 318
65   BAK, NS8 – 117
66   *Traum und Tragoedie*, op. cit., p.81
67   Diary, 16 September 1940
68   BAK, NS8 – 132
69   *The Story of Rosenberg's Mythus*, B. Lakebrink (Wiener Library Bulletin, Vol. VII, No.5/6, 1953)


Chapter 6 (pages 105–133)

1    *The Kersten Memoirs*, F. Kersten (London, 1956) p.32
2    *Mythus*, op. cit., p.482
3    BAK, NS8 – 99
4    ibid.; see also NS8 – 121
5    ibid.
6    *Traum und Tragoedie*, op. cit., p.85
7    *Blut und Ehre*, op. cit., p.65
8    ibid., p.89
9    *I Spied on Hitler*, W. de Ropp (Daily Mail, 28 October 1957 – November 1957)
10   *Traum und Tragoedie*, op. cit., p.218
11   *Memoirs*, F. v. Papen (London, 1952) p.261
12   *Katholische Kirche und National-Sozialismus*, ed. H. Mueller (Munich, 1965) p.129

13   Friends of Europe pamphlet No.64 of 1938, Archives of Royal
     Institute of International Affairs, London
14   *VB*, 16 August 1933
15   *VJH fuer Zeitgeschichte*, 1968, i: article by K. Scholder
16   BAK, NS8 – 157
17   *Nazi Persecution of the Churches*, J.S. Conway (London, 1968) p.95
18   *Hitler's Speeches*, op. cit., p.485
19   *Gestaltung der Idee*, op. cit., p.53
20   *Das Amt Rosenberg*, op. cit., p.53
21   ibid., p.54
22   Quoted in *Das Amt Rosenberg*, op. cit., p.56
     See also USNA, EAP99 – 398
23   ibid., op. cit., p.69
24   ibid.
25   USNA, EAP99 – 30a
26   Diary, 22 May 1934
27   BAK, NS8 – 99
28   *Mythus*, op. cit., p.525
29   *VB* of 9 January 1934, quoted in *Behemoth*, F. Neumann (London,
     1967) p.63
30   Diary, 28 June 1934
31   *Traum und Tragoedie*, op. cit., p.76
32   Diary, op. cit., 2 August 1934
33   *Traum und Tragoedie*, op. cit., p.160
34   ibid., p.178
35   ibid., p.166
36   Diary, 19 August 1934
37   *Kampf gegen den Mythus*, W. Neuss (Cologne, 1947)
     See also *Wiener Bulletin*, Vol. VII, Nos. 5-6, 1953
38   *Katholische Kirche und National-Sozialismus*, op. cit., pp.249–50
39   *Traum und Tragoedie*, op. cit., p.106
40   BAK, NS8 – 150
41   *Katholische Kirche und National-Socialismus*, pp. 324–27
42   CDJC, CXLVi – 2
43   Diary, 25 April 1936, cited in *Der Monat*, 1, No.X, 1949
44   Diary, 16 July 1941, cited in *Der Monat*, op. cit.
45   R. Bollmus believes that the observer was a Dr Brachmann; but see
     TMWC, Vol. XI, p.514
46   BAK, NS8 – 179. See also *VJH fuer Zeitgeschichte* (1956) Hans Buch-
     heim, p.307
47   TMWC, Vol. XI, p.514
48   This conclusion is not shared by R. Bollmus. . . . *Das Amt Rosenberg*,
     op. cit., p.291
49   *Der Monat*, No.10: entry of 18 January 1937
50   BAK, NS8 – 184
51   *VJH fuer Zeitgeschichte*, 1968: article by K. Scholder
52   *Das Amt Rosenberg*, op. cit., pp.98–99
53   ibid., p.101

54  *VB*, special supplement of 5 September 1937
55  Typescript by Sir W. Teeling, Archives of Royal Institute of
    International Affairs, London
56  BAK, NS8 – 7
57  *Der Monat*, No.10: entry of 10 October 1938
58  *Nazi Persecution of the Churches*, op. cit., p.216
59  Diary, 22 August 1939
60  USNA, EAP99 – 254
61  BAK, NS8 – 50
62  *Der Monat*, No.10: entry of 25 April 1936
63  TMWC, 098 – PS
64  TMWC, 1749 – PS
65  ibid.
66  Quoted in *Nazi Persecution of the Churches*, op. cit., p.232
67  USNA, EAP99 – 398
68  Diary, 19 January 1940
69  *Der Monat*, No.10: entry of 14 December 1941
70  USNA, EAP99 – 360
71  BAK, NS8 – 131
72  *Der Monat*, No.10: entry of 14 December 1941
73  *Traum und Tragoedie*, op. cit., p.205
74  ibid., p.206
75  Diary, 24 September 1939
76  ibid., 1 November 1939
77  BAK, NS8 – 131
78  Diary, 3 March 1940
79  USNA, EAP99 – 401
80  BAK, NS8 – 131
81  CDJC, CXL – 72
82  *Germany's Revolution of Destruction*, H. Rauschning, (London, 1939)
    p.165


Chapter 7 (pages 134–161)

1  *The Last Days of Hitler*, op. cit., pp.89–90
2  *Mythus*, op. cit., p.215
3  ibid., p.517
4  ibid., introduction
5  Quoted in *Fuehrung und Verfuehrung*, H.J. Gamm (Munich, 1964)
    p.188
6  *Origins of Totalitarianism*, op. cit., p.457
7  *Wesen, Grundsaetze und Ziele* in *Reden und Schriften*, op. cit., p.172
8  ibid., p.123
9  *Mythus*, op. cit., p.634
10 Quoted in *Education and Society in Modern Germany*, H. Samuel and
    H. Thomas (London, 1949) p.38

11   *Nazi Persecution of the Churches*, p.216
12   *Katholische Kirche und National-Sozialismus*, op. cit., p.297
13   *Traum und Tragoedie*, op. cit., p.197
14   ibid., p.110
15   Quoted in *Fuehrung und Verfuehrung*, op. cit., p.187
16   Typescript by Sir W. Teeling, Archives of Royal Institute of International Affairs, London
17   TMWC, Vol. XI, p.460
18   *Mythus*, op. cit., p.21
19   ibid., p.513
20   *Mythus*, op. cit., p.81
21   Quoted in *Der Nazismus: Ursprung und Wesen*, op. cit., p.65
22   Diary, 9 April 1940
23   *Deutsches Geistesleben and Nazismus*, op. cit., quoted by A. Flitner, p.231
24   CDJC, CXLVI – 11
25   CDJC, CXLV – 594
26   *Hitler's Speeches*, op. cit., Vol, I, p.104
27   *Gestaltung der Idee*, op. cit., p.158
28   *Mythus*, op. cit., p.634
29   *Gestaltung der Idee*, op. cit., p.303
30   Quoted in *Fuehrung und Verfuehrung*, op. cit., p.211
31   TMWC, 1749 – PS
32   *Gestaltung der Idee*, op. cit., p.35
33   CDJC, CXLV – 577
34   USNA, EAP99 – 360
35   *Deutsches Geistesleben und National-Sozialismus*, op. cit., chapter by H. Rothfels, p.103
36   USNA, EAP99 – 398
37   *Das Amt Rosenberg*, op. cit., pp.211–35
38   Quoted in *Wenn die Gotter den Tempel Verlassen*, op. cit., p.20
39   *Der Fuehrer*, op. cit., p.308
40   'Die NS-Ordensburgen', H. Scholz (*VJH fuer Zeitgeschichte*, No. 3, 1967)
41   BAK NS8 – 127
42   *Traum und Tragoedie*, op. cit., p.195
43   'Die NS-Ordensburgen', op. cit.
44   *Traum und Tragoedie*, op. cit., p.139
45   *Fuehrung und Verfuehrung*, op. cit., p.425. See also article by G.A. Rowan-Robinson in International Affairs, No.17, 1938
46   'Die NS-Ordensburgen', op. cit.
47   *Fuehrung und Verfuehrung*, op. cit., p.431
48   ibid., p.416
49   ibid., p.414
50   BAK, NS8 – 231
51   Quoted in *Wenn die Goetter den Tempel verlassen*, op. cit., p.120
52   *Account Rendered*, op. cit., p.79
53   Quoted in *Fuehrung und Verfuehrung*, op. cit., p.70
54   *Himmler als Ideologe*, op. cit., p.101
55   ibid., p.103

56   *So Hat Es Sich Zugetragen*, op. cit., p.307
57   *Mythus*, 1930 edition, p.527
58   ibid., 1938 edition, p.559
59   ibid., 1938 edition, p.546
60   *Germany's Revolution of Destruction*, op. cit., p.267
61   *Gestaltung der Idee*, op. cit., pp.79–83
62   USNA, EAP99 – 398
63   CDJC, CXLV1 – 11. See also Diary of 7 February 1940
64   CDJC, CXL111 – 269
65   Diary of 30 April 1940
66   BAK, NS8 – 129
67   Diary of 6 September 1940
68   BAK, NS8 – 129
69   *Hitler was my Friend*, H. Hofmann (London, 1955) p.180
70   *The Trial of the Germans*, E. Davidson (London, 1966) p.139
71   CDJC, CXL111 – 328
72   USNA, EAP99 – 360
73   CDJC, CXL111 – 269
74   CDJC, CXXX11 – 209
75   Quoted in *The Face of the Third Reich*, op. cit., p.168
76   *The Goebbels Diaries*, ed. L. Lochner (London, 1948) 27 February 1942

Chapter 8 (pages 162–186)

1   *Die Spur des Juden*, op. cit., p.84
2   *VB*, 8 May 1921
3   *Pest in Russland*, op. cit., pp.59–60
4   *Der Zukunftsweg der deutschen Aussenpolitik* (Eher Verlag, Munich, 1927)
5   *Der Zukunftsweg*, op. cit., p.87
6   ibid., p.87
7   *Pest in Russland*, op. cit., p.63
8   BAK, NS8 – 209
9   *Schriften und Reden*, op. cit., p.154
10   *Mythus*, op. cit., p.534
11   ibid., p.550
12   BDC, Rosenberg to Darré of 20 August 1930
13   *Germany's Revolution of Destruction*, op. cit., p.266
14   *Mein Kampf*, op. cit., p.389
15   *Hitler's Weltanschauung*, E. Jaeckel (Tuebingen, 1969) p.35
16   ibid., p.38
17   *Mein Kampf*, op. cit., p.533
18   *Hitler's Secret Book*, ed. T. Taylor (New York, 1961) p.135
19   ibid., p.210
20   ibid., p.215

21  *I Spied on Hitler*, W. de Ropp (Daily Mail, London, 28 October –
    1 November 1957)
22  BAK, NS8 – 117
23  USNA, EAP99 – 358
24  CDJC, CXLV – 622
25  *I Spied on Hitler*, op. cit.
26  *Secret and Personal*, F.W. Winterbotham (London, 1969) p.25
27  TMWC, Vol. XI, p.454
28  *Der Zukunftsweg*, op. cit., p.141
29  *Blut und Ehre*, op. cit., p.296
30  *I Knew Hitler*, op. cit., p.514
31  *Germany's Revolution of Destruction*, op. cit., p.255
32  *Traum und Tragoedie*, op. cit., p.283
33  *The Missing Years*, op. cit., p.197
34  *Lucifer ante Portas*, R. Diels (Stuttgart, 1950) pp.104–5
35  *Trail Sinister*, S. Delmer (London, 1961) pp.185–6
36  *I Knew Hitler*, op. cit., p.570
37  ibid., p.651
38  CDJC, CXXIXa – 720
39  Diary, 14 May 1934
40  BAK NS8 – 117
41  *Documents of British Foreign Policy*, 2nd series, Vol. V No.138
42  ibid., No.118
43  *Daily Telegraph*, 13 May 1933
44  *The Times*, 12 May 1933
45  *Documents on German Foreign Policy*, series C, Vol. 1, No.237
46  *The Mist Procession*, R. Vansittart (London, 1958) p.475
47  *I Knew Hitler*, op. cit., p.534
48  *Documents on German Foreign Policy*, op. cit., No.245
49  BAK, NS8 – 117
50  *Traum und Tragoedie*, op. cit., p.80
51  *Secret and Personal*, op. cit., pp.38 – 39
52  ibid., p.28
53  *Documents on British Foreign Policy*, second series, Vol. V, No.262
54  *Secret and Personal*, op. cit., p.64
55  Diary, 28 June 1934
56  ibid., 2 February 1935
57  ibid., 12 March 1935
58  'The Final Fight between Europe and Bolshevism' (1936) CDJC,
    CXLV – 637
59  *Traum und Tragoedie*, op. cit., p.133
60  TMWC, Vol. XI, p.584
61  *Traum und Tragoedie*, op. cit., p.283
62  Diary, 'mid-May'
63  ibid., 21 May 1939
64  TMWC, 1365 – PS
65  Diary, 19 July 1939
66  USNA, EAP99 – 399
66a Diaries of Sir A. Cadogan, ed. D. Dilks (London, 1971) p. 193

67  *Documents on German Foreign Policy*, series D, Vol. VIII, No.74
68  Diary, 22 August 1939
69  ibid., 25 August 1939
70  ibid., 24 September 1939
71  ibid., 29 September 1939
72  ibid., 5 October 1939
73  *Documents on German Foreign Policy*, series D, Vol. VIII, No.235
74  *Memoirs*, E.V. Weizsaecker (London, 1951) p.228
75  Diary, 9 April 1940
76  *Prisoner of Peace*, Ilse Hess (London, 1954) pp.19–20
77  *Meldungen aus dem Reich*, ed. H. Boberach (Munich, 1968) p.146


Chapter 9 (pages 187–214)

 1  *Im Hauptquartier der deutschen Wehrmacht*, W. Warlimont (Frankfurt, 1962) p.126
 2  ibid., p.166
 3  USNA, EAP99 – 110
 4  RKFDV, *German Resettlement Policy*, R.L. Koehl (Harvard, 1957) p.230
 5  TMWC, 1058 – PS
 6  ibid., 1030 – PS
 7  *The House Built on Sand*, G. Reitlinger (London, 1960) p.130
 8  *So Hat Es Sich Zugetragen*, op. cit., p.627
 9  TMWC, 1058 – PS
10  ibid., 1017 – PS
11  *The House Built on Sand*, op. cit., p.99
12  USNA, EAP99 – 1232
13  *So Hat Es Sich Zugetragen*, op. cit., p.401
14  *Nationalsozialistische Polenpolitik*, M. Broszat (Frankfurt, 1965) p.27
15  TMWC, 1019 – PS
16  ibid., 865 – PS
17  Quoted in *German Rule in Russia*, A. Dallin (London, 1957) p.37
18  TMWC, 1039 – PS
19  *So Hat Es Sich Zugetragen*, op. cit., p.345
20  *The House Built on Sand*, op. cit., p.129
21  *So Hat Es Sich Zugetragen*, op. cit., p.299
22  *Mein Kampf*, op. cit., p.533
23  Quoted in *The House Built on Sand*, op. cit., p.364
24  Diary, 21 May 1939
25  *So Hat Es Sich Zugetragen*, op. cit., p.390
26  ibid., p.391
27  RKFDV, op. cit., p.109

28 *So Hat Es Sich Zugetragen,* op. cit., p.437
29 *German Rule in Russia,* op. cit., p.276
30 *Im Kampf um die Macht,* W. Jochmann (Frankfurt, 1960) p.80
31 RKFDV, op. cit., p.196
32 ibid., op. cit., p.123
33 *So Hat Es Sich Zugetragen,* op. cit., p.412
34 ibid., op. cit., p.486
35 *European Tragedy,* op. cit., p.125
36 *Hitler's Table Talk,* op. cit., pp.572–686
37 *So Hat Es Sich Zugetragen,* op. cit., p.711
38 ibid., op. cit., p.312
39 ibid., p.307
40 ibid., p.313
41 TMWC, 1017 – PS
42 *Im Hauptquartier,* op. cit., p.176
43 ibid., p.181
44 TMWC, 1017 – PS
45 ibid., 1018 – PS
46 ibid., 1039 – PS
47 ibid., 1058 – PS
48 *Documents on International Affairs* (1939–46), RIIA, ed. A. Toynbee, Vol. II, p.230
49 ibid., p.367
50 *Der Monat,* No. 10, entry of 16 July 1941
51 *The House Built on Sand,* op. cit., p.183
52 *So Hat Es Sich Zugetragen,* op. cit., p.434
53 USNA, EAP99 – 110
54 *Hans Frank's Diary,* ed. S. Pietrowski (Warsaw, 1961) pp.132–33
55 TMWC, 1517 – PS
56 ibid., 081 – PS
57 *The Goebbels Diaries,* op. cit., 8 February 1942
58 ibid., 22 May 1942
59 TMWC, 1520 – PS
60 *So Hat Es Sich Zugetragen,* op. cit., p.452. See also USNA, EAP99 – 1075
61 TMWC, 1520 – PS
62 CDJC, CXLVa – 14
63 USNA, EAP99 – 1232
64 *Hitler's Table Talk,* op. cit., p.589
65 TMWC, 042 – PS
66 TMWC, Vol. XI, pp.545–46
67 *The House Built on Sand,* op. cit., p.323
68 BDC, Berger to Himmler of 23 September 1942
69 *Der Monat,* No. 10, entry of 25 January 1943
70 USNA, EAP99 – 30; also – 1119
71 ibid., EAP99 – 110
72 TMWC, 032 – PS
73 CDJC, CXLIV – 442
74 *German Rule in Russia,* op. cit., p.163

75  CDJC, CXLIV – 440
76  *So Hat Es Sich Zugetragen*, op. cit., p.611
77  USNA, EAP99 – 487
78  *The House Built on Sand*, op. cit., p.213
79  USNA, EAP99 – 40
80  *Lagebesprechungen*, op. cit., entry 8 June 1943
81  *So Hat Es Sich Zugetragen*, op. cit., p.613
82  ibid., p.624
83  *The Goebbels Diaries*, op. cit., entry 28 September 1943
84  *Traum und Tragoedie*, op. cit., p.116
85  *The House Built on Sand*, p.149
86  USNA, EAP99 – 40
87  *Traum und Tragoedie*, op. cit., p.104
88  USNA, EAP99 – 399 and 402
89  BAK, NS8 – 132
90  CDJC, LX11 – 29
91  USNA, EAP99 – 44
92  TMWC, 743 – PS
93  CDJC, CXL11 – 279
94  TMWC, Vol. XLI, Ros. – 14
95  ibid., Vol. XI, p.508


Chapter 10 (pages 215–230)

1   *Traum und Tragoedie*, op. cit., p.179
2   ibid., p.227
3   ibid., p.179
4   *So Hat Es Sich Zugetragen*, op. cit., p.713
5   *Traum und Tragoedie*, op. cit., p.180
6   ibid., p.172
7   *Rude Pravo*, Prague, 14 January 1971
8   *Traum und Tragoedie*, op. cit., p.182
9   ibid.
10  *Inside the Third Reich*, op. cit., p.498
11  Information from source mentioned on p.2
12  *Traum und Tragoedie*, op. cit., p.184
13  ibid., p.184
14  ibid., p.251
15  ibid., p.115
16  *Inside the Third Reich*, op. cit., p.515
17  Quoted from the papers of Col. B.C. Andrus
18  ibid.
19  *The Infamous of Nuremberg*, op. cit., p.134
20  ibid., p.91
21  *Traum und Tragoedie*, op. cit., p.165
22  ibid., p.178

23  ibid., p.204
24  TMWC, Vol. XXII, p. 382
25  TMWC, Vol. XVIII, p. 118
26  *The Infamous of Nuremberg*, op. cit., p. 172
27  ibid., p. 100
28  TMWC, Vol. I, p. 28
29  *Traum und Tragoedie*, op. cit., p. 269
30  TMWC, Vol. XXII, p.383
31  ibid., Vol. XI, p.498
32  *The Trial of the Germans*, op. cit., p.6
33  TMWC, Vol. I, p.296
34  Reproduced in *Portraet eines Menschheitsverbrechers*, S. Lang and
    E. Schenk (St Gallen, 1947) pp.8–9
35  TMWC, Vol. XI, p.460
36  TMWC, Vol. XI, p.584
37  TMWC, Vol. XXVI, 1058 – PS
38  TMWC, Vol. XIX, p.552
39  TMWC, Vol. XI, p.545
40  See particularly USNA, EAP99 – 110
41  TMWC, Vol. XVIII, p.9
42  *The Trial of the Germans*, op. cit., p.304
43  TMWC, Vol. XI, p.478
44  TMWC, Vol. XI, p.502
45  *So Hat Es Sich Zugetragen*, op. cit., p.475
46  Quoted in *Race and Reich*, J. Tenenbaum (New York, 1956) p.247
47  CDJC, CXXXII – 210
48  CDJC, CXLVI – 23
49  TMWC, Vol. XXII, p.382
50  *Traum und Tragoedie*, op. cit., p.187
51  TMWC, Vol. XXII, p. 541
52  *Traum und Tragoedie*, op. cit., p.283
53  ibid., p.238
54  TMWC, Vol. XI, p.449
55  Quoted in *Race and Reich*, op. cit., p.364
56  *Correspondence Tocqueville – Gobineau* (Paris, 1959) p.203
57  *So Hat Es Sich Zugetragen*, op. cit., p.714
58  *The Infamous of Nuremberg*, op. cit., p.185

# BIBLIOGRAPHY

## Rosenberg's Works:

A bibliography up to 1941 is contained in *Das Werk Alfred Rosenbergs: Eine Bibliographie*, compiled by Karlheinz Rüdiger (Munich, 1941). A complete bibliography will be found in *Das Amt Rosenberg und seine Gegner*, by R. Bollmus (Stuttgart, 1970). Both contain separately published editions of his speeches, extracts from *Der Mythus*, etc. These have been omitted from the shortened bibliography given below.

| | |
|---|---|
| 1920 | *Die Spur des Juden im Wandel der Zeiten* (München) |
| | *Unmoral im Talmud* (München) |
| 1921 | *Das Verbrechen der Freimaurerei* (München) |
| 1922 | *Pest in Russland* (München) |
| | *Der staatsfeindliche Zionismus* (Hamburg) |
| 1923 | *Wesen, Grundsätze und Ziele der NSDAP* (München) |
| | *Die Protokolle der Weisen von Zion* (München) |
| 1924 | *Der völkische Staatsgedanke* (München) |
| 1925 | *Die internationale Hochfinanz* (München) |
| 1927 | *Houston Stewart Chamberlain* (München) |
| | *Dreissig November – Köpfe* (Berlin) |
| | *Der Weltverschwörerkongress zu Basel* (München) |
| | *Der Zukunftsweg deutscher Aussenpolitik* (München) |
| 1929 | *Freimaurerische Weltpolitik im Lichte der kritischen Forschung* (München) |
| 1930 | *Der Mythus des 20. Jahrhunderts* (München) |
| | *Der Sumpf* (München) |
| 1934 | *Das Wesensgefüge des Nationalsozialismus* (München) |
| 1935 | *Blut und Ehre* (Collection of writings and speeches) (München) |
| | *An die Dunkelmänner unserer Zeit* (München) |
| 1936 | *Gestaltung der Idee* (Collection of writings and speeches) (München) |
| 1937 | *Kampf um die Macht* (Collection of writings and speeches) (München) |
| | *Protestantische Rompilger* (München) |
| 1941 | *Tradition und Gegenwart* (Collection of writings and speeches) (München) |
| 1943 | *Schriften und Reden* (Collection of writings and speeches) (München) |

## Posthumous Publications

| | |
|---|---|
| 1947 | *Porträt eines Menschheitsverbrechers*, ed. S. Lang and E. Schenk (St Gallen) |
| 1948 | *Testament Nazi: Mémoires de Rosenberg*, ed. S. Lang and E. Schenk (Paris) |

R*

1949  *Memoirs of Alfred Rosenberg*, ed. S. Lang and E. Schenk (New York)
1955  *Letzte Aufzeichnungen*, ed. H. Härtle (Göttingen)
1956  *Das politische Tagebuch Rosenbergs*, ed. H.G. Seraphim (Göttingen)
1970  *Grossdeutschland: Traum und Tragödie*, ed. H. Härtle (München)


Introductions by Rosenberg

1921  *Der Totengräber Russlands*, D. Eckart (München)
1928  *Dietrich Eckart: ein Vermächtnis* (München)
1938  *Jüdische Weltpolitik in Selbstzeugnissen*, G. Leibbrandt (München)


Translated by Rosenberg

1923  *Der Jude, das Judentum, und die Verjudung der christlichen Völker*
       (from the French of Gougenot de Mousseaux) (München)


Unpublished Documents

*Andrus*, B.C. – private papers concerning detention at Nuremberg
*Anon.* MS quoted on p.2 and p.217 in the author's possession
*Archives* of Berlin Document Centre (BDC)
    Centre de Documentation Juive Contemporaine (CDJC)
    Federal German Government, Koblenz (BAK)
    US National Archives, Alexandria (USNA)
*Teeling*, Sir W. – Typescript in RIIA, Chatham House, London


Published Documents

HMSO London, Documents on British Foreign Policy: Second Series
    (1929–38), Vol. V
Documents on German Foreign Policy: Series C, Vol. I
                                     Series D, Vol. VIII
RIIA London, Documents on International Affairs (1936–46), Vol. II
TMWC Nuremberg Vols, I, II, VIII, XI, XV, XVIII, XIX, XXII,
    XXV – XXVII, XLI of the Trial of the Major War Criminals

Pamphlets, Periodicals and Newspapers

Contemporary Review, London (See J.P. Fox 1968)
Daily Mail, London (28 Oct – 1 Nov 1957): W. de Ropp reminiscences
Der Monat, Berlin (No. 10, 1949): R.M.W. Kempner
Friends of Europe pamphlets: Religious Series, RIIA, London (especially
　　Nos. 12, 26, 27, 44, 46, 48, 51, 54, 66, 67)
International Affairs, RIIA, London (See G.A. Rowan – Robinson 1938)
The Times, London (9 – 12 May 1933)
Vierteljahreshefte für Zeitgeschichte, Stuttgart
Völkischer Beobachter, München and Berlin (1921–44)
Wiener Library Bulletin, London
(especially Nos. 5–6, 1950; 1–2, 1951, Nos. 5–6, 1953, No. 4, 1966).

Selected list of Secondary Sources

Ackermann, J., Himmler als Ideologe (Göttingen, 1970)
Andrus, B.C. (with Zwar, D.), The Infamous of Nuremberg (London, 1969)
Ancelet-Hustache, J., Master Eckhart (New York, 1957)
Arendt, H., The Origins of Totalitarianism (London, 1958)


Barth, K., The German Church Conflict (London, 1965)
Bayles, W.D., Caesars in Goosestep (London, 1941)
Baynes, N. (ed) The Speeches of A. Hitler (Oxford, 1942)
Billig, J., A. Rosenberg dans l'action idéologique, etc. (Paris, 1963)
Boberach, H. (ed), Meldungen aus dem Reich (München, 1968)
Bollmus, R., Das Amt Rosenberg und seine Gegner (Stuttgart, 1970)
Booth, M., See Hess, Ilse
Bracher, K.D., Die deutsche Diktatur (Köln, 1969)
　　(et al), Die Machtergreifung (Köln, 1960)
Bramsted, E., Goebbels in National-Socialist Propaganda (London, 1965)
Braeutigam, O., So Hat Es Sich Zugetragen (Wurzburg, 1968)
Broszat, M., Der Nationalsozialismus. Weltanschauung, etc. (Hannover, 1960)
　　Nationalsozialistische Polenpolitik (Stuttgart, 1961)
　　Der Staat Hitlers (München, 1969)
Buchheim, H. (et al), The Anatomy of the SS State (London, 1968)
Buchheit, G., Soldatentum und Rebellion (Rastatt, 1961)
Bullock, A., Hitler, A Study in Tyranny (London, 1962)
　　(ed), The Ribbentrop Memoirs (London, 1954)
Burden, H.T., The Nuremberg Party Rallies (London, 1967)
Butler, R., The Roots of National Socialism (London, 1941)


Calvocoressi, P., Nuremberg; The Facts, The Law, etc. (London, 1947)
Carsten, F.L., The Reichswehr and Politics (London, 1966)
Cassirer, E., The Myth of the State (New York, 1945)
Chamberlain, H.S., Die Grundlagen des 19ten Jahrhunderts (München, 1899)
　　Mensch Und Gott (München, 1921)

Chandler, A.R., *Rosenberg's Nazi Myth* (Cornell U., 1945)
Clark, A., *Barbarossa (1941–45)* (London, 1965)
Cohn, N., *Warrant for Genocide* (London, 1967)
Colvin, I., *Vansittart in Office* (London, 1965)
Conway, J.S., *Nazi Persecution of the Churches* (London, 1968)
Crankshaw, E., *Gestapo* (London, 1956)
Cross, C., *The British Fascists* (London, 1961)


Dallin, A., *German Rule in Russia* (London, 1957)
Davidson, E., *The Trial of the Germans* (London, 1966)
Delmer, S., *Trail Sinister* (London, 1961)
Diels, R., *Lucifer ante Portas* (Stuttgart, 1970)
Diem, H. (et al), *Deutsches Geistesteben and Nationalsozialismus*
    (Tübingen, 1965)
Dietrich, O., *Mit Hitler in die Macht* (München, 1934)
Dinter, A., *197 Thesen, etc.* (Leipzig, 1921)
Dutch, O., *Hitler's Twelve Apostles* (London, 1939)


Eckart, D., *Bolshevismus von Moses bis Lenin* (München, 1924)
Eilers, R., *Die Nationalsozialistische Schulpolitik* (Köln, 1963)


Fest, J.C., *The Face of the Third Reich* (London, 1970)
Fleiss, P.J., *Freedom of the Press in the German Republic* (Louisiana U. 1955)
Frank, H., *Im Angesicht des Galgens* (München, 1953)
Fraenkel, H. (with Manvell, R.), *H. Himmler* (London, 1965)
    *H. Goering* (London, 1962)
Franz-Willing, G., *Die Hitlerbewegung* (Hamburg, 1962)
Frey, A., *Cross and Swastika* (London, 1938)


Gamm, H.J., *Der Braune Kult* (Hamburg, 1962)
    *Führung and Verführung* (München, 1964)
Gilbert, G.M., *Nuremberg Diary* (London, 1948)
Gilbert, M.J., *The Roots of Appeasement* (London, 1966)
    (with Gott, R.), *The Appeasers* (London, 1963)
Gisevius, H.B., *A. Hitler* (München, 1963)
Gott, R., *See* Gilbert, M.J.
Granzow, B., *Mirror of Nazism* (London, 1964)
Grebing, H., *Der Nationalsozialismus: Ursprung und Wesen*
    (München, 1959)
Gros, O., *850 Worte: Erläuterung zu dem Mythus, etc.* (München, 1938)


Hale, O.J., *Captive Press in the Third Reich* (Princeton U. 1964)
Hanfstaengl, E., *The Missing Years* (London, 1957)
    *Zwischen weissen und braunen Haus* (München, 1970)

Hart, F.T., *A. Rosenberg, Der Mann und sein Werk* (München, 1939)
Hartshorne, E.Y., *German Universities and National Socialism* (London, 1937)
Hedin, S., *German Diary* (Dublin, 1951)
Heiber, H. (ed), *The Early Goebbels Diaries* (London, 1962)
  *Lagebesprechungen im FHQ* (München, 1962)
Heiden, K., *History of National Socialism* (London, 1934)
  *Der Führer* (Boston, 1944)
Heller, E., *The Disinherited Mind* (Cambridge, 1952)
Hermelink, H. (ed), *Kirche im Kampf* (Stuttgart, 1950)
Hess, Ilse (with Booth, M.), *Prisoner of Peace* (London, 1954)
Heyer, K., *Der Staat als Werkzeug des Bösen* (Freiburg, 1965)
Hilger, G. (with Meyer, A.), *The Incompatible Allies* (New York, 1953)
Hildebrandt, K., *Deutsche Aussenpolitik* (Mainz, 1971)
Hitler, A., *Mein Kampf* (London, 1939)
Hofer, W. (ed), *Der Nationalsozialismus: Dokumente* (Frankfurt, 1957)
Hofmann, H., *Hitler was my Friend* (London, 1955)
Hoehne, H., *The Order of the Death's Head* (London, 1969)


Ilnytzkj, R., *Deutschland und die Ukraine* (München, 1955)


Jacobsen, H.A., *Nationalsozialistische Aussenpolitik – 1933–38* (Frankfurt, 1968)
Jarman, T.L., *The Rise and Fall of Nazi Germany* (New York, 1964)
Jaeckel, E., *Hitlers Weltanschauung* (Tübingen, 1969)
Jochmann, W. (ed), *Im Kampf um die Macht* (Frankfurt, 1960)
  *Nationalsozialismus und Revolution* (Frankfurt, 1963)


Kelley, D., *Twenty-two Cells at Nuremberg* (London, 1947)
Kersten, F., *The Kersten Memoirs* (London, 1956)
Kessler, H., *Tagebücher* (Frankfurt, 1961)
Kleist, P., *European Tragedy* (London, 1965)
Klemperer, K.v., *Germany's New Conservatism* (Princeton U. 1968)
Koehl, R.L., *RKFDV: German Resettlement Policy* (Harvard U. 1957)
Kogon, E., *Theory and Practice of Hell* (New York, 1950)
Kohn, H., *The Mind of Germany* (New York, 1960)
Krebs, A., *Tendenzen und Gestalten der NSDAP* (Stuttgart, 1959)
Krosigk, S.v., *Es Geschah in Deutschland* (Tübingen, 1951)


Laqueur, W., *Young Germany* (London, 1962)
  *Russia and Germany* (London, 1965)
Leasor, H.J., *Hess* (London, 1962)
Lerner, D., *The Nazi Elite* (Stanford U. 1951)
Lewy, G., *The Catholic Church and Nazi Germany* (London, 1964)
Lochner, L. (Ed), *The Goebbels Diaries* (London, 1948)
Lohalm, U., *Völkischer Radikalismus* (Hamburg, 1969)

Loock, H.D., *Quisling, Rosenberg and Terboven* (Stuttgart, 1970)
Ludendorff, E., *Auf dem Weg zur Feldherrnhalle* (München, 1937)
Luedecke, K., *I Knew Hitler* (London, 1938)


Manvell, R., *See* Fraenkel, H.
Maschmann, M., *Account Rendered* (London, 1964)
Maser, W., *Die Frühgeschichte der NSDAP* (Frankfurt, 1965)
  *Mein Kampf: An Analysis* (London, 1970)
Meinecke, F., *The German Catastrophe* (Boston, 1950)
Meyer, A., *See* Hilger, G.
Meyer, H.C., *Mitteleuropa* (The Hague, 1955)
Micklem, N., *National Socialism and the Roman Catholic Church*
  (Oxford, 1939)
Mosse, G.L., *The Crisis of German Ideology* (London, 1966)
Mosse, E. (ed), *Entscheidungsjahre 1932* (Tübingen, 1966)
Mueller, H. (ed), *Die Katholische Kirche und Nationalsozialismus*
  (München, 1965)
Muenzenberg, W., *Nazi Führer Sehen Dich An* (Paris, 1934)
Mullally, F., *Fascism Inside England* (London, 1946)


Neumann, F., *Behemoth* (London, 1946)
Neuss, W., *Der Kampf gegen den Mythus* (Köln, 1947)
Niemoeller, W., *M. Niemöller* (München. 1952)
  *Hitler und die evangelischen Kirchenführer* (Bielefeld, 1959)
Nolte, E., *The Three Faces of Fascism* (London, 1965)
Norden, G.v., *Kirche in der Krise* (Düsseldorf, 1963)
Nyomarkay, J., *Charisma and Factionalism in the Nazi Party*
  (Minneapolis, 1967)


O'Neill, R.J., *The German Army and the Nazis* (London, 1966)
Orlov, D., *History of the Nazi Party* (Pittsburgh U. 1969)


Papen, F.v., *Memoirs* (London, 1952)
Peterson, E.N., *The Limits of Hitler's Power* (Princeton U. 1969)
Pietrowski, S. (ed), *Hans Frank's Diary* (Warsaw, 1961)
Plamenatz, J., *German Marxism and Russian Communism* (London, 1954)
Pois, R. (ed), *Alfred Rosenberg: Selected Writings* (London, 1970)
Poliakov, L. (with Wulf, J.), *Das Dritte Reich und Seine Denker*
  (Berlin, 1959)


Rauschning, H., *Hitler Speaks* (London, 1939)
  *Germany's Revolution of Destruction* (London, 1939)
Reitlinger, G., *The Final Solution* (London, 1953)
  *SS—Alibi of a Nation* (London, 1950)

*The House Built on Sand* (London, 1960)
Roberts, S., *The House that Hitler Built* (London, 1937)
Robertson, E.M., *Hitler's Pre-War Policy and Military Plans*
(London, 1963)
Roehm, E., *Geschichte eines Hochverräters* (München, 1933)
Rossi, A., *The Russo-German Alliance* (London, 1950)


Salomon, E.v., *Die Geächteten* (Berlin, 1931)
Samuel, H. (with Thomas, H.), *Education and Society in Modern Germany*
(London, 1949)
Schacht, H., *My First 76 Years* (London, 1955)
Schellenberg, W., *Memoirs* (London, 1956)
Schirach, B.v., *Die HJ: Idee und Gestalt* (Leipzig, 1934)
*Ich Glaubte an Hitler* (Hamburg, 1967)
Schoenbaum, D., *Hitler's Social Revolution* (London, 1967)
Schubert, G., *Anfänge der Nationalsozialistische Aussenpolitik* (Köln, 1963)
Sebottendorff, R.v., *Bevor Hitler Kam* (München, 1933)
Speer, A., *Inside the Third Reich* (London, 1970)
Stein, G.H., *The Waffen SS* (London, 1966)
Stern, F., *The Politics of Cultural Despair* (California U. 1961)
Stirk, S.D., *The Prussian Spirit* (London, 1941)
Strasser, O., *Gangsters Around Hitler* (London, 1942)


Taylor, T. (ed), *Hitler's Secret Book* (New York, 1961)
Tenenbaum, J., *Race and Reich* (New York, 1956)
Thomas, H., *See* Samuel, H.
Thyssen, F., *I Paid Hitler* (London, 1941)
Toynbee, A. (ed), *Survey of International Affairs. Hitler's Europe*
(Oxford, 1954)
Trevor-Roper, H., *The Last Days of Hitler* (London, 1947) (Ed.) *Hitler's
Table Talk* (London, 1953)


UNESCO Symposium: *The Third Reich* (London, 1955)


Vansittart, Lord, *The Mist Procession* (London, 1958)
Viereck, P., *Metapolitics* (New York, 1961)


Waite, R.G.L., *Vanguard of Nazism* (Harvard U. 1952)
Warlimont, W., *Im HQ der deutschen Wehrmacht* (Frankfurt, 1962)
Weinberg, G.L., *Germany and the Soviet Union* (Leyden, 1954)
Weinreich, M., *Hitler's Professors* (New York, 1946)
Weizsaecker, E.v., *Memoirs* (London, 1951)
Wheeler-Bennett, J., *The Wooden Titan* (London, 1936)
*The Forgotten Peace* (London, 1938)

Winterbotham, F.W., *Secret and Personal* (London, 1969)
Wiskemann, E., *Germany's Eastern Neighbours* (London, 1956)
  *Europe of the Dictators* (London, 1966)
Woolf, S. (ed), *European Fascism* (London, 1968)
  *The Nature of Fascism* (London, 1968)
Wulf, J., *See* Poliakov, L.


Zahn, G.C., *German Catholics and Hitler's Wars* (London, 1963)
Zeman, Z.A.B., *Nazi Propaganda* (London, 1964)
Zipfel, F., *Kirchenkampf in Deutschland* (Berlin, 1965)
Zwar, D., *See* Andrus, B.C.

# INDEX